MINNESOTA

A

HISTORY

MINNESOTA

A
HISTORY

SECOND EDITION

WILLIAM E. LASS

W. W. NORTON & COMPANY

NEW YORK / LONDON

Copyright © 1998 by William E Lass Copyright © 1977 by
American Association of State and Local History
First published as a Norton paperback 2000

For information about permission to reproduce selections from this book, write to Permission
W W Norton & Company, Inc , 500 Fifth Avenue, New York, NY 10110

The text of this book is composed in Garamond No 3
with the display set in Poster Bodoni Compressed
Desktop composition by Platinum Manuscript Services
Manufacturing by The Courier Companies, Inc
Book Design by JAM Design

Library of Congress Cataloging-in Publication Data
Lass, William E
Minnesota a history / William E Lass —2nd ed
p   cm
Includes bibliographical references and index
ISBN 0-393-04628-1
1 Minnesota—History I Title
F606 L35   1998
977 6—dc21   97-34650
CIP

ISBN 0-393-31971-7 pbk

W. W. Norton & Company, Inc.
500 Fifth Avenue, New York, N.Y. 10110
www.wwnorton.com

W. W. Norton & Company Ltd.
Castle House, 75/76 Wells Street, London W1T 3QT

4 5 6 7 8 9 0

To the memory
of my wife,
Marilyn J. Lass
(1932–94)

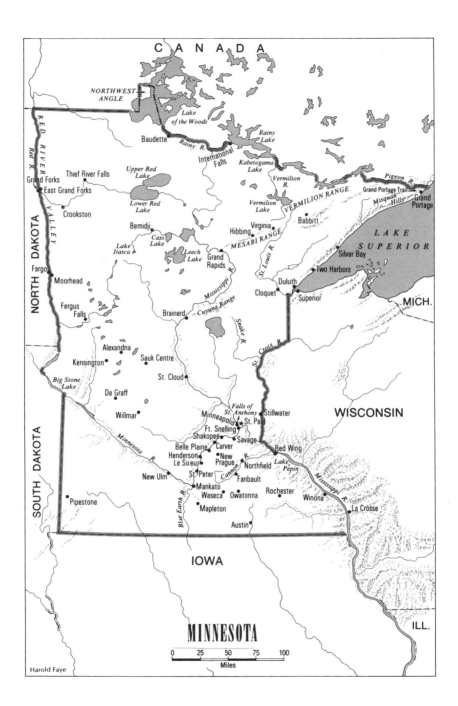

CANADA

NORTHWEST
ANGLE

*Lake
of the Woods*

RED RIVER VALLEY

Red R.

Baudette

Rainy R.

*Rainy
Lake*

International
Falls

*Kabetogama
Lake*

Pigeon R.

Thief River Falls

*Upper Red
Lake*

Grand Forks
East Grand Forks

*Vermilion
R.*

VERMILION RANGE

Grand Portage Trail

*Misquah
Hills*

Grand
Portage

Crookston

*Lower Red
Lake*

*Vermilion
Lake*

Babbitt

Bemidji

Virginia

Hibbing

MESABI RANGE

St. Louis R.

*LAKE
SUPERIOR*

*Cass
Lake*

*Lake
Itasca*

*Leech
Lake*

Grand
Rapids

Mississippi R.

Silver Bay

Two Harbors

Fargo

Duluth

Moorhead

Cloquet

Superior

MICH.

Fergus
Falls

Brainerd

Cuyuna Range

Snake R.

NORTH DAKOTA

Alexandria

Sauk Centre

St. Croix R.

Kensington

*Big Stone
Lake*

De Graff

St. Cloud

WISCONSIN

Willmar

*Falls of
St. Anthony*

Stillwater

Minneapolis
Ft. Snelling
Shakopee
Belle Plaine
Henderson
Le Sueur
St. Peter

St. Paul

Savage

Carver

New
Prague

Cannon R.

Northfield

Red Wing

*Lake
Pepin*

SOUTH DAKOTA

Minnesota R.

Faribault

New Ulm

Mankato
Waseca
Mapleton

Blue Earth R.

Owatonna

Rochester

Winona

Mississippi R.

La Crosse

Pipestone

Austin

IOWA

ILL.

MINNESOTA

0   25   50   75   100
Miles

Harold Faye

CONTENTS

LIST OF ILLUSTRATIONS

Maps

PREFACE

THE EARLIER VERSION of this book, titled *Minnesota: A Bicentennial History*, was published in 1977 as part of the States and the Nation series. Like it, this volume is not intended to be a comprehensive history, but rather a survey that emphasizes the historical interplay of Minnesotans and their ever-changing environment. During the score of years that has elapsed since the book first appeared, I have continued teaching, researching, and writing the history of my adopted state. Like all historians engaged in the everlasting quest to have the last word, I have strived to keep apace of the elusive present.

Much has happened in Minnesota and elsewhere in the last twenty years. As the cumulative effects of events have evolved into trends, perspectives about the past have been adjusted. Some aspects of Minnesota's development, such as concern for environmental protection and accelerating metropolitanism, have demonstrated strong continuity. But others have featured changes far greater than those generally anticipated in the bicentennial year. Certainly, the conservative resurgence has altered the way Minnesotans collectively look at their relationship with government.

In preparing this edition I have both revised and expanded the original book. Certain aspects have been changed to reflect today's perspective, scholarship, and word usage. The coverage of the last two decades concentrates on recent economic and political developments.

The writing of this history has been greatly facilitated by the extensive collections of the Minnesota Historical Society and the holdings of the Marilyn J. Lass Center for Minnesota Studies at Mankato State University. I am particularly grateful to Robert (Skip) Drake, site manager of the Minnesota Historical Society's Forest History Center at Grand Rapids, and Deborah L. Miller, research supervisor of the Minnesota Historical Society. Both read and critiqued portions of the manuscript and assisted in other ways. Jean A. Brookins, the Minnesota Historical Society's assistant director for publications and research, and Anne R. Kaplan, editor of *Minnesota History*, kindly suggested sources of information. Dana H. Miller of the Mineland Division of the Iron Range Resources and Rehabilitation Board cordially answered many of my questions about the iron industry and arranged tours of two taconite plants for me.

In obtaining information on Minnesota's forest industries I benefited from the assistance of a number of individuals. John Krantz and Bruce Zumbahlen of the Forestry Division of the Minnesota Department of Natural Resources graciously responded to my inquiries. Jack LaVoy, executive vice president of both the Minnesota Forest Industries and the Minnesota Timber Producers Association, gave me invaluable insights into present-day forestry. Bob Behr, area forestry coordinator of the Forestry Division of Blandin Paper Company, introduced me to the current forest harvesting technology and helped explain a number of the technical aspects of forestry. Ronald A. Herbig, the supervisor of employee relations, and Alan Barse, both of the Potlatch Corporation Oriented Strand Board Plant in Grand Rapids, were genial hosts during my plant tour. John Chell, manager of public relations for the Blandin Paper Company, provided information on the forest industry, and Jack I. Rajala and John Rajala of the Rajala Companies at Deer River enthusiastically explained recent changes in wood-products production and marketing.

I gained a better understanding of recent developments in the taconite industry by visiting with Wayne E. Brandt, the president of the Iron Mining Association of Minnesota. The highlight of my taconite research was a personal tour conducted by John Rowe of the National Steel Pellet Company's mine and plant at Keewatin. I benefited immensely from his extensive knowledge about the transition of Minnesota's iron industry during his thirty-five years of experience with it.

Several of my Mankato State University colleagues assisted in various ways. Bruce L. Larson, professor of history, facilitated my understanding of Scandinavian aspects of Minnesota's history. Peter Jarnstrom, the interlibrary loan librarian, was enthusiastic and prompt in processing my requests, and Alan O. Wiese, professor of political science, shared his research on Minnesota gambling with me. In readying the manuscript I received invaluable assistance from Yvonne Schmeling, administrative secretary of the College of Graduate Studies, whose typing and computer skills are greatly appreciated.

I also appreciate the assistance and interest of James L. Mairs, vice president of W. W. Norton. He edited the manuscript, helped in locating and selecting illustrations, and cordially directed all stages of the book's production. Nearly all of the illustrations were obtained from the splendid photographic collection of the Minnesota Historical Society. Obtaining them was greatly facilitated by the enthusiastic cooperation of various Minnesota Historical Society personnel. In particular I thank Bonnie G. Wilson, Curator of Sound and Visual Collections, Ann Christensen and Angie Noyes of the copy center, and Bridgit White of the photo lab.

Lastly, I thank my children, Barbara and Bill, for their continued encouragement and support.

—WILLIAM E. LASS
Mankato, Minnesota
November 1996

MINNESOTA

A
HISTORY

1

THE LAND AND FIRST PEOPLE

DURING THE SPRING of 1965, Minnesota reeled under a succession of blizzards, floods, and tornadoes. Through it all the state legislature debated daylight saving time with great fervor. Residents took it all in stride, quipping that Minnesotans were people with snow in their yards and water in the basements of their roofless houses who did not know what time it was. The experience reminded them of nature's impact throughout the state's history.

Minnesotans have always been close to nature. The geographic forces that influenced the past are still very much a part of their lives, for geography is active and evolving. Minnesotans have been shaped by the land, and they in turn have shaped it. Through this interaction the people and the institutions of today's Minnesota have emerged.

Minnesota's bountiful waters have molded the state's character just as surely as the search for scarce water has influenced much of the Great Plains and the American Southwest. Because Minnesota's waters contribute to three distinct drainage basins, the state is sometimes called the "Mother of Three Seas." Most of the state's land is drained by the Mississippi and its tributaries, which flow to the Gulf of Mexico; but the land that lies to the north and west is drained northward to Hudson Bay, while the area about Lake Superior lies in the Gulf of St. Lawrence drainage. If Minnesota had been landlocked, her history would be far different: the water connections were the paths to the interior for French and British explorers and for the American frontiersmen, and they are plied yet today by modern vessels.

The Mississippi River flows from its small beginnings in Lake Itasca past Bemidji, Grand Rapids, St. Cloud, over the Falls of St. Anthony in Minneapolis, on past Hastings, Red Wing, Winona, and out of Minnesota on to the gulf. It was important to the Indians who plied it for hundreds of years before white men set eyes upon it, but they did not comprehend its grandeur. Tribes living along its banks called it by various names and used that portion of it which served their purposes; but white men popularized the name Mississippi, an Algonquin word that, when applied to rivers, meant "great water."

Those who traveled on the Mississippi River in Minnesota found that when they reached the Falls of St. Anthony, they had to portage before they could resume navigation. Thus the falls were the practical head of Mississippi River navigation. Indians congregated at the falls; fur traders built their posts there. This in turn led the United States Army to build its first installation in Minnesota—Fort Snelling—near the falls. Two of Minnesota's greatest industries, sawmilling and flour milling, developed about the Falls of St. Anthony because of the water power available there. When manmade aqueducts, dams, and canals threatened to destroy the falls, they were dressed with a concrete apron that makes them look today very much like a large spillway. More than any other geographic feature, the Falls of St. Anthony contributed to the development of the state's only truly metropolitan area.

The Mississippi below the Falls of St. Anthony has always been more or less navigable, but it has not always had a deep channel. Steamboats, which were the heart of Minnesota's economy for almost half a century, often had to stop running by August or early September because the river was so low. The river, like the falls, has been altered: the Army Corps of Engineers must provide a nine-foot navigation channel. The project, dating from 1928, has stimulated commercial barge traffic, but it has created problems that distress ecologically-minded Minnesotans and Wisconsinites. Because the deposits of dredged silt that were piled onshore posed serious threats to vegetation and wildlife habitat, environmentally safer techniques were developed by the River Resources Forum, a cooperative arrangement between the Corps of Engineers and the affected states. Through this effort and such agencies as the Minnesota-Wisconsin Boundary Area Commission, which was created in 1965,

Minnesotans have struggled to bring about an awareness of the need to achieve a balance between economic use of the river and preservation of its natural features.

The Mississippi River above the falls was a major canoe route for the fur traders, and it had its steamboat era in the 1860s and 1870s in the St. Cloud–Little Falls area, but it is best known for the years of mystery surrounding its source. In their struggle for empire in North America, the great powers of Europe—France, Great Britain, and Spain—used the Mississippi as a natural boundary to demark their claims even though its source was unknown. At the close of the Revolutionary War, Great Britain and the United States made the unknown source of the river an important factor in determining the northwestern boundary of American claims. After years of wrangling, the boundary was settled diplomatically, resulting in that odd configuration of the northern boundary of Minnesota known as the Northwest Angle. Not until 1832 did Henry Rowe Schoolcraft trace the Mississippi to its origin in Lake Itasca, about thirty miles southwest of Bemidji. Schoolcraft put together knowledge about the nature of the Mississippi, which whites had collected piecemeal—often from Indians—since the Spaniard Hernando de Soto first saw the river in 1541.

Despite the ravages of steamboatmen who cut untold quantities of wood for fuel along its banks, and lumbermen who leveled the white pine along the Mississippi above the falls, the river has retained much of its natural beauty. The broad valley, the swiftly moving water, and the verdant islands and banks are not so greatly changed from the time of early explorers, and there remain places along the river where there is no sound other than that of flowing water or leaves moving in a summer breeze. The Mississippi, like many of Minnesota's other waters, offers the opportunity to be with nature—something that means a great deal to Minnesotans.

The longest tributary to the Mississippi in Minnesota is the Minnesota River, which drains much of southern Minnesota and runs in a rough V from Big Stone Lake on the South Dakota border to its juncture with the Mississippi several miles below St. Anthony Falls. The French called it St. Pierre's River; British and early Americans, St. Peter's. The Dakota Indians, however, had a more descriptive name, "Minnesota," whose literal translation is whitish water. Because of the silt it carries, the stream has a cloudy appearance. Missionaries translated the name as "somewhat clouded water," which prompted some historians to interpret that romantically to mean "sky-tinted water." In recent times, Minnesota, because of its many lakes, has been heavily promoted as the "land of sky-blue water." This has led to a widespread assumption that the advertising slogan is the meaning of the state's name. The Dakota name was given to Minnesota Territory, and three years later Congress, responding to a petition from the territorial legislature, officially changed the river's name from St. Peter's to the Minnesota.

The Minnesota, like the Mississippi, was an important route for fur traders and explorers and was thought by both the French and the British to be a possible link in the fabled Northwest Passage—the mythical all-water route through the continent. The beauty and fertility of the land in the Minnesota River Valley was extolled from the beginning of its exploration in accounts of men such as Jonathan Carver, Joseph Nicollet, and William Hypolitus Keating. When the valley was wrested from the Dakota by the United States government in the famous treaties of 1851 and subsequently opened for settlement, throngs of pioneers rushed to establish claims in "Suland."

The Minnesota River provided pioneers with access to southern Minnesota and was plied by steamboats in the years before railroads, but it has never really been profitable for commercial navigation purposes. Steamboats could usually ascend no farther than New Ulm or Mankato in early spring when the water was high, and by late June the head of navigation would be yet farther downstream—at St. Peter, Henderson, Chaska, or Shakopee. Despite numerous suggestions and proposals for river improvement over the years, only the very lower portions have been improved enough to permit barge traffic. In recent times Savage has become headquarters for huge grain terminals, which are fed by caravans of trucks from throughout southern Minnesota, and the barges haul the grain downstream from there.

The St. Croix River, yet another major tributary to the Mississippi and part of the Minnesota-Wisconsin boundary, was followed by fur traders and explorers as they moved from the north-south highway of the Mississippi to the east-west thoroughfare of the Great Lakes. Because of the immense stands of white pine on its upper reaches, the St. Croix Valley was one of the first areas to be claimed when the land was legally opened to settlement. And at Stillwater, lumbering's "Queen of the St. Croix," a loose assemblage of Yankee lumbermen, fur traders, and other frontier boosters met in 1848 at the Stillwater Convention, which led to the formation of Minnesota Territory. Their action earned Stillwater the reputation as the "Birthplace of Minnesota."

The Upper St. Croix, one of eight original components of the National Rivers System under the federal Wild and Scenic Rivers Act of 1968, is one of the most scenic rivers on the continent. Its cascading waters, sometimes clifflike banks, and numerous parks and natural areas have become focal points for outdoor activities—fishing, camping, canoeing, hiking, climbing, cross-country skiing, snowshoeing—which are important to Minnesotans not only recreationally but economically as well.

Minnesota shares the St. Croix Valley with Wisconsin because Congress believed that the river was a natural boundary, a sentiment not shared by the original settlers of the St. Croix. They believed that there should be unity in the valley, and they fought vigorously to have the entire valley left outside Wisconsin (and thus potentially in Minnesota) when Wisconsin became a state. The movement failed, but the sense of regional identity remains. For once, hindsight and foresight agree, for political unity as envisioned by the pioneer politicians of the St. Croix Valley would be an obvious advantage to the many thousands of Wisconsinites who work in the Twin Cities.

Every river has a valley, but the dictates of custom have reserved a special place for the Red River Valley. It is "the Valley" to Minnesotans. Only the uninitiated call it by more formal names. Students of geography feel compelled to refer to the Red River as the Red River of the North to distinguish it from the Red River that separates Oklahoma and Texas. And they also must explain that the name comes from the spectacular sunset-lit Red Lakes whence the main tributary to the Red River flows.

The Great Plains are flat, but even Kansans or Nebraskans will concede that they have not seen flat until they have seen the Valley. The rich black soil is the bed of the gigantic glacial Lake Agassiz, whose remnants are still evident in Red Lake, Lake of the Woods, and Lake Winnipeg in Manitoba. Furs and land were the magnets that drew settlers to the Red River Valley. Usually there was a certain order in the frontier process, with the fur traders passing on before the pioneer farmers arrived. But because of the visionary Scottish earl Lord Selkirk, this pattern was violated in the Red River area. Selkirk brought English, Scottish, and Swiss settlers to his New World colony near Winnipeg as early as 1812, at a time when fur traders believed that part of the world to be theirs. The Selkirkers found the soil fertile enough, but they also found hostile mixed-bloods, droughts, floods, grasshoppers, and great suffering and tragedy. Many of these disillusioned colonists fled upstream into the United States, and thus the Valley became one of the paths into

The *Dakota* (above) and other small steamboats and barges were operated on the
Red River in the 1860s and 1870s.
Courtesy of the Minnesota Historical Society

Minnesota. Later it was the route of the famed Red River carts used by
American traders who linked St. Paul and Fort Garry (Winnipeg) in commercial alliance long before the railroad age. But the Valley is best known
for the advent of bonanza farming in the 1870s, when, in the golden age
of wheat, it became one of the greatest breadbaskets in the United States.
Today the Valley is recognized as the producer and processor of a diversity of agricultural products—wheat, sugar beets, sunflowers, potatoes,
canola, and a variety of vegetables.

The state's other great waterway in the Hudson Bay drainage area is
the system of lakes and streams connecting North Lake west of Lake
Superior to Lake of the Woods—the border watershed that is the legal
boundary separating Minnesota and Canada. French and British explorers, in their persistent search for the Northwest Passage, traveled over the
boundary waters and, as they did so, claimed vast hinterlands for their
countries. For a long time these waterways were the world's greatest fur-

trade route, and the lore of the area speaks of the voyageurs who paddled hundreds of miles through unmapped wilderness in search of beaver. Much later these waters were important to lumbermen for the movement of logs and the processing of lumber and paper-pulp products. Today, the meaning of the boundary water region lies beyond the diplomatic and the economic. Much of that heavily forested zone is in such areas as the Superior National Forest and Voyageurs National Park. Most of the Boundary Waters Canoe Area within Superior National Forest is a designated wilderness that provides a glimpse of this land the way it was before the advance of European civilization.

The St. Louis River is the dominant stream in that part of Minnesota which lies in the Great Lakes watershed. Fur traders used the river to move from Lake Superior to the Mississippi by way of the Savannah Portage, and they also traveled up it and then down the Vermilion River to reach the boundary waters. Like most of the rivers that drain into Lake Superior, however, its natural head of navigation is only several miles inland, and those coming off Lake Superior into the St. Louis were soon challenged by a series of cataracts that rushed through the dells that are now part of Jay Cooke State Park southwest of Duluth. Voyageurs could portage their canoes around the falls, but no one ventured onto the St. Louis with larger boats. Millions of logs were moved down it, but even they could not be passed through the dells without sluices. As a result, important sawmilling centers such as Cloquet developed upstream to challenge Duluth, the Lake Superior port situated not far from the outlet of the St. Louis.

Minnesotans who travel to less watery places will often find strangers staring at their automobile license plates and asking: "Are there really ten thousand lakes in Minnesota?" A precise answer would be, "No, there are actually fifteen thousand two hundred ninety-one." Minnesotans have always made an effort to count the lakes, but they have not been consistent in defining one. The ten-thousand-lakes tradition is rooted in the promotional literature of Minnesota Territory—a tradition reinforced by mapmakers and geologists. The motto was put on the license plates nearly half a century ago as an inexpensive and effective way of publicizing one of Minnesota's outstanding features. But since that time the definers have been at work. Today in Minnesota, any basin of at least ten acres that is partially or completely filled with water is a lake.

Not every Minnesotan fishes, but it often seems as if that were so. Many Minnesotans will settle for nothing less than the best game fish—

The Dayton Company's Aquatennial float, Minneapolis, 1941. The annual aquatennial celebrates the city's water tradition. Minneapolis translates literally from a
combination of Dakota Indian and Greek words as "water city."
Courtesy of the Minnesota Historical Society

the walleye, which is the official state fish. They shun the bullheads,
which are so common in the shallow lakes of southern Minnesota, leaving
those "Iowa trout" to Iowans, children, and other amateurs. Minnesotans
are inclined to make the most of what they have, so the small community of Waterville as the self-proclaimed "Bullhead Capital of the World"
celebrates "Bullhead Days" every summer and hosts hundreds of Iowans
who make regular pilgrimages to the nearby bullhead-infested lakes.

A visitor to the state might sometimes get the impression from over-
hearing Minnesotans that there is only one lake in the state: "the Lake."
On summer weekends and holidays many communities seem deserted as
Minnesotans throng to "the lake"—whichever one is most convenient—
pulling motorboats behind them. Long before recreational boating
became popular, most of the lakeshores fell into private hands, so public
access has been a lively issue in Minnesota. Major lakes now have public

access, but often not much more than a spot from which to launch or land a boat. The motorboat has for many become almost a necessity. Motorboating and its accompanying waterskiing boomed during the last half-century, but there also has been a sharp revival in canoeing. The birch-bark canoes of the Ojibwe Indians and the voyageurs have been replaced by aluminum craft, and that which once was a necessary mode of transportation has become a form of recreation and relaxation. Minnesotans find that canoeing toughens the body while it soothes the mind—that it has a naturalness in harmony with the elements.

If there is a single distinctive lake in Minnesota, it is Lake Superior, which Minnesota shares with Wisconsin, Michigan, and Canada. Lake Superior, one of the world's largest freshwater lakes, has a certain awesomeness. To the Ojibwe it was "Kitchi Gamma"—great water—and to Henry Wadsworth Longfellow in *The Song of Hiawatha* it was "shining Big-Sea-Water." The surface of the lake can be mirror smooth one day, and on the next roll in waves violent enough to break up the largest ships.

Split Rock Lighthouse on the North Shore Drive of Lake Superior, which was operated from 1910–69, is now a historic site in a state park.
Courtesy of the Minnesota Historical Society

The beaches of Lake Superior are strewn with curious flat, oval rocks that fit into the palm of the hand—rocks fashioned by thousands of years of water action. Even the shores suggest its enormity. In places such as Palisade Head the lake laps and pounds away at the foot of vertical cliffs rising hundreds of feet to the rocky terrain above. Tradition has it that Ojibwe warriors, as a test of manliness, tried to shoot arrows up the escarpment.

French adventurers first crossed Lake Superior in the mistaken belief that it led to yet greater seas, and for nearly two centuries it was navigated by French, British, and American traders who were the cutting edge of the white man's inexorable push into the wilderness. Later the lake was important in the movement of Minnesota wheat, lumber, and iron ore to eastern markets; and in recent times, with the completion of the St. Lawrence Seaway in 1959, the world has been brought to Minnesota's door at Duluth, the western terminus of the seaway. Minnesota seems to be a midland state, a notion dispelled when one stands at the waterfront in Duluth and watches freighters bearing the flags of Japan, Norway, the Netherlands, Great Britain, and a host of other nations.

Lake Superior is used for boating and fishing, but most visitors see it from the strikingly beautiful North Shore Drive running from Duluth to the Canadian boundary. Every summer the highway, from which one can almost constantly see the lake, is filled with thousands of vehicles and sightseers. There is, however, a less attractive side to the Lake Superior story. The lake, because of its great breadth and depth and the absence of major industrial centers on its shores, was unspoiled by manmade pollutants for many years. But for nearly two decades after a taconite plant was opened at Silver Bay in 1955 it was threatened by vast deposits of taconite waste that were shoved into its waters. This pollution of Lake Superior became a highly emotional issue—a classic case of conflict between economic interests and environmental concerns.

Minnesotans' appreciation of the value of their environment is not a recent development. The first state park, Lake Itasca, was started in 1891 before the lumbering frontier had run its rampant course; public funds purchased thousands of acres of land to protect the area about the headwaters of the Mississippi. Visitors to Lake Itasca State Park today can see virgin stands of red pine and view the source of the Mississippi much as it presented itself to Henry Rowe Schoolcraft more than a century and a half ago. The same principle that guided the selection of Itasca as a park site before its desecration has been applied to other sites in Minnesota.

Throughout the state, one may visit parks that preserve virgin stands of timber, waterfalls and unimproved streams, and natural vegetation.

Minnesota's frontier economic diversity was based on its three greatest natural resources—fertile soil, forests, and iron ore. There is a tendency, though it is not accurate, to associate the first one with southern Minnesota and the other two with the northern part of the state. Minnesota, in a broad sense, has only two parts—north and south—in much the same way as South Dakota has an east-of-the-Missouri area and a west-of-the-Missouri, or Nebraska has a south-of-the-Platte area and a north-of-the-Platte. In Minnesota, however, there is no physical demarcation separating north and south. There are, instead, rough categorizations suggested by the shape of the state—which is nearly twice as long north-south as it is wide east-west—and solidified through customs and activities. Minnesotans think of the Twin Cities as being the borderland between north and south, when in fact Minneapolis and St. Paul are well south of the state's midpoint, near Brainerd. But to southern Minnesotans Brainerd is north, because there is no well-developed concept of central Minnesota. Northern Minnesotans, who admittedly are closer to the North Pole than are southern Minnesotans, delight in promoting their regional identity.

North means an area not so rich in terms of dollars nor so heavily settled as the south; but it also means more lakes, more forests, and more wilderness areas. The south in many ways is more like neighboring Iowa than it is like northern Minnesota. It is predominantly intensively cultivated farmland that is very much a part of the Corn Belt.

North and south in Minnesota are not all-inclusive. The Red River Valley, which is really in the northwest, is within the geographical north but not the colloquial north. It is the Valley, agriculturally oriented and therefore unlike most of the forest and mining sections of the north. Likewise, there tends to be a north-of-north area in much the same way that the United States has a west of the west: if Wyoming is west, California is somehow beyond the west. In the same way, Minnesota has a boundary area that is usually described in those terms. People traveling from southern Minnesota who say they are going north really mean someplace like Bemidji or Grand Rapids, but if they go farther north, to Baudette or International Falls, they are "up on the boundary."

Other parts of the north also have a regional identity. Shape and promotional literature clearly identify as "the Arrowhead" that northeastern triangle bounded by Lake Superior, the St. Louis River, and the international boundary. And Minnesotans talk of "the Range" and "the Range Towns." The Range is not a cattle range, nor a mountain range, like the Big Horns or the Grand Tetons; rather, it is the Mesabi Iron Range. There are, of course, three iron ranges in Minnesota—the Mesabi, the Vermilion, and the Cuyuna—but only the largest and the richest is the Range. The others, except in the very immediate locale, are always called by their proper names. As the notion of range is deeply embedded, so also is the idea of the Range Towns. It is not necessary to enumerate Chisholm, Hibbing, and Virginia. They are distinct enough, to be sure, but to Minnesotans the meaning of the Range Towns is clear.

With the exception of the northeast, where the Misquah Hills formation provides a rugged landscape, the hilly portions of the southeastern part of the state, and the Coteau des Prairies in the southwest, the land is gently rolling. These contours are the result of glaciation, for over a period of about two million years most of Minnesota was gouged, shaped, and leveled by four distinct glaciers that not only graded the land but deposited a rich topsoil as well. In the postglacial period, forests developed over about 70 percent of the state and the remainder was open prairie. The forest was an extension of the eastern forest belt that stretched from the Atlantic beyond the Mississippi. In Minnesota all of the area east of the Mississippi was forested, with the exception of the excessively swampy areas, and the forest extended west of the river irregularly for about 30 to 125 miles. Within the timbered area there were both coniferous and deciduous forest zones. The zone in which the large conifers, such as white and red pine, spruce, and tamarack, were the dominant trees encompassed most of the area east of the Mississippi and roughly north of Pine City. There were some coniferous stands west of the Mississippi, but generally the western fringe of the forest belt from Canada south was composed of deciduous trees. At about the latitude of St. Cloud, south of the coniferous forest, the deciduous belt widened considerably. Within the deciduous zone there was one particularly distinctive area—the Big Woods, so named because of its extent and the massiveness of its trees. The Big Woods lay in an irregular triangle, its corners at St. Cloud, Mankato, and Northfield.

Minnesota's pioneer farmers first looked to the Big Woods. They had come from the forested areas of the eastern United States and western Europe, and the Big Woods, in which elm, oak, maple, and other hardwoods commonly grew more than one hundred feet tall, proved to them that the land was fertile. But these pioneers were interested in farming, not lumbering; so they cleared the land rapidly by burning, and most of the hardwood forest was soon devastated. For those today who want to know what the Big Woods were like, they may visit Nerstrand State Park, an area set aside because of its stand of virgin timber.

Because of the coniferous forest, much of Minnesota was a lumberman's frontier—a frontier that started before agriculture and then developed apace with the farming frontier. The lumberman's assault on the vast stands of white pine undid thousands of years of nature's bounty in less than a century. As the coniferous forests were cleared, the agricultural belt pushed northward into the cutover area, so that today the relative proportions of forested and open land have been nearly reversed from that of those zones before settlement.

Iron mining, Minnesota's third frontier activity, developed within the coniferous forests. All three of the iron ranges were in heavily timbered regions; when iron ore was found on the Mesabi, its discoverers scraped away layers of pine needles to reveal the iron-laden red soil beneath. Pine trees were stripped away as the great open-pit mines of the Mesabi were developed, and all of the pioneer mining companies operated lumber camps for a time.

Pioneer farmers were not attracted to Minnesota's prairie area. Perhaps they believed that it, like the rest of the Great Plains, was the Great American Desert. Because there were other places with wood and water, they saw no need to challenge a treeless land that lacked navigable streams. Not until the advent of railroads, liberal land laws, and an enticing wheat market in the 1870s and 1880s were farmers led out of the wooded areas onto the prairie.

Little of the prairie described so aptly by Ole Rölvaag in his *Giants in the Earth* remains. There are a few small tracts in Minnesota that settlers did not disturb because they were too rocky, and there are some others— such as the small preserve about the Jeffers Petroglyphs and the Ordway Prairie near Glenwood—that were deliberately left as pioneers found them. Although the prairie is now mostly cropped and trees have been planted where none grew naturally, there is yet a recognizable openness and contour to the land. Looking across the corn and soybean fields, one still sees the land roll and slope gently to distant horizons, and the trees in shelter belts or around the farmsteads seem artificial. Man-planted prairie trees are like so many large cornstalks, symmetrically arranged in neat rows, reaching for a sky that seems much too high for them.

North Dakotans and Canadians understand Minnesota's climate, but

In 1936 a touring car on the Gunflint Trail between Grand Marais and Gunflint
Lake passed through a fairly typical coniferous forest.
Courtesy of the Minnesota Historical Society

Iowans are glad that Minnesota stands between them and northern winters. And people in yet warmer climes enjoy the anecdote about the Minnesota farmer who was informed that, as a result of a land resurvey, he was now living in Wisconsin instead of Minnesota. "Thank God, no more cold winters," he wrote in his diary. In like vein, Mark Twain wrote that the coldest winter he ever spent was a summer in Duluth, and Duluthians themselves tell about the cab driver who, when asked by a visitor, "How is summer in Duluth?" responded, "I don't know yet. I've only lived here fourteen months."

Territorial newspapers, promotional literature, and letters sent back east by new Minnesotans exuberantly proclaimed the invigorating healthfulness of the climate and the purity of the dry winter air. During the 1860s and 1870s health seekers by the thousands sought restoration at Minnesota's resorts and spas. Even after medical opinion shattered the notion that climate neither spawned nor discouraged disease, Minnesota resorts and spas continued to exist, but with a changing emphasis. Resorts originally began in the southern part of the state and along the Mississippi River, but they gradually spread northward into the cutover area left by the lumbermen, springing up alongside the deep, cold glacial lakes so ideally suited to game fish.

Modern Minnesotans are more subtle than the pioneer boosters; when they boast, they speak of the theater of seasons—the verdant growth of spring, the water sports of summer, the brilliantly colored autumn leaves, and the diverse winter sports. Minnesotans have adapted to their climate. They ski, and they send skiers to the Winter Olympics. They invented the snowmobile and have used it until it has become an ecological issue. They fish through the ice, entering into the spirit of it so wholeheartedly that entire villages of fish houses, ranging from shacks to carpeted, heated cabins, spring up almost before the lakes are completely frozen over. Hockey and ice-skating are favorite winter sports. St. Paul has since 1886 sponsored a Winter Carnival complete with King Boreas and oftentimes a spectacular ice palace.

Minnesotans nevertheless are still defensive about their climate, and they were offended during World War II when a newscaster, in attempting to put the awfulness of winter on the Russian front into meaningful terms, said that Minnesotans at least would understand it. More recently, in response to the metric trend, weather forecasters began citing temperatures in both Fahrenheit and Celsius scales, and many Minnesotans protested. On the Celsius scale, Minnesota could easily record temperatures below zero most of the winter.

There was more truth in the likening of Minnesota to Russia than Minnesotans care to admit, for the temperatures of St. Paul, Duluth, and Moscow are roughly comparable. Like all the interior land masses of the Northern Hemisphere, Minnesota is a land of temperature extremes. Winter's cold has reached a low of -60°F, but summer's heat has soared as high as 114 degrees. Minnesota is dry compared to Seattle, but wet by the standards of Miles City, Montana; and during all seasons the winds blow across Minnesota's flat terrain. Windiness, like the other elements, is relative. Most of Minnesota is windier than the "Windy City" of Chicago, but not as windy as North Platte, Nebraska; Clinton, Oklahoma; or hundreds of other places on the Great Plains.

Climate, however, is not simply something that people live in. Climate is formative. Cold winters made possible the furs that attracted Minnesota's first businessmen. Lumbermen used the snow and ice to move logs economically. Hard winters and short growing seasons showed immigrant farmers from milder climates that the customary plants, animals, and methods were not suited to Minnesota. Through trial and error, and

Cold weather and sometimes heavy snows are characteristic of Minnesota's winters. This photo (February 8, 1936) is of a crew struggling to open state Highway 60 between Mountain Lake and Windom.
Courtesy of the Minnesota Historical Society

Ice harvesting on Minnesota's lakes was commonplace until the use of block ice for cooling was replaced by refrigeration. This photo was taken on Whitefish Lake in Crow Wing County during the 1920s.
Courtesy of the Minnesota Historical Society

with professional assistance from the University of Minnesota and the United States Department of Agriculture, Minnesotans shifted from winter to spring wheat, developed regional varieties of alfalfa, corn, and soybeans, and adapted dairying to the rigors of the land. As agriculture has been adapted to climate, so too have industry and all other aspects of life. Cold winters and hot summers necessitate large heating and cooling plants, more insulation, and the construction of basements. Because of the demands of both heat and air-conditioning, there are heavy drains on energy. Minnesota has not produced its own supply of energy since the days when wood was the common fuel.

Even in their politics and government, Minnesotans have been influenced by geography, for geographic factors were determinants in the drawing of political boundaries and in the development of diverse economic sections with all the attendant political interplay. Sectionalism is as old as Minnesota politics, stemming from the time when a small group of fur traders and lumbermen, loyal to the small area between the Mississippi and the St. Croix, channeled their sectional cohesiveness into a political activism that divorced them from Wisconsin and led to the formation of Minnesota Territory.

Since Minnesota became a state in 1858, north-south division has been the most evident. It originated because of the great length of the state and was nurtured as the interests of a predominantly agricultural people collided with those of people whose livelihood depended on shipping, iron mining, and tourism. Lawmakers from the north and from the south have always been conscious of their own sectional interests; thus, the legislature has a long history of political compromises that have affected numerous acts and plans of state agencies. Through the years roads, schools, and state institutions have been built or located in open recognition of the natural interests of both north and south.

Urbanization has created yet another kind of sectionalism. With industrialization in the generation following the Civil War, Minneapolis and St. Paul became the core of an urban area that far surpassed any other in the state. Because of this single large metropolitan area, Minnesotans have developed concepts of "the Cities" and "outstate." To go to the Cities means to go anywhere in the metropolitan area, be it Minneapolis, St. Paul, or one of the numerous suburbs, but the boundaries of the outstate are not quite so clear—except that anything removed from the immediate environs of the metropolitan area is in it. If outstaters take the term too literally, they are offended, but outstate does not really mean that there is an "instate" in Minnesota; it only suggests that modern Minnesota has both a rural and an urban identity. And it further suggests that the rural-urban character has caused some strain. Throughout much of the state's history, metropolitan residents resented the political clout of the outstate legislators—often thought of as farmers even if they happened to be lawyers, doctors, or businessmen. But rapid population growth in the urban area and one person—one vote representation have reversed the roles. Today there is concern in outstate Minnesota about what sometimes appears to be the oppressive will of the majority, which has resulted in the use of state funds for improvements or programs in the Twin Cities, something justified by metropolitan legislators on the grounds that "What's good for the Cities is good for the state."

The land that is now Minnesota was first inhabited thousands of years ago by the ancestors of modern American Indians. America's first people migrated from Asia. Making their way across Beringia, the land bridge that then connected Russia and Alaska, they gradually moved southward through glacial corridors. Their migration, which evidently spanned a period of several thousand years, was ended by the inundation of Beringia when the glacial meltdown raised ocean levels.

Archaeologists generally agree that Indians living before about 5000 B.C. were of the Big Game or Paleo culture. Their livelihood depended on the hunting of large animals, such as mastodon, giant bison, and giant beaver. Living before knowledge of the bow and arrow, they relied on spears, whose points were shaped by chipping rather than grinding stone. Over a long period of time the spear was made a more effective weapon by the development and popularization of the atlatl, or spear thrower. The Paleo Age ended with the extinction of the large mammals. The disappearance of these animals was apparently caused by a complex of climactic and vegetative changes, but it was obviously accelerated by overhunting.

Evidence of Paleo Indian activity has been derived mainly from artifacts and hunting sites, but there has been one significant discovery of human bones. In 1933 an amateur archaeologist found the skeletal remains of a Paleo Indian and associated projectile points and knives at the southern outlet of glacial Lake Agassiz. Browns Valley Man, as the subject has come to be called, was an adult male who lived about 6000 B.C.

Browns Valley Man was older than the skeleton found near Pelican Rapids in 1931. In the terminology of anthropologists and archaeologists, those remains of a teenage girl were identified as Pelican Rapids Man. Radiocarbon dating indicates that she lived somewhere between 5000 B.C. and 1000 B.C. The most recent date would clearly place her near the end of the Eastern Archaic culture, which succeeded the Paleo Age.

Ranging over four millennia, the Eastern Archaic culture was marked by significant advances. In this period hunters preyed on modern animals with projectiles fashioned by grinding stones. Their hunting and warfare were revolutionized by the introduction of the bow and arrow. They also developed such woodworking tools as stone axes and adzes and made some metal implements by cold-hammering copper. Evidently the first Indians to use copper were those who lived near the deposits in Upper Michigan, but pieces of copper were also found in glacial deposits. Probably through intertribal trading, the copper culture was extended into Minnesota. In 1966 a major copper culture site was excavated in Mille Lacs—Kathio State Park

Based on artifactitious evidence, archaeologists have concluded that the transition from the Eastern Archaic Age to the Woodland culture happened about 500 B.C. Like its predecessor, the Woodland culture was a hunting and gathering society, but it was clearly distinguishable from the Eastern Archaic because of the extensive use of pottery and burial mounds. Numerous pottery finds have enabled archaeologists not only to identify various phases of the Woodland culture but to gain insights into intertribal trade patterns, the use of natural resources, and a sense of aesthetics as well. Woodland burial mounds, which have been found throughout Minnesota, usually contained human remains, tools, ornaments, and food. The characteristically low, conical mounds were normally about thirty-five feet in diameter and two feet high. Before the incursion of white farmers there were some effigy mounds in southeastern Minnesota, which represented the western extension of an effigy mound phase centered in southern Wisconsin.

Most of the thousands of mounds built in Minnesota were destroyed when pioneers cultivated the land. However, some of the largest ones were preserved, such as those in St. Paul's Mounds Park. Grand Mound, near International Falls, is maintained as a historic site by the Minnesota Historical Society. This massive structure is nearly 140 feet long, 100 feet wide, and about 40 feet high. The mounds have provided invaluable insights into Woodland lifestyle, social structure, and religious concepts.

Large Woodland Indian burial mounds are located in Mounds Park, St. Paul.
Courtesy of the Minnesota Historical Society

By about 800 A.D. Woodland Indians were gathering wild rice throughout the Minnesota range. Use of this grain, which supplemented the traditional hunting mode, caused a population surge by providing a greater and more constant food source.

About 1000 A.D. the Woodland culture in southern Minnesota was replaced by the Mississippian. Demonstrating Mexican influences, the Mississippian emphasized agriculture by cultivating such crops as maize, beans, squash, and sunflowers. Their farming was augmented by fishing, gathering and hunting. While tilling small fields in river bottomlands, they had easy access to massive buffalo herds.

The origin and meaning of the Jeffers Petroglyphs in Cottonwood County is a mystery, but archaeologists have determined they were carved by Indians who lived in southwestern Minnesota before the Dakota.

Courtesy of the Minnesota Historical Society

When the French first entered Minnesota, the Mississippian and Woodland peoples were in a state of flux. The Mississippian Indians moved southwestward to the Missouri River, where they were organized and identified by such modern tribes as the Ponca and Otoe. Modern tribes evolving from the Woodland tradition included the Dakota, Assiniboine, and Cheyenne.

Unlike previous cultures, the activities of modern tribes were documented by written records. Although the French obviously did not fully understand Indian civilization, they nonetheless observed Indian life before it had been greatly affected by European influences. Thus, their accounts significantly augment archaeological and anthropological evidence.

The Dakota and Ojibwe were Minnesota's dominant modern tribes. When first encountered by the French, the Dakota were dwelling in the forests of northwestern Wisconsin and eastern and northern Minnesota. Composed of seven council fires, or tribes, they lived as "allies," which was the meaning of their name. Although they used the name Dakota to describe themselves, in time they generally came to be identified as Sioux.

As the French advanced westward, they naturally learned from Indians about more distant tribes. They were told by the Ojibwe that the next people westward were the Nadouessioux, meaning "little viper" or "lesser enemy." The large Iroquois confederation to their east was the traditional enemy, or viper, to the Ojibwe. No doubt alert to the derogatory meaning of Nadouessioux, by the late seventeenth century the French had abridged it to the meaningless "Sioux." Following the French, the British and Americans reinforced the name Sioux to such a degree that it was widely used until comparatively recent times.

The seven Dakota groups comprised three branches—western, middle, and eastern—which as they were being dispersed developed somewhat different dialects. Using variants of Dakota, the western branch became the Lakota, and the middle division, the Nakota. Within a century of initial French contacts, the Lakota, one of the seven council fires, were ranging west of the Missouri River through the Black Hills region. Following in their wake, the Nakota, consisting of Yankton and Yanktonai, occupied the area near the Big Sioux and James Rivers in present-day eastern South Dakota.

The Dakota, who remained in Minnesota, were variously known to American government officials and settlers as Minnesota Sioux, Sioux of the Mississippi, Eastern Sioux, and Santee Sioux. Santee, which was apparently derived from the Dakota words *isan*, for knife, and *ti*, for dwell,

Dwellings in permanent Dakota villages were made of saplings, tree limbs, and bark. Photo of a painting (about 1850) by Seth Eastman, artist and Fort Snelling commandant.

Courtesy of the Minnesota Historical Society

seems to have been first commonly used by the Dakota to describe themselves about the time of the Dakota Conflict of 1862. Missionary Stephen Return Riggs wrote that the name was initially applied to the Dakota by their western kin, who may have been influenced by the residency of some Dakota at Knife Lake or the proximity of all Dakota to the "Long Knives"—the Americans. The four original council fires of the Dakota were the Mdewakanton, Wahpekute, Sisseton, and Wahpeton. Dakota history was dominated by the Mdewakanton, the mother tribe, according to Dakota tradition. Their name translates as "People of the Spirit Lake" or "People of the Mystic Lake," in reference to their occupancy on Lake Minnewaukon, which the French renamed Mille Lacs. The Wahpekute, or leaf shooters, normally lived near the Mdewakanton, and may have been the last group to divide from the mother tribe. The Sisseton ("People of the Swamp") and the Wahpeton ("Leaf Dwellers" or "Forest Dwellers") at the time of first French contacts lived north and west of Mille Lacs.

Dakota history was profoundly influenced by their relations with their neighbors and enemies—the Ojibwe. Calling themselves the Anishinabe,

This photo of an 1850 painting by Seth Eastman shows a Dakota Indian council
next to a tipi or temporary dwelling.
Courtesy of the Minnesota Historical Society

"The First People," the Ojibwe were concentrated in the Sault Ste. Marie
vicinity of Upper Michigan when the French met them. Initially the
French called them Saulteurs—people of the Sault—but soon they became
known as Chippewa, or its variant, Ojibwe. Meaning to "roast until puckered up," Ojibwe probably referred to their puckered moccasin seams that
were hardened by fire. Historically, the commonest name for them has
been Chippewa, but Ojibwe and Ojibwa now have wider acceptance.

Located between the Dakota and the French, the Ojibwe were the first
important partners of French fur traders in the Lake Superior region.
After beginning direct trade with the French, they soon seized the opportunity to become middlemen between the French and the Dakota. In this
role the Ojibwe entered Dakota lands in northeastern Minnesota beginning in the late seventeenth century. Since the Dakota benefited from
the influx of French weapons and other goods, they permitted the Ojibwe
to gather furs and hunt on their land.

The system worked as long as the Dakota depended on Ojibwe traders

Expert canoeists, the Ojibwe navigated Minnesota's lakes and streams with birch bark
canoes. This photo is of Ojibwe men on Lake Itasca during the pageant of June 2, 1933.
Courtesy of the Minnesota Historical Society

to deliver French goods, but French advancement ruined it. With the
establishment of Fort Beauharnois on Lake Pepin in 1727 and the construction of Fort St. Charles on Lake of the Woods five years later, the
French came in direct contact with the Dakota and their enemies to the
north—the Cree and Assiniboine. Angrily responding to French supplying of the Cree and Assiniboine, a Dakota war party killed some
Frenchmen on a Lake of the Woods island in 1736. Choosing to cement
their alliance with the French, the Ojibwe attacked the Dakota.

The 1736 incident opened a long period of hostilities featured by intermittent raids. Initially, because of more concentrated forces, French supplies,
and, apparently, French military advice, the Ojibwe succeeded in forcing the
Dakota southward. Fortunately for the Ojibwe, the Dakota were somewhat
disunited because the middle and western branches had migrated well away
from the conflict zone. About 1750 Ojibwe warriors struck at the heart of
Mdewakanton lands and forced the Dakota to abandon their villages on
Mille Lacs. The last major Dakota counterattack failed when they lost a skirmish fought near the mouth of the Crow Wing River in 1768.

The dome-shaped wigwam, with a sapling frame covered by birch bark, as shown in this photograph of about 1870, was a typical Ojibwe dwelling.
Courtesy of the Minnesota Historical Society

After the Crow Wing setback, the Dakota reconciled themselves to the loss of their ancestral domain. Subsequent Ojibwe advances forced the Dakota to find new homes along the Minnesota River and the Mississippi below the Falls of St. Anthony. In this range the Mdewakanton established their principal villages on the lower reaches of the Minnesota and along the Mississippi downstream to the Winona vicinity. The Wahpekute occupied the adjacent Cannon River area. Their proximity to the lower portion of the Minnesota River caused Americans to collectively call the Mdewakanton and Wahpekute the Lower Sioux. Because their villages were generally located along the Minnesota River upstream from about present-day Chaska, the Sisseton and Wahpeton came to be known as the Upper Sioux.

By about 1780 the Dakota and Ojibwe had reached an approximate military balance. Ojibwe gains after that were modest, in part because of a calamitous smallpox epidemic in northern Minnesota in 1781–82, and in part because of the British supplying of the Dakota. With British support the Dakota were able to range into the lower St. Croix valley, the Mississippi valley above the falls, and the region stretching northwestward to near the juncture of the Red and Red Lake Rivers.

The Dakota were variously affected by their movement into southern Minnesota. The Mdewakanton and Wahpekute continued to be forest people who relied on deer hunting, fishing, and the gathering of wild fruits and berries. Sometimes their hunting forays carried them into the grasslands to the west, where they killed buffalo and gathered wild potatoes and wild turnips. The lifestyle of the Sisseton and Wahpeton changed more drastically, because they became prairie hunters. From their villages on the Minnesota they could conveniently hunt buffalo on prairies to the west. Dependence on the prairie isolated them somewhat from the Mdewakanton and Wahpekute and brought them in closer contact with the Yankton. It is impossible to determine exact Dakota populations, but from 1834 to the Dakota Conflict of 1862, missionaries and government officials generally placed their number at six to seven thousand.

Like all Indian tribes the Dakota were radically changed by invading whites. Prior to the French trade they were basically self-sufficient, but the appeal of such conveniences as guns, steel knives, and hatchets, and iron kettles, blankets, and cloth, soon made them dependent on traders. While the Dakota seemingly benefited from these new goods, their civilization was debased by the introduction of hard liquor, ravaging diseases, and miscegenation.

Like other American Indians the Dakota generally clung to their traditional ways after they accepted white goods and technology, but ultimately their culture was eroded. Frontier whites tended to interpret Dakota culture from the standpoint of their own society. As a result they saw Dakota religion as wrong rather than mystifying. Coming from a monotheistic religious tradition, whites looked disparagingly on people who had a lexicon of gods and spirits. The Dakota conceived of a creating god, who had shaped the universe. But the various forces of nature—the sun, the moon, the wind, and the rain—were manifestations of other gods. Ignoring Dakota religion, whites saw them as pagans, who were likely subjects for conversion to Christianity.

Indian-white differences were epitomized by the clash between a hunting society and an agricultural one. Whites regarded hunting as an inefficient use of land and could not comprehend the degree of physical effort required. With a deeply ingrained work ethic, whites had little appreciation for a society that did not require long hours of toiling in fields and tending livestock. Their irreconcilable differences were partially responsible for the Dakota Conflict.

The Ojibwe and whites in Minnesota never warred against each other, but Ojibwe society was gradually changed by the intrusive majority white culture. As the Ojibwe expanded south and west, those who came to occupy parts of Minnesota, western Wisconsin, the Turtle Mountains area of North Dakota, and sites in northeastern Montana were generally identified as the Southwestern Ojibwe. As with the Dakota, the various Ojibwe bands shared a tribal identity because of common language, culture, and history. However, during their dissemination they lost political unity, so in Minnesota they became identified by bands at particular locations such as Leech Lake and Mille Lacs. However, in negotiating nineteenth-century treaties with them, the United States found it convenient to group bands into such divisions as the Lake Superior, Mississippi, and Pembina. Consequently, treaties had the effect of restoring some degree of political unity.

Like the Dakota and other hunting societies, the Ojibwe had a relatively small population. An 1843 census showed forty-eight hundred Ojibwe in what became Minnesota, and thirteen years later six thousand of them were reported to be living in Minnesota Territory, which would have included the Turtle Mountains band.

The Dakota and Ojibwe, like similar peoples throughout the Western Hemisphere, left an indelible impression. On a hemispheric scale American Indians contributed knowledge of crops and farming techniques, hunting, trapping, and geography. Their languages enriched and enlarged European languages, and their oral traditions became part of American literature. Dakota and Ojibwe tales influenced Henry Wadsworth Longfellow's *The Song of Hiawatha,* the most famous piece of literature inspired by the Lake Superior cultures.

Dakota and Ojibwe contributions to Minnesota place-naming are evident throughout the state. Dakota names that have been perpetuated include Chanhassen (sugar maple), Hanska (long and narrow), Mankato (blue earth), Kandiyohi (place where the buffalo fish come from), and Watonwan (fish bait). Ojibwe influences in central and northern Minnesota are shown by the naming of Bemidji (cross lake, as in having a current run across it), Chisago (large and lovely), Kanabec (snake), and Winnibigoshish (miserable, bad, filthy water).

Much of Minnesota's history has been the story of its first people, who evolved through successive cultures into modern tribes. After their initial contacts with the French, the Dakota and Ojibwe became primarily concerned with Indian-white relations.

INTERLUDE

THE VIKING MYTH

MAGNUS ERICKSON, RULER of all Norway and Sweden and a militant Catholic, received word in 1354 that the Scandinavian colonists in far-off Greenland were falling away from the faith. He dispatched Baron Paul Knutson on an expedition to bring the errant ones back into the fold. When Knutson finally reached western Greenland, he found the settlements abandoned, so he went on to Vinland on the North American continent to find the colonists. He and his men searched three or four years about the Gulf of the St. Lawrence, but to no avail. Then Knutson reasoned that the colonists might have sought a place that more nearly resembled Greenland, so he moved north along the Atlantic coast for a thousand miles until he turned the tip of Labrador and entered Hudson Strait. Passing through the five-hundred-mile strait, Knutson skirted the shores of Hudson Bay for another fifteen hundred miles, finally reaching the mouth of the Nelson River. Knutson spent the long winter ice-bound in that vicinity. When summer at last arrived, the Vikings decided on a yet bolder course. Some were left with the ship, but most went up the Nelson River, determined now not only to continue the search for the lost colonists but to claim new lands for the Crown. The men moved into the interior by way of the Nelson, Lake Winnipeg, and the Red River. Traveling eastward from the Red River they reached what is now Douglas County, Minnesota, in 1362.

One day some of the party returned from fishing and found ten of their companions killed by Indians. The frightened survivors fled but then halted to leave a record of their presence. They selected a slab of gray rock some two and a half feet long, sixteen inches wide, and about six inches thick, and the rune master was asked to inscribe it appropriately. Working on the two-hundred-pound rock for about two days, he chiseled out this message: "8 Swedes and 22 Norwegians on an exploration journey from Vinland westward. We had our camp by 2 rocky islets one day's journey north of this stone. We were out fishing one day. When we came home we found 10 men red with blood and dead. AVM save us from evil. We have 10 men by the sea to look after our ships, 14 days' journey from this island. Year 1362."[1]

The inscription on the Kensington Rune Stone has stirred lively debate about its authenticity.

Courtesy of the Minnesota Historical Society

After placing their handiwork on a little knoll about three miles northeast of the site of the future Kensington, Minnesota, the Vikings moved on. Despairing of ever seeing their homeland again, or even of reaching their ship, they decided to spend the rest of their days in the wilderness. They moved west of the Red River, met the Mandan Indians in central North Dakota, and became the progenitors of blue-eyed, fair-skinned Indians.

This intriguing tale of Minnesota's discovery was the outgrowth of the unearthing of the Kensington Rune Stone in November 1898 by Olaf Ohman, a Swedish immigrant farmer. While clearing land Ohman and his ten-year-old son found the stone among the roots of an aspen tree. The reticent Ohman, never at ease except when speaking his native tongue, showed the strange stone to some neighbors and permitted some Kensington merchants to see it, but he did not invite the attention of outsiders. Then, several months after the discovery, a Kensington lumber dealer solicited opinions about the nature of the stone. The initial responses were both voluminous and critical. Norse language experts immediately recognized the runic symbols but pronounced them to be a modern forgery done very shortly before the stone was found.

After the first flurry, interest in the stone lapsed. Ohman kept it on his farm, using it as a granary stepping-stone, and there it languished until 1907, when it was rediscovered by Hjalmar R. Holand—the greatest champion of its authenticity. Holand, who had a long-standing interest in pre-Columbian Viking explorations, probably first learned of the stone in 1899 when he was a student of the University of Wisconsin. Eight years later, while researching a history of Norwegian immigrants, Holand visited Ohman and acquired the stone. Until his death in 1963, Holand publicized and defended the stone through numerous books and articles, letters and speeches.

Soon after acquiring the rune stone, Holand tried to buttress its validity with the opinions of European runologists, but Scandinavian-language experts questioned the stone because a number of the symbols that appeared on it were unknown in 1362. Holand, undaunted, complained that "there is in Europe, a number of educators who tied down to their narrow little round of duties have been led to believe, through an unfortunate superstition, that all things American are tinged with humbug."[2]

Over the years Holand further developed his defense of the stone. Reacting to criticism that there was no Viking activity in North America in the mid-fourteenth century, he seized on the historical fact that

Magnus Erickson had ordered Paul Knutson to Greenland to reassert control over apostates, and on this fact alone wove the Viking saga. Other than the king's order, there is no record of Knutson, but Holand, working almost entirely from assumption and supposition, carried the Viking odyssey into the heart of North America, where the stone was placed and where the Norsemen, by his reasoning, intermarried with the Mandans. In espousing the Mandan theory, Holand chose to ignore preponderant scientific opinion that the seemingly white features of the Mandans resulted from inbreeding rather than from mixing with itinerant Europeans. Holand's ingenious case for the stone was given a wide audience with the publication of his book, *The Kensington Stone: A Study in Pre-Columbian American History*, in 1932.

The book gave those who believed that the stone was an authentic record of Viking discovery a satisfactory explanation of the Kensington mystery, and it also won some converts to Holand's cause. For those unfamiliar with the nature of historical proof and hoaxes, Holand had built a persuasive case. Within a few years after the book's appearance, one critic predicted in alarm that if the enthusiasm for the stone "be not stayed by an exposition of the facts concerning it, it may reasonably be anticipated that the zealots responsible for the myth will ere long procure the enactment of a law requiring it to be taught as true history in the public schools of Minnesota and other neighboring states."[3]

Although Holand had sold the stone to a group of Alexandria businessmen before his book was published, he continued as its chief advocate. When critics attacked his theories, Holand responded with an emphatic retelling of his old arguments. Holand saw himself, like Knutson's men, a crusader, and he took a particular delight in quarreling with academically trained critics who were unimpressed with his logic and his selective use of evidence.

Holand and other believers had some moments of elation when the stone's alleged validity was given boosts from other sources. Some enthusiasts, reasoning that it dealt with the discovery of America and not merely with a small part of Minnesota, arranged to have it exhibited at the Smithsonian Institution in 1948. Although officials of the national museum stopped short of declaring it to be an authentic record, they certainly left a favorable impression when one of them described it as "probably the most important archaeological object yet found in North America."[4] The exhibit in the minds of many was an implied endorsement, and because of it the stone was nationally publicized—including coverage in

National Geographic, which pictured the Smithsonian's curator of archae-
ology studying the stone and included the statement that "later studies
indicate that it was carved by white men who had traveled far into North
America long before Columbus's first voyage."[5] With this backing, the
stone was returned triumphantly to Minnesota and ceremoniously
unveiled by Governor Luther W. Youngdahl on March 3, 1949, as part of
the commemoration of Minnesota's Territorial Centennial.

By this time even those who thought the stone was a hoax had to rec-

This replica of the Kensington Rune Stone, about five times larger than the
actual stone, was erected in Alexandria in 1951.
Courtesy of the Minnesota Historical Society

ognize its significance in the public mind. Residents of Alexandria, the county seat of Douglas County and the possessor of the stone, began advertising their city as the "Birthplace of America," and under the leadership of the Alexandria Kiwanis Club a granite replica about five times the size of the Kensington stone was placed at the east entrance of the city in August 1951. The stone itself, however, was still not appropriately displayed. Then, during 1958, the centennial year of Minnesota's statehood, the Alexandria Chamber of Commerce solicited donations from its businesses and civic groups for the erection of an area historical museum, where the stone has been enshrined ever since. The stone's boosters displayed it as part of Minnesota's exhibit at the World's Fair in New York in 1964–65, a move that contributed nothing to resolving the question of its authenticity but made the stone and Alexandria yet more famous.

Although the Kensington Rune Stone has enlivened discussions about Minnesota's beginnings, and though there will always be those who believe in its authenticity, there is overwhelming evidence that the stone was a hoax. Generally, authorities in runic languages have pronounced the inscription to be modern and are agreed that those who chiseled it were amateurs who probably had nothing more than some rather elementary runic sources at their command. Historians too, particularly Erik Wahlgren and the late Theodore C. Blegen, the most eminent Minnesota historian of his day, challenged the stone's authenticity, primarily because of the circumstances under which it was found. They thought it rather a strange coincidence that the stone was found by a Scandinavian in one of the most Scandinavian parts of a state heavily peopled by Scandinavian immigrants at a time when there was great popular interest in Viking explorations of North America. In addition, Olaf Ohman and his minister friend, Sven Fogelblad, had a strong interest in romanticized Viking history and, like many Scandinavian immigrants, were familiar with nineteenth-century runic writing. Furthermore, Ohman and Fogelblad were fun-loving and quite capable of perpetrating a hoax to confound academicians. There was a local rumor too, immediately after the discovery, that the whole matter was a prank.[6]

From the perspective of the late twentieth century, it is apparent that the Kensington Rune Stone will remain controversial. The very existence of the stone is sufficient proof of its authenticity to those who embrace Holand's contrived historical context, but believers will always be challenged by critics, who are mainly professional archaeologists, historians, and linguists.

The most recent debate has centered on two pro-stone books by Robert A. Hall, Jr. His *The Kensington Rune-Stone Is Genuine: Linguistic, Practical, Methodological Considerations* (1982) presented, among other things, the novel premise that the stone's inscription was a type of provincial runic writing known in the fourteenth century. Hall repackaged his main ideas and supplemented them with an unqualified endorsement of Holand's contentions in his *The Kensington Rune-Stone, Authentic and Important: A Critical Essay* (1992), written with the collaboration of Richard Nielsen and Rolf M. Nilsestuen. The titles are imposing, but probably only those with the temperament of medieval scholastics will have the determination to cope with the pedanticism of these books. Although they are hardly casual reading, Hall's books will undoubtedly appeal to rune stone supporters.

Anyone who consults Hall's first book would be well advised to look at a review of it by Brigitta Linderoth Wallace, the most prominent recent critic of the stone and Holand. Challenging Hall on all fronts, Wallace concluded that the book was "marred by a lack of research into basic source material, a poor grasp of the disciplines of Scandinavian linguistics and runology, and a naïve acceptance of secondary sources. As a result, *The Kensington Stone Is Genuine* does not live up to its initial promise of being an objective study; it is a contribution to the perpetuation of perfidious fiction rather than to serious knowledge."[7]

Wallace, who had written two highly critical essays before writing the review,[8] has become the latest bête noire to the stone's defenders, who have been bolstered by the recent publication of Rolf M. Nilsestuen's *The Kensington Runestone Vindicated*. While attacking Wallace and other rune stone detractors, Nilsestuen reiterated all of Holand's suppositions. These recent writings, if nothing else, illustrate the continuance of irreconcilable viewpoints.

However, even those who insist that the stone was a hoax acknowledge that the Viking myth has become deeply ingrained in Minnesota's popular culture. As an object of great curiosity it will continue to be of interest even to the disbelievers who may, as Erik Wahlgren suggested, come from afar to Alexandria, where they will "witness, not an ancient runic monument, but a memorial to the pioneer settlers of Douglas County— and to the good sportsmanship of their present day descendants."[9]

2

EUROPEANS IN THE WILDERNESS

LIKE MUCH OF North America, Minnesota was first claimed by the French who pushed westward into the heart of the continent by way of the Great Lakes. Their movement was part of an intense French rivalry with England and Spain for control of the vastness of North America. Goaded by this rivalry, and led yet farther by the elusive dream of finding a northwestern all-water route to the Far East, the French navigator Jacques Cartier made important discoveries. After finding the mouth of the St. Lawrence River in 1535 he ascended the stream to the later site of Montreal. He passed the winter with Indians on the St. Lawrence, and before turning homeward issued a proclamation on May 3, 1536, claiming the entire valley of that mighty river for France. Having learned from Indians that great bodies of water lay to the west, he obviously concluded that he had found the beginnings of a convenient water route to Asia.

Costly European wars prevented the French from pursuing this waterway, so they turned their interests to fishing. Commercial fishermen hauled in enormous catches from the Grand Banks of Newfoundland, established numerous stations onshore to salt and dry their fish, and began trading steel knives and other items to Indians for furs—becoming the first fur traders in North America. When European buyers recognized that beaver pelts from the wilds of Canada compared favorably to furs imported from boreal Russia, the French monarchy decided that the fur trade was a feasible commercial venture in its own right and chartered the Company of New France to colonize the lower St. Lawrence.

Under the vigorous leadership of Samuel de Champlain, who dominated New France for years, the company founded Quebec in 1608. Though menaced by the English, the Dutch, and the powerful Iroquois confederation to the south, Champlain pushed his agents into the interior to stimulate the fur trade and to seek the ever-beckoning water route through the continent. The goals complemented each other, for in seeking furs new tribes were discovered, peoples who might have information about western waters; and as the waterways became known, they benefited the extractive and transitory fur trade. The agents of Champlain's policy were his "Young Men"—men such as Étienne Brule and Jean Nicolet, whom he sent to live among the Indians to learn their languages, to cement alliances, to carry on the fur trade, and to gather information about other bodies of water to the west.

The discovery of the Great Lakes excited Champlain; he thought it was the beginning of the route to the East. Outfitted with native guides, Champlain had traveled up the Ottawa River and discovered Lakes Huron and Ontario. Then, when Quebec was about a decade or so old, he

Landfall of Jean Nicolet near Green Bay, 1634. Painting by Edward Willard Deming.
Courtesy of the State Historical Society of Wisconsin

learned of Lake Superior—the largest and westernmost of the great inland
seas. Late in his career Champlain heard of yet another great sea southwest of Lake Huron upon whose shores lived people who might be Asiatic
or, if not Asiatic, Indians who had met Asian traders. Aged and infirm,
Champlain could not undertake this trip himself, but he sent out an expedition led by Nicolet. Though Nicolet's primary instructions were to
extend the French alliance to western tribes and to lay the foundations for
trade, Champlain also had the passage to Cathay in mind. Therefore,
Nicolet was outfitted with "a grand robe of China damask, all strewn
with flowers and birds of many colors."[1] The robe was sure to impress any
Indians he met and would make him doubly welcome if the distant people proved to be Orientals.

Champlain's remote waters proved to be Lake Michigan, and the "people of the sea" were Ho-Chunk Indians (formerly called Winnebago),
whom Nicolet met at the site of Green Bay, Wisconsin, in 1634 when he
debarked from his canoe garbed in the brilliant Chinese robe. Although
he enriched the storehouse of knowledge about the interior and added the
fourth of the Great Lakes to French maps, Nicolet brought back questions
as well as answers. For at Green Bay, on the mouth of the Fox River, the
Winnebago told him that three days distant there was another stream
issuing from a lake which led to a great water. That stream was probably
the Wisconsin River or the Illinois River, and the second great water was
apparently the Mississippi; but Nicolet could report to Champlain only
that he had learned of yet more water to the west—water that flowed
south.

Champlain died a few months after Nicolet's return, and with his
death, French dreams of quickly penetrating the mystery of the unknown
area west of Lake Michigan faded. Without Champlain, the Company of
New France drifted into a long time of troubles—warring with the
Iroquois, unsuccessfully fending off creditors, and striving to control the
rebellious *coureurs de bois*, those unlicensed traders who often dealt with
the Dutch and English. Of the dozens of men who defied the company,
two, Pierre Esprit Radisson and Médart Chouart, the Sieur des
Groseilliers, won enduring fame.

Groseilliers began his trading career in 1654. In 1656–57 he and
young Radisson went on an unlicensed but lucrative expedition into the
Superior country. Two years later, emboldened by their first successful
foray, they set out again. The second trip, undertaken in secrecy, carried
them along the south shore of Lake Superior to Chequamegon Bay, where

they built a rough log hut to cache some of their provisions. Moving inland, they wintered among the Ottawa on Lac Court Oreilles near present Hayward, Wisconsin, and there they learned of the Dakota to the west. Enticed because no Frenchmen had ever before visited this powerful tribe, Radisson and Groseilliers traveled southwestward to meet the "nation of the Beef,"[2] or the buffalo-hunting Indians. After this rendezvous Radisson and Groseilliers worked their way to the Apostle Islands in Lake Superior. From there they paddled across the lake to near the mouth of the Cross River, thus becoming the first whites to enter Minnesota.

Radisson and Groseilliers retraced their path to Montreal in 1660, confident that because they carried back quantities of furs and brought reports of new country and new Indians, their unlicensed adventures would be forgiven. Instead of the heroes' welcome they expected, they were detained and stripped of their furs. Embittered, the two worked their way to England, where they helped organize the Hudson's Bay Company and thus contributed to the downfall of the French empire in North America.

Although outside the law in the eyes of French officials, Radisson and Groseilliers contributed significantly to later exploration. They added much to the knowledge about Lake Superior and revealed the importance of the fur trade in that region. Further, they learned from the natives of Lake Superior about the interior route from Hudson Bay to Lake Winnipeg and correctly presumed that it was the easiest passage to the interior of the continent; and they learned that rivers from Lake Winnipeg led westward, perhaps even to the "Western Sea." As the first white men to visit the Dakota, they observed these Indians before they had been influenced by the ways and tools of Europeans. Radisson, the diarist of the expedition, captured the exhilaration of young men in the wilderness—men in control of their own destiny—with his classic observation that "We weare Cesars being nobody to contradict us."[3] He found a certain comfort in the pristine wilderness, describing Lake Superior as the "delightfullest lake in the world" and wondering if the surrounding area might be a future "laborinth of pleasure" for the crowded masses of Europe who warred over "a rock in the sea."[4]

Men like Radisson and Groseilliers hastened the demise of the Company of New France, whose holdings were taken over by the royal government in 1663. Capable executives of Royal New France soon revived Champlain's dreams. Jean Talon commissioned the youthful

explorers Louis Jolliet and Father Jacques Marquette to push inland from
Green Bay in search of the Mississippi. On their famous trip of 1673 this
pair, after crossing Wisconsin by way of the Fox and Wisconsin Rivers,
reached the Mississippi a few miles downstream from present Prairie du
Chien and followed it southward for a month to the mouth of the
Arkansas. In disappointment they concluded that it led to the Gulf of
Mexico, not to a South Sea that connected with the Pacific Ocean. But
still, they had discovered the mouth of the Missouri River, which was a
larger stream than the Mississippi at the point where the two rivers
joined. Was the Missouri, then, the way to a western sea? Leaving that
question unanswered, the two men, led by native guides, returned to Lake
Michigan by way of the Illinois and Chicago Rivers, thus pioneering two
routes from that lake to the Mississippi for later explorers to follow.

The royal governor, Count Frontenac, was aggressive and soon French
traders moved westward along the Chicago-Illinois, Fox-Wisconsin, and
Lake Superior paths. While Robert Cavalier, Sieur de la Salle, was establishing posts in the Illinois country, the trade of Lake Superior, dormant
since the time of Radisson and Groseilliers, was revived by Daniel
Greysolon, Sieur Duluth. Duluth, sponsored by Quebec and Montreal
merchants, set out from Montreal in 1678. After wintering among the
Ojibwe near Sault Ste. Marie, Duluth moved on to a rendezvous with the
Dakota near where the city of Duluth now stands. The tribesmen escort-
ed him inland to their principal village on the south shore of Lake Mille
Lacs, and there, on July 2, 1679, he formally claimed the country for
Louis XIV.

Satisfied that he had extended French suzerainty over the Dakota,
Duluth returned to Lake Superior, leaving behind three engagés who were
to visit other Dakota villages seeking information about the western sea.
These men met Dakota warriors who told of having been on a campaign
twenty days' travel westward to a great lake that had salty waters.
Ignorant of the breadth of the continent and equally ignorant of Great
Salt Lake, Duluth assumed that his men had been told about the Pacific.
Duluth wintered at the mouth of the Kaministiquia (present-day
Thunder Bay, Ontario), convinced that a water route to the Pacific lay
through the Dakota country.

Duluth's plans to find the saltwater reported by his men were thwarted. While journeying down the St. Croix River in 1680, Duluth learned
that a band of Dakota warriors was holding three white captives.
Believing they were French and realizing that no French lives were any

safer than those of the captives, Duluth overtook the Dakota hunting party and effected the release of the prisoners. The men proved to be emissaries of La Salle, led by Michel Accault and sent from the Illinois River to explore the Upper Mississippi. Near the mouth of the Illinois they had been seized by the Dakota party, which had carried them northward into Minnesota. Realizing the gravity of the situation, Duluth returned to the Dakota villages on Mille Lacs and upbraided the assembled chiefs for their effrontery to the Sun King's subjects, insisting that they abide by their alliance. Then he returned to Montreal. Although Duluth failed to find a way to the Pacific, he did reopen the Lake Superior fur trade, and he added the Dakota to the French alliance. His explorations also fed the French expansionist mania with yet another story about a saltwater lake to the west.

Father Louis Hennepin, the European discoverer of St. Anthony Falls, wrote the first book about Minnesota.
Courtesy of the Minnesota Historical Society

Father Louis Hennepin, a Belgian who was diarist and cartographer for the Accault expedition, became an instant celebrity. He had carefully noted the actions and customs of his captors, who carried him past the picturesque falls of the Mississippi, which he named in honor of his patron saint, Anthony of Padua. In 1683, only a year after he returned to France, he published his *Description of Louisiana*. With a keen sense of the reading appetite of Europeans, who were fascinated by the natives of North America, Hennepin emphasized those things that would seem bizarre to his readers. Though he was not overly concerned with geography, he did introduce the Upper Mississippi and its falls to thousands because his book was a best-seller in its time. Unfortunately, Hennepin fell victim to an inclination to exaggerate; by 1699, in a later edition, he was describing the sixteen-foot falls of St. Anthony as having a drop of fifty or sixty feet.

In a sense, Hennepin exploited the wilderness, but most Frenchmen who ventured among distant tribes were interested in economic exploitation through the fur trade. During the 1680s, Nicholas Perrot, who had long traded in the Lake Michigan area, extended his operations to the Upper Mississippi. He established Fort St. Antoine on the Wisconsin side of Lake Pepin, the widening of the Mississippi above the mouth of the tributary Chippewa River, and began trading with the Dakota. When the English announced a claim to the area and Dakota loyalty appeared to be wavering, French officials ordered Perrot to claim the Upper Mississippi for France again, even though Duluth had already done so and La Salle, upon reaching the mouth of the Mississippi in 1682, had claimed its entire drainage basin for Louis XIV. Intent upon overawing the Dakota, Perrot arranged an elaborate ceremony at Fort St. Antoine on May 8, 1689. There, to the sound of muskets, Latin chants, and shouts of "Long live the king," Perrot claimed the lands adjoining the Fox, Wisconsin, and Upper Mississippi as well as the country of the Dakota and the rivers St. Croix and St. Pierre's; and lest some undiscovered area of value should escape the French grasp, Perrot also laid claim to "other places more remote."[5]

Throughout much of his career on the Upper Mississippi, Perrot was accompanied by his young lieutenant, Pierre Charles Le Sueur. Le Sueur stayed with Perrot from 1683 until at least the mid-1690s, trading not only with the Dakota but with the Ojibwe on Lake Superior as well. During this time he met Dakota, who smeared their faces and bodies with a greenish-blue clay they extracted from the banks of a stream that entered St. Pierre's River from the south. Intrigued by the possibility that copper ore might be found along with the clay, Le Sueur visited the "mine" site along the stream that he called the Green River (the modern Blue Earth River).

Le Sueur brought out specimens of the clay and purportedly had them assayed in France, where they were proclaimed to be copper-bearing. Le Sueur's desire to return to the Blue Earth River was frustrated for several years by difficulties in obtaining a royal permit: he also wanted to trade in furs, and the French market was glutted with beaver pelts. Ultimately, however, he received a patent to search for mineral wealth in the Upper Mississippi region and to trade with the Indians for peltries and hides other than beaver. He was delayed yet another year when his ship was seized by belligerent English; then Canadian colonial officials, mistrustful of his purpose, also blocked his expedition.

In an extraordinary move, Le Sueur decided to reach the Upper Mississippi by way of the Gulf of Mexico. His path was at last made smooth through the fortune of being related by marriage to the Sieur de Iberville, the founder of Biloxi, Mississippi, and it was from there that Le Sueur undertook his voyage early in 1700. He and his party of about two dozen men reached the mouth of the Blue Earth early in October and constructed a small stockade named Fort L'Huillier, after a French official who had befriended Le Sueur.

Working out of the fort, Le Sueur's men almost immediately began taking out the blue earth from the mine site a few miles upstream, scraping it out with knives and loading it onto canoes. Le Sueur seems to have come well equipped with trade goods, for he also struck up a lucrative business with the Dakota in which he gathered nearly four thousand beaver pelts. He and his men lived well, killing and butchering hundreds of buffalo, which were numerous on the prairies west of the Blue Earth. He left Fort L'Huillier after less than a year, taking with him a reported two tons of blue earth—as well as the furs. Leaving behind a portion of his party, who abandoned the post the following year because of the threatening Fox Indians, he was back in France within a few months; but he did not return to his homeland bearing untold mineral wealth. The blue earth apparently never reached France. Whether it was cast into the Father of Waters or simply abandoned someplace no one knows. But Le Sueur successfully perpetuated the myth that he had worked a copper mine. Later, chroniclers, particularly Bénard de la Harpe, one of the first historians of Louisiana, reported Le Sueur's intention as an accomplish-

ment, and as a result tales of Le Sueur's copper mine on the Blue Earth
River persisted for years. The mine was not finally declared bogus until
it was visited by the Anglo-American geologist George Featherstonhaugh
in 1835.

Surely Le Sueur should have been able to identify copper, for when
trading among the Ojibwe and Dakota he had seen float copper, those
pieces scattered by glacial action; and he had seen objects the Indians
shaped from this copper, including musket balls fashioned when lead was
unavailable. Given this knowledge Le Sueur should have had no difficulty in making a distinction between copper and the blue earth because of
the difference in color, heft, and consistency.

Le Sueur was not without critics in his day. The intendant of New
France suspected deceit in Le Sueur's expedition, speculating that "the
only mines that he seeks in those regions are mines of beaver skins."[6]
Because of Le Sueur's subsequent trade with the Dakota even though his
license excluded beaver, this may have been the most accurate statement
ever written about the first explorer of the Minnesota and Blue Earth
Rivers. But Le Sueur still must be credited with contributing to the geographical knowledge of the area in which he traveled. He sketched the
region between Lake Superior and the Blue Earth River, and he obtained
information from Indians who had been on the plains to the west. He cal-
culated as best he could the latitude and longitude of significant stream
junctures. He reported his findings to the famous Royal geographer
Claude Delisle, who issued a 1703 map showing much of the Upper
Mississippi area.

Le Sueur's expedition marked the end of an era in the fitful history of
New France in the northwest. The exigencies of the War of the Spanish
Succession, which found France again pitted against her age-old foe Great
Britain, caused the Royal government to abandon all posts and activities
in the western Great Lakes region. The area lay dormant while armies in
Europe struggled for control of North America. Peace was finally restored
in 1713 with the treaty of Utrecht, by which France surrendered the
Hudson Bay region to Great Britain.

This reversal proved to be a stimulant, and the French launched a
broad campaign to strengthen their remaining hold in North America.
The settlement of New Orleans was begun in 1718, and at the same time
the French reoccupied the Lake Superior posts, hoping to draw the Indian
fur gatherers away from the British at Hudson Bay. With the revival of
trade, the French awakened anew to the task of finding an all-water route

through the continent to the Western Sea. It was a long way to the Pacific, and the French pinned their hopes on that Western Sea, which would provide easy passage from the Great Lakes and the Mississippi River to the ocean.

Thus it was that the government of New France authorized a reconnaissance by the Jesuit priest Pierre François Charlevoix. To prevent the British from discovering his real purpose, Charlevoix conducted his business under the guise of a tour of missions. He questioned Indians at Green Bay about routes west of Lake Superior and the Upper Mississippi and then canoed across Wisconsin and down the Mississippi to the gulf. In his report of this 1721 trip he recommended two possible ways of reaching the Western Sea, which he believed lay southwest of Lake of the Woods. One suggested avenue was by way of the Missouri River; the other was overland from a location on the Upper Mississippi. In the interest of economy the government chose the Upper Mississippi route without knowing that an expedition up the Missouri would have borne more fruit.

The Upper Mississippi expedition was launched in 1727 by the government of New France headed by Charles de la Boische, Marquis de Beauharnois, whose rule, like Frontenac's, was marked by westward expansion. Merchants underwrote the costs of constructing a post in return for a three-year monopoly of the fur trade, and Beauharnois provided a military escort. The fleet of canoes carried not only Beauharnois's men but also Jesuit missionaries, sent because the Dakota had told Charlevoix that they would welcome the Black Robes.

After a three-month trip, which carried them through the lands of the hostile Fox Indians in Wisconsin, the group selected a site on the Minnesota side of Lake Pepin, about two miles from present-day Frontenac. There, on low ground along the Mississippi, they erected an enclosure "a hundred feet square surrounded by stakes twelve feet high with two good bastions."[7] The fort was named Beauharnois, and in November the men celebrated Beauharnois's birthday with a fireworks display, which wrought terror among the Indians. But Fort Beauharnois was a failure. The Fox Indians made war, trade with the Dakota was not realized, and no expeditions set forth for the Western Sea. The fort was occupied intermittently for a decade and then abandoned.

When Beauharnois realized that the Fox Indians would prevent any expeditions from Lake Pepin, he looked for another way of reaching the west. His interests soon melded with those of Pierre Gaultier de Varennes, Sieur de la Vérendrye, whom history remembers as the last of

the important French explorers in North America—and the only one who
was a native of Canada. He had served with distinction in the French
army in the War of the Spanish Succession, and after the war he was
rewarded with various commands, including that of a post on Lake
Nipigon, north of Lake Superior. Here, on the border of an expanse dot-
ted by thousands of lakes and laced with streams, he listened eagerly to
Indian tales of water routes and the great sea that could be reached from
Lake Superior.

La Vérendrye was aware of the route inland by way of the
Kaministiquia from Thunder Bay to Lac la Croix—it had first been used
by Jacques de Noyon in 1688—and he learned of the route along the
present Minnesota-Ontario boundary from the Assiniboine Indians, one
of whom sketched the border lakes for him on birch bark. Indian guides
showed La Vérendrye a trail, later known as the Grand Portage, leading

The High Falls of the Pigeon River was the principal impediment to navigation on the stream's lower portion. This 1937 photo shows in the lower right a
wooden flume used to carry logs around the falls.
Courtesy of the Minnesota Historical Society

from Lake Superior to the Pigeon River above the series of falls that blocked its lower reaches, and led him on an arduous canoe route that had some three dozen other portages and carried him across the Lake Superior–Hudson Bay divide on Height of Land Portage and through numerous lakes and the Rainy River. At last, before him lay Lake of the Woods.

Lake of the Woods could easily have been described as an inland sea, but La Vérendrye knew the Western Sea he sought lay yet ahead, so he thought of Lake of the Woods as a likely halfway point between Montreal and his unknown destination. Therefore, to provide himself with a base of operations and a way station, La Vérendrye built Fort St. Charles during the summer of 1732. The small stockade was erected on the Minnesota side of Northwest Angle Inlet about halfway between Rainy River's entry into the lake and the lake's outlet into the Winnipeg River.

La Vérendrye could have profited immensely from the fur trade in that unexploited wilderness had he been content to limit himself to that activity, but his belief in the Western Sea drove him on. The outflow from Lake of the Woods led him to Lake Winnipeg, a massive remnant of glacial Lake Agassiz, and canoe routes from that lake drew him westward by way of the Saskatchewan and Assiniboine Rivers. La Vérendrye's quest took him all the way from present-day Winnipeg, Manitoba, across the prairies to the Mandan villages on the Missouri River. Always, the Western Sea lay beyond. Later two of his sons explored through North Dakota and into Montana, Wyoming, and South Dakota in the futile search for saltwater. Debts and personal tragedy at last defeated La Vérendrye, and he abandoned his search in 1744. Fort St. Charles lives to the present day, for in reconstructed form it stands on the ground where La Vérendrye stood and saw the Western Sea beyond Minnesota's horizon.

There is a certain sadness in La Vérendrye's story; New France had little time to use the western lands added by the La Vérendryes. The defeat of General Edward Braddock's redcoats by the French and their Indian allies in the forests of western Pennsylvania ignited the last of four Anglo-French wars that ultimately brought the end of New France and the French phase of Minnesota's history. The fate of the vast lands placed under the *fleur-de-lis* by the Champlains, the Duluths, and the La Salles was decided on the Plains of Abraham before Quebec, and four years later, in 1763, France formally relinquished its North American holdings, including Minnesota east of the Mississippi, to Great Britain.

French flags were taken down with the end of the struggle for the continent; but, through activities spanning a century, the French introduced Minnesota to the world. They did not find the seas they sought, but they found major waterways, and they left as least some legacy of maps. The traders made a beginning in the fur trade and, whether for good or for bad, they began the process of making the Indians dependent on the white man's goods and tools.

Minnesota's French tradition has been perpetuated by names left upon the land—some of them given by the French themselves, others in memory of them. Thus there are counties named Mille Lacs, Roseau, and Lac Qui Parle, and another called St. Louis, after the river named by La Vérendrye in honor of King Louis IX. Hennepin became the name of a county and a major avenue in Minneapolis, and Le Sueur had a county, a river, and a city named in his honor. Although many French names have been lost through translation—Lac la Pluie to Rainy Lake and Lac du Bois to Lake of the Woods—and some changed beyond recognition, such as the transformation of the Riviere des Embarrass to the Zumbro—others are still evident in Lake Pepin, Lac la Croix, Grand Marais, Frontenac, Pomme de Terre, Belle Plaine, and Faribault.

Though French influence in the fur trade technically ended with the British conquest, it lingered nonetheless. French remained the essential language of the trade, and the British and, later, American fur companies were filled with the French Canadian voyageurs who carried their names and their culture among the tribes. These French Canadians soon found that Great Britain, like France, encouraged but two activities in its new kingdom—the fur trade and exploration for a route to the Pacific. The year before the British legally acquired that portion of Minnesota east of the Mississippi, the lands across the river, called Louisiana by the French, had been transferred to Spain. Minnesota is said to have been under four flags—those of France, Great Britain, Spain, and the United States—but though most of Minnesota was part of Spanish Louisiana for nearly four decades, the Spanish flag never waved above it. The Mississippi in the north was not a firm boundary, and British traders and explorers ventured into Spanish Louisiana at will.

The annals of British exploration in Minnesota are not nearly so long as those of the French, but they are colorful, and the highlight of them has to be the adventures of Jonathan Carver. Carver was yet another pawn in the game of seeking the Northwest Passage. His career as a traveler was inextricably bound with that of his sponsor, Robert Rogers, a rugged New Englander whose heroic deeds as a frontier ranger during the French and Indian War made him known from the colonies to Great Britain. While serving at Detroit, Rogers heard tale after tale from French voyageurs and Indians about the unknown interior and the myriad water routes. His interest was further piqued through conversations with Arthur Dobbs, the aged governor of North Carolina. Dobbs, a testy Irishman, had devoted much of his life to the search for a Northwest Passage; years before meeting Rogers, he had concluded absolutely that there was a connecting strait from Hudson Bay to the Pacific. Dobbs not only was convinced that the strait existed but believed that the Hudson's Bay Company knew of it. Dobbs was dedicated to the point of sending a party of explorers to Hudson Bay and fanatical enough to denounce the leader of the expedition as part of a conspiracy of silence when he reported that he could find no strait to the Pacific. It did not take long for Dobbs's zeal to conjure up for Robert Rogers visions of marching from the Upper Mississippi overland to the Pacific, skirting the ocean's shores, and finding at last the elusive strait to Hudson Bay. But for such an enterprise Rogers wanted Royal backing. Though he had powerful friends in England, he was not able to win support for his expedition from British ministers who were struggling with the staggering debt of the recent European war. Instead, he received the command of the military post at Michilimackinac. Once back in Boston, the undaunted Rogers schemed to use this command to launch a small private expedition.

For leader of the expedition, Rogers chose a former ranger associate, James Tute, known for his courage and resourcefulness. Second in command was James Stanley Goddard, a veteran fur trader, well known among the Indians of the western Great Lakes. As mapmaker and draftsman, Rogers engaged the unemployed Jonathan Carver, then fifty-six, whom he had first met during the recent war when Carver was an officer in a colonial unit. Some of Dobbs's suspicious nature must have communicated itself to Rogers, for he never revealed the expedition's real purpose to Carver but merely instructed him to winter near the Falls of St. Anthony and map the area west of the Mississippi in that sector. Carver made his way from his Massachusetts home to Michilimackinac at the western end of Lake Huron, and in September 1766 he left with some traders on a journey that carried him across Wisconsin from Green Bay to Prairie du Chien. From Prairie du Chien he paddled upstream, accompanied by only two companions—a French Canadian and a Mohawk Indian. He arrived among the Dakota Indians near St. Anthony Falls in November and wintered with them on the Minnesota River.

Capt:JONATHAN CARVER.

Jonathan Carver, who explored in Minnesota, 1766–67, later wrote the first
English language book about the region.
Courtesy of the Minnesota Historical Society

Tute and Goddard, who had left Michilimackinac some two weeks
after Carver, wintered among Indians near Prairie du Chien. Rogers had
instructed Tute that his goal was to move from Lake Huron to the Pacific,
which he would finally reach by following the great river "Ourigan" after
wintering twice en route. But Rogers also had more immediate aims,

which account for the separation of Tute and Goddard from Carver. Penniless and hounded by creditors, Rogers hoped to recoup himself through the Indian trade, so Tute and Goddard at Prairie du Chien were to persuade the tribesmen to meet with Rogers in a grand conclave at Mackinac.

Whatever hope these men had of reaching the Pacific was lost after the first winter. Carver was completely out of touch with the other two for months, and Tute and Goddard, away from the infectious enthusiasm of Rogers, grew increasingly skeptical of the scheme of crossing the Dakota lands to a second winter's destination far out on the Canadian prairies. Tute was also well aware of Rogers's slim purse and wisely decided not to gamble on his getting provisions to the second wintering ground. After Carver joined him and Goddard at Prairie du Chien in the spring, Tute decided to move far northward to the fur trade rendezvous of Grand Portage in the hope of receiving further word and supplies from Rogers.

The trio found Grand Portage bustling with dozens of traders, none of whom bore goods from Rogers. At last, after a three-week wait, word arrived. Rogers could not send supplies, but still he urged his men to carry out their grand mission. Under these circumstances, the thought of starting for the Pacific held no appeal for the demoralized explorers, and Carver noted that they "universally agreed to return to Michilimackinac and give over our intended expedition."[8]

For Carver, however, the end had not yet come. He made his way to England, where his life changed drastically. Separated from his homeland and his family, he married an English woman, fathered a second family without divorcing his American wife, and spent the rest of his days hoping to persuade the Crown to reward him for his services as an explorer.

In 1778, Carver's *Travels Through the Interior Parts of North America, in the Years 1766, 1767, and 1768* was published and became instantly popular. It soon appeared in other editions and ultimately was translated into many foreign languages. As the first book in English about the Upper Mississippi, it became one of the classic accounts of the region. The book was really two books in one. The first section was authentic, although it suffered for want of accuracy since Carver evidently wrote it without having at hand the diaries he had written en route. Even in this section his account sometimes surpassed belief, as when he described the hissing snakes of Lake Erie or the forty-pound trout caught two at a time through the ice. But the second part, a lengthy exposition of Indian manners and customs followed by descriptions of wilderness plants, animals, and birds, was another matter. In writing this section, Carver liberally copied ver-batim passages from the accounts of Charlevoix, Hennepin, and others. Perhaps Carver can be forgiven his plagiarism, since in his day it was common and aroused no particular ire among readers, and perhaps his enthusiastic exaggerations of the natural wonders of the wilderness can also be excused; but Carver was less than honest about his part in the expedition, and that is more difficult to forgive. Rogers was not men-tioned except as "governor" of Michilimackinac, Tute was not mentioned at all, and, said Carver, Goddard was "a gentleman that desired to accom-pany me."[9] It may have been that Carver hoped through such deception to dupe government officials into rewarding him for his enterprise.

It is no wonder that Europeans read Carver's account avidly. His descriptions were often vivid—the terrain in the Lake Pepin vicinity he saw as "the most beautiful and extensive prospect that imagination can form. . . . Verdant plains, fruitful meadows, numerous islands, and all these abounding with a variety of trees that yield amazing quantities of fruit, without care or cultivation."[10] And St. Pierre's River, he said,

> flows through a most delightful country, abounding with all the neces-saries of life . . . wild rice grows here in great abundance; and every part is filled with trees bending under their loads of fruits, such as plums, grapes, and apples; the meadows are covered with hops, and many sorts of vegeta-bles; whilst the ground is stored with useful roots, with angelica, spike-nard, and ground-nuts as large as hens eggs. At a little distance from the sides of the river are eminences, from which you have views that cannot be exceeded even by the most beautiful of those I have already described; amidst these are delightful groves, and such amazing quantities of maples, that they would produce sugar sufficient for any number of inhabitants.[11]

Not content to limit himself to the country he had actually seen, from Indian reports and his own speculations Carver made intriguing though not always accurate comments on western geography. He had information that the sources of the Minnesota and Missouri Rivers lay within a mile of each other, and he had learned from the Dakota and Assiniboine that the four great rivers of North America all started from the same high-lands, with the Mississippi flowing south, the St. Lawrence east, the Bourbon (Nelson) north to Hudson Bay, and the Ourigan west. Like Rogers, Carver believed in the great river of the west. He may have been writing about the stream that was later named the Columbia, but neither it nor any other river of the far west was ever known to the natives as the Ourigan. Many years later Carver's Ourigan became Oregon.

Carver also popularized the belief that there was a great mountain range in the west. It was three thousand miles long in its extent north from Mexico, he said, and it divided the waters of the Gulf of Mexico and the Gulf of California. Could this have been anything other than the Rocky Mountains? Carver called them the Shining Mountains, "from an infinite number of crystal stones, of an amazing size, with which they are covered, and which, when the sun shines full upon them sparkle so as to be seen at a very great distance."[12]

Carver's obsession with his great adventure lived beyond him not only because of his book. Shortly after his death, Carver's first biographer revealed a deed under which Carver purportedly had been granted a huge triangle of land in western Wisconsin by the Dakota. But the deed was obviously fraudulent, and efforts by his heirs and others to have the grant honored were ultimately rejected by Congress. Still, in the Minnesota River Valley, where Carver lived with the Dakota, a community and a county bear his name.

Great Britain was not monopolistic, as France had been, and the fur trade was open to all comers to increase competition and encourage productivity. Soon Scots and New Englanders became the lords of the wilderness, and they dominated it until the close of the War of 1812. Most of the British trade centered on Lake Superior, but some traders canoed from Lake Michigan to the Mississippi by the Fox-Wisconsin passage and worked from Prairie du Chien along the Upper Mississippi and its tributaries, especially the St. Croix and the Minnesota.

One of the earliest British traders in this Mississippi trade was Connecticut-born Peter Pond, who was in his early thirties when he led a trading party to the Minnesota River in 1773–74. Pond was a ruffian, but he had a sense of history and he kept a diary of this trip. Virtually uneducated, Pond spelled instinctively, phonetically, his writing unencumbered by punctuation. "On account of the fase of the Cuntrey & Soile the Entervales of the River St. Peter," he observed in describing the Minnesota River Valley, "is Exsaland & Sum Good timber the Banks Bend the Intervals are high and the Soile thin & lite the River is Destatute of fish But the Woods & Meaddoues afords abundans of annamels Sum turkeas Buffeloes are Verey Plentey the Common Dear are Plentey and Larg."[13] Pond later joined the North West Company and traded in the distant Athabascan country. He had, and deserved, a bad reputation because he was a known murderer, but he also had an uncommonly strong interest in geography.

Of the dozens of British trading posts built in Minnesota, none compare in magnitude to Grand Portage, at the start of the nine-mile "great carrying place" connecting Lake Superior and the Pigeon River. For nearly four decades this post, situated in a sweeping bay on Lake Superior with the rugged pine-clad hills of northeastern Minnesota rising above it, was probably the single most important fur-trade location in the world. From here large canoes and other vessels that hauled the rum, guns, powder, ammunition, blankets, cloth, tobacco, kettles, axes, and beads out from Montreal could go no farther, and it led to the start of a two-thousand-mile-long canoe route into the Canadian interior.

Jonathan Carver observed that it was the place where Indians customarily awaited traders, though it was but a bare meeting ground, and the British first used it as a rendezvous site without benefit of stockades. During the next decade independent traders built houses with stockades around them, until by 1778 Grand Portage was a virtual village in the wilderness, with as many as five hundred people coming and going throughout the season.

Grand Portage took on a new importance during the 1780s and 1790s under the influence of the North West Company. The company erected a huge stockade enclosing sixteen buildings, including a great hall. The post was occupied year-round, but every July and August it burgeoned with the arrival of canoes from Montreal laden with goods that had been sent out many months before from London. The boatmen for the Montreal–Grand Portage trip were usually young French Canadians who returned to Montreal the same year. These men were called *mangeurs du lard*, or pork eaters, because they cooked their dried corn and peas in grease, and the name came also to signify their status as greenhorns. Each year some of the pork eaters stayed in the fur-trade country and thus became *hiverants*, or winterers (in common fur-trade parlance, "northmen"). The social distinction between the pork eaters and the northmen was so strong that they did not even occupy the same campgrounds. Most of the voyageurs, whether *mangeurs du lard* or *hiverants*, were legally engagés: apprenticed servants, bound to the company by the advancement of an outfit and trade goods. Some of the more enterprising engagés worked their way out of debt and became independent traders, but others stayed bound for many years as their debts to the company accrued with each passing season. It was difficult to succeed in a situation where

Grand Portage (showing the reconstructed great hall, about 1979) was Minnesota's
ranking fur-trade post during the British era.
Courtesy of the Minnesota Historical Society

prices paid for pelts were meager and trade goods cost ten to twelve times
the original London prices.

The bourgeois, or director of the fur-trading post, and his clerks
packed the goods for the overland trip to Fort Charlotte on the Pigeon
River, where the North canoes were assembled for the western trade, but
the voyageur carried them. With two or even more ninety-pound packs
held high on his back by a portage strap secured around his head, the
voyageur would toil through the hilly terrain, ascending nearly eight
hundred feet as he traversed the nine-mile path. Mud, rocks, and swarms
of mosquitoes must have caused these men to give voice to more than the
chansons for which they are so well remembered. Those who toiled over
the great carrying place surely must have wished for a better way, but
there was none: carts and wagons required roads and animals, impractical
in a business that was both seasonal and transitional.

At Fort Charlotte the birch-bark canoes that had come in from distant

Partridge Falls, about two miles upstream from the west end of the Grand Portage
Trail, was the westernmost of the cascades on the Pigeon River.
Courtesy of the Minnesota Historical Society

posts deposited their beaver, weasel, mink, fisher, and marten pelts along
with bearskins and buffalo hides and took on a cargo of trade goods. Each
of the large North canoes could carry almost a ton and a half of cargo and was
manned by four or five men. When the canoes were loaded for trade, the
Northmen departed for the interior once more. Many times the voyageurs
who had carried trade packs uphill to Fort Charlotte would make the
return trip bearing packs of furs downhill, back to Grand Portage. These
furs were taken to Montreal and then to the great market in London,
which attracted buyers from all across Europe. Some of the Grand Portage
furs were caravaned across Russia and sold eventually in China.

Grand Portage's glory was brief, for it was abandoned by the North West Company in 1803. The boundary drawn between the United States and Canada at the end of the Revolutionary War was vague in the region west of Lake Superior, and the partners of the North West Company became increasingly uneasy about the possibility that the post was really on American soil and thus subject to American customs officials. When the British removed themselves from Detroit and Mackinac in 1796, Grand Portage seemed alone and unprotected, and the North West Company sought an alternate depot. The Kaministiquia waterway from Thunder Bay to Lac la Croix had been known for many years, but it was longer and more rigorous than the Grand Portage way. Nevertheless, the North West Company built Fort William at the mouth of the Kaministiquia and moved its base of operations.

For the British and for the North West Company, Grand Portage had been something more than a fur-trading post. It was an outpost to adventure. Alexander Mackenzie, the partner in the North West Company who followed the river named after him to the Arctic, and who was the first man to cross North America, used the post as the starting point for both his expeditions. David Thompson, astronomer and surveyor employed by the North West Company who was responsible for mapping much of northern Minnesota and western Canada (and the Pacific Northwest), worked out of Grand Portage during his search for the northern source of the Mississippi, as did Dr. John McLoughlin, another North West Company partner, who gained fame in the Oregon country.

The shift to Fort William signified increasing recognition by the British of America's intent to assert herself in that enormous country, which was hers by diplomatic right. The French and the British who explored and exploited Minnesota had as goals the development of commercial routes and trade with the Indians. These men were removed from their native governments by thousands of miles of ocean; their posts were outposts of civilization. But American aims were vastly different. America was a young nation, a growing nation, concerned with placing her stamp on that which was hers; concerned with the fur trade, yes, but also with determining and enforcing permanent boundaries and exploring for the sake of ascertaining potential economic wealth. The Indians had to be dealt with—not just as trade contacts or as allies, but in such a way that they would not impede the settlement that was inevitable.

Although the British abandoned Grand Portage, they did not desert their posts in the interior of the Old Northwest. They stayed on at Fond du Lac, near the mouth of the St. Louis River; at Sandy Lake, near the western end of the Lake Superior–Mississippi canoe route through Savannah Portage; at Leech Lake; at Pembina in the Red River Valley; and wherever else they had a foothold. But those footholds were challenged time and again by an American government determined to control the Northwest country.

3

—

AMERICAN ASCENDANCY

WITH THE EXCEPTION of George Rogers Clark's expedition through southern Illinois and Indiana, there was little American military activity in the Old Northwest during the Revolutionary War; and even Clark's venture only temporarily interrupted British control of the Illinois country. British traders in the western Great Lakes area paid scant attention to the war. It was inconceivable to them that Great Britain would ever surrender the west, and they were bitter when they learned of the provisions of the Treaty of Paris. Under it, American claims were extended to the very heart of the continent and Great Britain agreed to a northern boundary that gave most of the Great Lakes trade region to the Americans.

Late in the war American diplomats Benjamin Franklin, John Jay, and John Adams met with Richard Oswald, the British envoy to the peace talks, to consider perplexing northern boundary settlements. Franklin had a simple solution—Great Britain could just relinquish the whole of Canada to the United States. The British countered with a suggestion that perhaps the Ohio River was a suitable demarcation. Serious discussion then dealt with the possibility of using the forty-fifth parallel westward from the Connecticut River to the Mississippi. There was legal precedent for such a line, since it was the southern boundary of the old province of Quebec, but it presented problems; if drawn to the

Mississippi, which it would have reached where Minneapolis now stands, it would have crossed the St. Lawrence River and the Great Lakes, leaving southern Ontario to the United States, and much of Michigan, Wisconsin, and central and northern Minnesota to Great Britain. The idea was finally abandoned because it did not respect the natural flow of waters and because of its inconvenience to British fur traders. Finally the diplomats agreed to the American suggestion that the boundary follow natural water routes leading from the St. Lawrence River to Lake of the Woods.

As described in the treaty, the northern boundary was to be drawn from the point where the forty-fifth parallel struck the St. Lawrence River through the middle of Lakes Ontario, Erie, and Huron,

> thence through Lake Superior northward of the Isles Royal & Phelipeaux, to the Long Lake; then through the middle of said Long Lake, and the water Communication between it and the Lake of the Woods, to the said Lake of the Woods, then through the said Lake to the most Northwestern point there of, and from thence on a due west Course to the River Mississippi.[1]

The Mississippi was to be the western boundary from the point of intersection west of Lake of the Woods south to the thirty-first parallel, which was believed to be the northern boundary of Spanish claims east of the Mississippi.

When the American peace commissioners left Paris, they were highly pleased with the northern boundary stipulation and totally oblivious to its flaws. And flawed the agreement was, for there was no Isle Phelipeaux in Lake Superior, no Long Lake west of Lake Superior; nor did the Mississippi River lie west of Lake of the Woods. The errors are understandable: the negotiators were a long way from the fur traders and others who were knowledgeable about the Lake Superior–Lake of the Woods area, and they were hurried, so they relied on the highly reputed Mitchell map of North America, which had been drawn nearly thirty years before the Paris deliberations. Mitchell's map was as good as any North American map of the day and far better than most; nonetheless, it showed all those nonexistent features mentioned in the boundary provisions, as well as other errors. It left the impression that Lake of the Woods was elliptically shaped, with a perceptibly narrow northwest end, and that it was the head of the St. Lawrence watershed; and it showed the source of the Mississippi rising in an area on the map covered by an inset, so it was not really located at all. The treaty makers apparently believed they were using two uninterrupted water lines for boundaries and closing them in the northwest with a straight line from Lake of the Woods to the Mississippi.

The Revolutionary War boundaries would stand, but they were tested because there were British who believed that their country had been far too generous in the peace settlement. The North West Company, with the aim of discrediting the northern boundary provision of the Treaty of Paris, dispatched David Thompson to map Lake of the Woods and locate the headwaters of the Mississippi. The company hoped not only to save Grand Portage but also to cause the boundary to be shifted far enough southward so that its future extension to the Pacific, which was sure to come, would retain the Columbia River basin for the British fur traders. In 1797–98, with the aid of Indian guides, Thompson found Turtle Lake (only about ten miles north of where Bemidji now lies) and proclaimed it the source of the Mississippi. Later explorers proved that Thompson had found only the start of the river's northern branch rather than the true source, but his activities did reveal the gap in the boundary, south rather than west of Lake of the Woods. An effort to close that gap was made in 1803 with the negotiating of the King-Hawkesbury line, drawn from the northwest point of Lake of the Woods to Turtle Lake.

When the King-Hawkesbury agreement was presented to President Thomas Jefferson, he was confronted with a dilemma. He had before him also the Louisiana Purchase Treaty, and both documents had to be forwarded to the Senate for consideration. Realizing that the boundaries of the Louisiana Purchase were extremely vague, Jefferson wanted to avoid any action that would perhaps limit American claims to the northern plains. He saw immediately that the King-Hawkesbury line could adversely affect the northern boundary of Louisiana, because the northern source of the Mississippi rather than the northwest point of Lake of the Woods might become the point of departure for a boundary extension. So not until the Louisiana Purchase was secure did Jefferson forward the King-Hawkesbury agreement, which the Senate approved after striking out the article calling for the line by which the northwest boundary gap was to be closed.

Jefferson saw a certain urgency in determining the northern boundary of the Louisiana Purchase, and he found it difficult to believe, despite French insistence, that there had never been a clear definition of it.

Finally, he found several sources that seemed to indicate that the forty-ninth parallel had been established as the northern extent of French possession by a commission appointed under the provisions of the Treaty of Utrecht in 1713. Great Britain evidently did not care to prove that this was not the case—though Jefferson's citations were erroneous—and finally, in 1818, the two countries agreed that the northern boundary would be extended to the continental divide by following the forty-ninth parallel from the point where a due north–south line from the northwest corner of Lake of the Woods touched it. Thus Minnesota's northern boundary was established in principle, though it was years before any of it was marked upon the ground.

The negotiation of the forty-ninth parallel boundary was part of joint efforts by Great Britain and the United States to resolve lingering issues from their two wars. An unsettled boundary was an open door to further troubles, so the Treaty of Ghent, which formally ended the War of 1812, provided for the surveying of the 1783 line. One of the joint boundary commissions was assigned the task of determining the boundary from upstate New York to the northwest corner of Lake of the Woods.

By 1822, after several years of work, the surveyors were ready to move into the Lake Superior area. In that uncharted wilderness they had to determine what was meant by the "Long Lake" mentioned in the peace treaty and where it was located, and they had to fix the northwest point of Lake of the Woods. Mitchell's Long Lake was located in the Pigeon River and appeared to be the middle water course leading from Lake Superior to Lake of the Woods. The American surveyors believed that the boundary should simply be drawn through the Pigeon River since it was obviously Mitchell's Long Lake, but Anthony Barclay, the British boundary commissioner, advanced the suggestion that the St. Louis River to the south should be the boundary. Ironically, nothing was known at the time of the vast mineral deposits that lay north of the St. Louis River area. Barclay seems to have advanced this claim so that a more desirable boundary through the water connection between Lakes Huron and Superior might emerge as a compromise. Barclay's tactics drove the American commissioner, Peter B. Porter of Buffalo, New York, to claim the Kaministiquia River to the north as the true Long Lake. After nearly five years of wrangling, the commissioners were finally able to agree that the Pigeon River was Long Lake, but they still disagreed over the details of a boundary from that river to the northwest point of Lake of the Woods. Barclay wanted the line to follow the traditional canoe route, which because of its numerous portages was partly a land route, but Porter insisted on a truly continuous water route, which lay somewhat north of the customary trade route in several places. Finally, in 1827, the boundary commission adjourned without having resolved the boundary from Lake Superior to the northwest corner of Lake of the Woods.

Determining the "true" northwest point of Lake of the Woods was perhaps even more of a challenge than locating the nonexistent Long Lake. In mapping Lake of the Woods, American surveyors became aware of its irregular shape. David Thompson, the principal British surveyor, was equally perplexed: he had identified four possible northwest points. Dissatisfied with Thompson's work, the British Foreign Office hired Johann Ludwig Tiarks, a German astronomer who had previously worked on the New York–Canada boundary, to proceed in secrecy to Lake of the Woods. Tiarks did so, and through scientific measurements determined that the head of the inlet later named Northwest Angle Inlet (which was one of Thompson's original points) was the most northwest point. His measurement preserved British control of the outlet of Lake of the Woods and established the point from which a due south line was to be drawn to the forty-ninth parallel. Tiarks's northwest point left a small portion of Minnesota, the Northwest Angle, separated from the mainland by Lake of the Woods. The Northwest Angle proved to be the northernmost point in the contiguous United States and is the inspiration for Minnesota's motto, "L'Étoile du Nord"—Star of the North.

Since the results of the survey had been negated by the dissolution of the boundary commission, the legalization of the northwest point of Lake of the Woods and the boundary from Lake Superior to that point did not occur until the Webster-Ashburton Treaty of 1842. Faced with a New England boundary controversy that threatened to plunge their countries into war, Daniel Webster and Lord Ashburton did not attach great significance to the boundary west of Lake Superior. Consequently, they affirmed without further question Tiarks's most northwest point and fixed the boundary through the Pigeon River and then by the historic traders' route to Lake of the Woods with the stipulation that the Grand Portage Trail remain free and open to subjects of both nations. This treaty ended the diplomatic phase of Minnesota's international boundary, but none of the boundary line east of Lake of the Woods was marked until the early twentieth century and then only after numerous conflicting claims between American and Canadian fishermen, lumbermen, and settlers.

While the United States was establishing its legal boundary west of

Lake Superior, it also moved to control the area physically. When the Louisiana Purchase was made, Jefferson knew that British fur traders in the area had a great deal of influence over the Indians, and he was determined to see American military posts established as counteractants. In 1805 twenty-six-year-old Zebulon Montgomery Pike, in command of a twenty-man party, was sent from St. Louis to reach the source of the Mississippi. On the way, Pike was to choose sites for army posts, gather intelligence about British traders on the Upper Mississippi, make alliances with the Indians, and, if possible, effect a truce between the Ojibwe and the Dakota.

At Prairie du Chien, Pike engaged two interpreters: Pierre Rousseau, who could speak to the Menominee and the Ojibwe, and Joseph Renville, who was to translate the Dakota language. Pike also crossed to the west bank of the Mississippi and selected ground for a possible military post on a hilltop that later became known, at least locally, as "Pike's Hill." On the first day of fall he reached the mouth of the Minnesota River and camped on an island that was later named for him. There he also met a band of Mdewakanton led by Little Crow, grandfather of the Little Crow of Dakota Conflict fame, and, in the first American treaty ever concluded with the Dakota, acquired title to two parcels of land, one at the mouth of the St. Croix and the other at the mouth of the Minnesota.

Zebulon Montgomery Pike (holding weapon) and exploring party in Crow Wing County, December, 1805. Photo of painting by Sarah Thorp Heald.
Courtesy of the Minnesota Historical Society

Satisfied that he had acquired grounds for an army post, Pike moved upstream until his boats were forced to halt, and he built a wintering post near present-day Little Falls. From this rough stockade he hiked in the dead of winter to the trading post of the North West Company on Leech Lake, which was supervised by Hugh McGillis, director of the company's affairs in that district. Pike had the British flag over the post shot down and warned McGillis of possible grave consequences for trespassing on American soil. Then Pike, attempting to carry out his order to find the source of the Mississippi, traveled finally to Upper Red Cedar Lake (later named Cass Lake), and designated it "the upper source of the Mississippi."[2]

Pike returned to St. Louis the following spring to report that he had broken the power of the British traders and had effected a truce between the Dakota and the Ojibwe. His accomplishments were not truly that grand, but he did contribute to topographical knowledge of the area, lay the foundations for a future army post, and make the United States presence known fleetingly to the Indians.

British traders were bothered by Pike's expedition: for all they knew, his was just the first of many American military expeditions. But, with a wait-and-see attitude, they stayed on American ground. It was a wise enough decision on their part because the United States was preoccupied with maritime difficulties with Great Britain and a host of frontier Indian problems in the Indiana country (which led to the outbreak of the War of 1812), and so was unable to follow the Pike expedition with the immediate development of armed posts.

Seizing on the war as an opportunity to regain the Northwest, British troops, assisted by Indian allies (including the Dakota and Ojibwe from the Upper Mississippi), reoccupied such strategic places as Detroit and Mackinac. At the end of the war the situation in the Great Lakes country was not greatly different from what it had been at the end of the Revolutionary War more than thirty years before: British traders and their Indian compatriots were firmly in control. But the Treaty of Ghent returned the British traders to the status of trespassers and left their Indian friends in even less desirable circumstances, for the establishment at last of American control presaged the agricultural invasion—something the free-roaming natives had not had to fear from the British.

After ratification of the Treaty of Ghent, American influence spread across the Northwest. Military posts were established at Green Bay, Prairie du Chien, and Rock Island, and the American Fur Company, headed by John Jacob Astor, purchased the North West Company posts in the United States. Astor and his chief lieutenants influenced Congress to pass the Foreign Intercourse Act of 1816, which provided that foreign subjects who had been trading in the United States had to either leave the country or become naturalized. Many of the foreign traders, including the well-known Jean Baptiste Faribault and Louis Provençalle, chose naturalization so that they could stay with their homes and their families.

Despite these actions British influence in great sections of the border area was still strong several years after the end of the war. Secretary of War John C. Calhoun thus moved to safeguard the Upper Mississippi and the Upper Missouri from the British traders and from possible encroachment of Lord Selkirk's colonists.

Anglophobic American nationalists were concerned, if not alarmed, by the seemingly imminent invasion of their nation's northern flank by British subjects. In 1811 a Scottish earl, Lord Selkirk, obtained a vast land grant—Assiniboia—from the Hudson's Bay Company. Assiniboia encompassed most of present-day southern Manitoba and a portion of southeastern Saskatchewan, as well as northeastern North Dakota and northwestern Minnesota. Selkirk was a humanitarian who wanted to give the poor of Europe an opportunity for a new life in his agricultural colony. While his motives were pure, to Americans he was a British imperialist. After his first settlers arrived at the confluence of the Red and Assiniboine Rivers (present-day Winnipeg, Manitoba) in 1812, Assiniboia struggled to survive. The colony's population after five years was at best several hundred, but American nationalists, through the press, portrayed the Selkirkers as a massive horde that threatened United States security.

To forestall British traders and Selkirkers, Calhoun launched another military expedition. This one was under the command of Stephen H. Long, topographical engineer. In 1817 Long reached the Upper Mississippi and inspected the two tracts of land Pike had purchased from the Dakota. He recommended the construction of a post on a high point overlooking the junction of the Mississippi and Minnesota Rivers, which would become the guardian of the entire northern Great Plains.

While Long was struggling vainly up the Missouri toward another potential site at the mouth of the Yellowstone, Colonel Henry Leavenworth arrived at the juncture of the Mississippi and Minnesota Rivers in August 1819. During the next year his dragoons lived miserably in temporary shelters. Leavenworth, believed by his superiors to have dallied too long in starting a permanent fort, was replaced by Colonel

Colonel Josiah Snelling supervised the construction of Fort Snelling, the north-westernmost military post in the United States for a generation.
Courtesy of the Minnesota Historical Society

Josiah Snelling, a career military officer who had served throughout the War of 1812 and had been present at the disastrous American defense of Detroit.

Because of its commanding view of the river junction, Snelling selected the very site recommended by Long for the post. Its walls, buildings, and blockhouses were constructed of cream-colored limestone quarried from the nearby bluffs, and it was artfully designed to repel attack from any direction. The diamond-shaped enclosure was bastioned by a hexagonal tower on the south corner, a semicircular battery on the east curve, a pentagonal tower on the north corner, and, as the last resort for defenders, a round tower on the west corner.

Fort Snelling
Courtesy of the Minnesota Historical Society

Constructing the fort was Snelling's greatest achievement, and in 1825 the War Department renamed it in his honor. Fort Snelling loomed above the wilderness like a medieval fortress, its stone walls and massive towers a symbol of American strength and permanence in an area accustomed to but small and temporary fur posts. The fort was never attacked, but it was maintained as a frontier post nearly to the time of the Civil War. Until the beginning of St. Paul, it was the principal center of white civilization in Minnesota. Its walls sheltered Minnesota's first hospital, its first school, and its first circulating library. The fort was a lively social center, hosting holiday dances and musical events. Much of Minnesota's Indian history revolved about Fort Snelling as well because it was the headquarters for the St. Peter's Agency, established in 1819. The agency was to take care of government payments to the Dakota under the terms of Pike's treaty with them, and it was to facilitate their transition to the white people's way of life.

Because it was at the head of navigation on the Mississippi River, Fort Snelling was commonly visited by both Americans and foreigners who came by steamboat, including the celebrated British novelist Frederick Marryat and the Swedish author Fredrika Bremer. President Zachary Taylor in his early career commanded the post for a time, and artist Seth Eastman was several times commander of the fort. Dred Scott, remembered for the Supreme Court case that split the nation in the late 1850s, made his bid for freedom on the basis of his temporary residence in free territory at Fort Snelling.

Even though nearly a century and a half elapsed between Duluth's explorations in Minnesota and the building of Fort Snelling, much of the area was still unexplored when United States troops first arrived. Observers such as Hennepin, Carver, and Pike had left vivid but general descriptions of areas along or near the Mississippi, but the source of that great river had not been determined. Virtually nothing was known about the prairie region or the Red River Valley, and no one had even considered the region's economic potential. There was no real knowledge of the Indian population or natural life, and there was no accurate map of the area. Even such a famed place as the pipestone quarries, where the Dakota and other tribes obtained the soft red stone from which they fashioned peace pipes, had not been seen by the eyes of whites.

Of all these challenges, none was more alluring than searching for the source of North America's longest river, for it was almost unthinkable that the course of the river first seen by Hernando de Soto nearly three centuries before was not yet fully known. Knowledge of the source was a vital bit of information for mapmakers and geographers because it was not really possible to draw accurate maps of the United States without it. Fame seemed assured for the man who would discover the source, so Lewis Cass, governor of Michigan Territory, traveled to the Upper Mississippi in 1820. Cass was also superintendent of Indian affairs for Michigan Territory, which then included that part of Minnesota east of the Mississippi, and he made his western trip ostensibly to remind his charges of the change from British to American sovereignty; but he was most interested in the Ojibwe who lived along the route that led him through Lake Superior and the Savannah Portage canoe route, connecting it and the Mississippi. Cass's party reached Pike's Upper Red Cedar Lake, and Cass, like Pike, concluded that this was the Mississippi's true source.

Henry Rowe Schoolcraft, whom Cass had taken along as the expedition's geologist, dutifully reported that Cass had found the Mississippi's "true source"; but he obviously did not believe it, for later in the same report he noted that two rivers entered the lake, the Turtle and a longer one which he called the "La Beesh" in the language of the voyageurs. The La Beesh, he wrote, was known by the voyageurs to be "the outlet of Lake La Beesh, which lies six days journey, with a canoe, west-northwest of Cassina Lake, and has no inlets."[3] Schoolcraft was content to leave matters as they were, though he was determined to return alone and follow the course of the La Beesh River to its end. It was twelve long years before he could achieve this ambition.

In the meantime, another adventurer came upon the scene—Giacomo Constantino Beltrami, an exiled Italian nobleman who came to Fort Snelling in 1823 on the *Virginia,* the first steamboat to travel on the Upper Mississippi. Beltrami accompanied Long on his expedition through the valleys of the Minnesota and Red Rivers, but he quarreled with the commander and left the party at Pembina in a huff to work his way back to Fort Snelling. Beltrami canoed through the area David Thompson had explored before him, and there purportedly discovered a lake that miraculously was both the "most southern sources" of the Red River "and the most northern sources of the Mississippi."[4] Although he believed Lake Julia, as he named it, to be landlocked, Beltrami asserted that its waters filtered through its banks both northward and southward. Beltrami recounted his madcap adventure in *Pilgrimage in America*, a work that captivated its European audience. Years later the Minnesota legislature named a county in the Lake Julia area after him.

After the Cass reconnaissance, Schoolcraft was appointed agent to the Ojibwe at Sault Ste. Marie. With the assistance of his well-educated wife, who was of Ojibwe-British descent, and her numerous Indian relatives, he mastered the Ojibwe language and recorded tribal legends. He also found time and energy to serve in the Michigan legislature; he helped start the Michigan Historical Society and organized the Algic Society to encourage Indian studies. But he had not forgotten about finding the Mississippi's source. From the Ojibwe Schoolcraft learned that the great river started from what they called Elk Lake, and he was assured that with an Indian guide he could proceed directly to it. All he needed was an opportunity to return to the country west of Lake Superior, and that came in 1832 when he received orders to visit the Ojibwe living in that region.

Confident that he would find the river's source, Schoolcraft turned his thoughts to naming it. The Ojibwe name, while descriptive because the lake's irregular shape resembled elk antlers, would not do. Neither would such commonplace names as Duck, Loon, or Turtle. So, while crossing Lake Superior, Schoolcraft asked his companion, the Reverend William

Boutwell, for the Greek or Latin words for true source. Boutwell could not recall his divinity school Greek, and the best he could do in Latin was *veritas caput*, for "true head." The thought of a "Veritas Caput Lake" was not appealing, but the imaginative Schoolcraft simply struck the first and last syllables of the phrase and, by combining the remains, coined "Itasca." Once he had the name he had only to reach the lake, so he engaged the knowledgeable Ojibwe Yellow Head as his guide.

After weeks of traveling, Schoolcraft felt exhilarated at the final approach to the Mississippi's source, noting that every step "seemed to increase the ardor with which we were carried forward."[5] His course led him

In 1832 Henry Rowe Schoolcraft discovered Lake Itasca, the source of the
Mississippi River.
Courtesy of the Minnesota Historical Society

The source of the Mississippi in Itasca State Park is a popular tourist attraction.
Courtesy of the Minnesota Historical Society

from Lake Bemidji up the eastern source of the Mississippi, later named
the Schoolcraft River, into a swamp. He followed Yellow Head overland

> with the expectation of momentarily reaching the goal of our journey.
> What had been long sought, at last appeared suddenly. On turning out of
> a thicket, into the small weedy opening, the cheering sight of a transpar-
> ent body of water burst upon our view. It was Itasca Lake—the source of
> the Mississippi.[6]

Schoolcraft spent only a few hours at Lake Itasca, his last as an explorer, but a long career of studying Indian languages, customs, and history
lay before him. He made a major contribution to American Indian eth-
nology by writing a multivolume study on the "history, condition and
prospects" of Indians in the United States, and he collected and recorded
hundreds of Indian legends. Henry Wadsworth Longfellow drew heavily
upon his collections in writing his romantic *The Song of Hiawatha*.

The Upper Mississippi area was not mapped adequately until 1836,
when Joseph Nicollet, a French émigré, determined the altitude and area

of Lake Itasca and mapped it and the surrounding region. Two years later he returned to Minnesota, sponsored by the United States government and accompanied by John C. Frémont. On this trip, he was to determine and record the nature and resources of the land that lay between the Missouri and the Mississippi. Nicollet's findings were published as a federal government document several years later along with his map, which was significant not only as the first accurate and detailed map of Minnesota but also because of its contribution to place-naming. Nicollet admired the Indian facility for capturing the essence of geographical or natural features with their names and usually adopted them in native or translated form. He was also impressed by the thousands of lakes he saw; one particularly watery region stretching from Redwood Falls through Mankato to Faribault inspired him to name it the Undine Region after the Teutonic water nymph. Unfortunately, less learned frontiersmen commonly believed that Undine was the name of a Sioux princess.

Other reports publicized the river valleys and the prairies both at home and abroad. Stephen H. Long was dispatched by the army in 1823 on a scientific reconnaissance from Fort Snelling that took him up the Minnesota and Red Rivers into Canada and across Lake Superior. Long was accompanied by William Hypolitus Keating, who was the diarist for the expedition. Keating had a broad background not only in history but in geology, botany, zoology, and entomology as well, and he wrote vivid descriptions of the area's terrain, natural life, and Indians in his *Narrative of an Expedition*. This work, which also included reports by other members of the expedition, provided a wealth of new information about the Minnesota and Red River Valleys.

Artist George Catlin was the first white man to make known to the world the famous quarries from which Indians for hundreds of years had been taking stone to carve their pipes. In the mid-1830s Catlin visited Fort Snelling to paint portraits of the Dakota and from there traveled up the Minnesota River and across the plains to the southwestern part of Minnesota, where he viewed the quarries and painted them. Catlin removed specimens of the stone, which were later analyzed by the Geologist of the United States and given the scientific name catlinite.

George W. Featherstonhaugh was assigned in 1835 to conduct a geological survey of the Minnesota River Valley and specifically to inspect Le Sueur's alleged copper mine. Featherstonhaugh, British-born and middle-aged, had been a gentleman farmer and had started the railroad that grew into the New York Central before going to work for the federal government as

The Pipestone Quarries in southwestern Minnesota yielded a relatively soft, red-dish-colored sedimentary rock from which Indians carved ceremonial pipes and other objects. This photo (about 1893) shows Indians quarrying stone from a characteristic shallow pit.

Courtesy of the Minnesota Historical Society

a geologist. He wrote an official report of his geological reconnaissance, then returned to England and wrote *A Canoe Voyage up the Minnay Sotor*, the first work to feature the future name of the state. Like many cultured European travelers of his day, Featherstonhaugh depicted frontiersmen as land-hungry barbarians. Most Minnesotans he met, with the exception of his French-Dakota guide and Henry Hastings Sibley, were slashed by his sharp pen.

The fur trade continued as the common thread that ran through the fabric of the region's history, but by the time the Americans gained control it had changed. American fur traders continued the credit system and depended heavily upon Indian fur gatherers, but their center of activity moved west, with their major outfitting points at Mackinac, the gateway to the western Great Lakes, and at St. Louis, the door to both the Upper Mississippi and the Missouri. The American Fur Company realized the advantages of steamboat navigation and pioneered the use of the boats on the Upper Mississippi, the Missouri, and the western Great Lakes. The steamboat not only facilitated the fur trade but enabled the American Fur Company to augment its business by transporting supplies and passengers for the army and the Indian service.

The beaver had been the mainstay of the British fur trade, but by the time the Americans dominated, the beaver was very scarce. The common animal on the Upper Mississippi by then was the muskrat. Millions of muskrats lived along the lakes and swamps and were comparatively easy to trap. They were attractive to the Indians too because muskrat flesh was a regular part of their diet. Thus the "rat" dominated the Minnesota business and became the medium of exchange between traders and Indians.

The Indians' situation too changed with the transition from British to American control. The British had traded with the Indians and used them as allies; but with a growing background of frontier experience, the American government recognized the transitory nature of the fur trade and the inevitable aftermath of settlement, and it tried to prepare the Indians for the future. When Fort Snelling was started, the United States sent Lawrence Taliaferro to serve as agent for the St. Peter's Agency. He was to try to protect the Dakota from exploitation by traders, to end their warring with the Ojibwe, and to convert them from hunters to farmers. This stiff, proud Virginian throughout nearly twenty years of service proved to be an exception in a bureau overridden by corruption and incompetence. He was honest and dedicated, but he was caught in a nearly impossible situation in which the traders and the government vied for control of the Indians.

Despite their differences, traders and the government both wanted to achieve their long-held dream of peace between the Dakota and Ojibwe. Intertribal raids detracted from the fur trade and made more difficult the attempt to convert the Indians to farming, so the United States sought a formalized boundary between the two tribes. In 1825, a grand conference was held at Prairie du Chien and hundreds of chiefs and headmen from the two tribes were entertained at government expense. Taliaferro appeared with a large delegation of Dakota and Ojibwe, and Schoolcraft came with other Ojibwe. As part of the treaty, which affected the major tribes from Lake Michigan to the Red River, the Dakota and the Ojibwe agreed to a boundary from near present-day Chippewa Falls, Wisconsin, that zigzagged northwestward to a point on the Red River about twenty miles downstream from present-day Moorhead. The boundary meant nothing to the Indians; but whether or not it accomplished the aim of pacifying them, it did legally describe tribal lands and thus laid the foundation for future Indian land cessions.

The American Fur Company recognized the boundary line as a sure sign that the Upper Mississippi area would soon be lost to the ax and plow, though the company temporarily strengthened itself by merging with its principal rival, the Columbia Fur Company, which had cut into the Upper Mississippi and Missouri trade. Rising costs, the increasing preference for silk rather than beaver hats in Europe, the loss of a vast area to advancing farmers, and his own poor health caused John Jacob Astor to quit the business in 1834. With his withdrawal, the company was divided. One division, headquartered in St. Louis, was sold to the Chouteaus and their associates, and the other division went to a group headed by Ramsay Crooks. These were separate companies, and although Crooks legally retained the old firm name, both of them continued to be known as the American Fur Company.

For some years Crooks had anguished over the inefficiency of many of the old traders who were fluent in Indian languages but unschooled in accounting and lacking in business acumen, so when the company became his he moved to revitalize it with young, educated men. With this in mind, he engaged Henry Hastings Sibley and Hercules Dousman to lead the Upper Mississippi trade. Sibley was twenty-three years old when he reached Mendota, across the Minnesota from Fort Snelling, in 1834. He had been given an academy education in his native Detroit, where his father was a judge and community leader. When still in his teens Sibley went to work for trader Robert Stuart at Mackinac and thus came to the attention of Crooks. Perhaps he did not equal Dousman in business savvy, but Sibley handled men well and won the respect of most of his Indian customers.

Sibley at Mendota and Dousman at Prairie du Chien formed a partnership with Old Joe Rolette—a partnership that controlled the trade in an area encompassing most of western Wisconsin and southern Minnesota. In the agreement the area controlled by the Dakota Indians was specially assigned to Sibley, and he, through his Sioux Outfit, had traders located at various stations. Sibley's men worked south of the region controlled by the Northern Outfit led by William Aitkin, who worked out of both La Pointe in the Apostle Islands and Fond du Lac.

Most of Sibley's first associates were inherited from the old American Fur Company. The veteran traders who had started under the North West Company and other British firms included Jean Baptiste Faribault, who became a close friend and Mendota neighbor of Sibley; Joseph LaFramboise, who traded for a number of years in southwestern Minnesota; Joseph Renville; and Louis Provençalle. Renville, fifty-five years old when Sibley assumed command, was native to the area. He was born of French-Dakota parentage at the Dakota village of Kaposia, which was south of present St. Paul, and served as a leader of Britain's Indian allies during the War of 1812. Following the war he lived for a time in Canada, and then, after returning to the United States, was one of the principal organizers of the Columbia Fur Company. After its merger with the American Fur Company, Renville was assigned the area about Lac qui Parle on the Upper Minnesota, where he built a rude stockade and presided like a feudal baron.

Provençalle, who traded from his post at Traverse des Sioux, the traditional Minnesota River crossing of the Dakota near present-day St. Peter, was known to travelers and Indians alike as Le Blanc, "The White Man." Provençalle epitomized the old order. He entered the trade as an illiterate young man and left it as an illiterate old man. His deficiency created some problems in keeping accounts, but he resolved them. Sibley observed that "he kept his Indian credit books by hieroglyphics, having a peculiar figure for each article of merchandise, understood only by himself, and in marking down peltries received from the Indians, he drew the form of the animal, the skin of which was to be represented." As for recording the names of Indian debtors, he developed a method "peculiar to himself." Sibley was gratified that the old trader at least "had mastered the mystery of figures sufficiently well to express by them the amount he wished to designate, and the general correctness of his account did not admit to question."[7]

Although he showed remarkable patience and tact with the old traders, Sibley gradually augmented them with young men. So Joseph Renshaw Brown, who had come to Minnesota as a fifteen-year-old army musician in 1820, became a Sibley associate and, in time, a confidant. In the same manner Sibley added to his retinue Norman W. Kittson, an aggressive Canadian he had first met while working for Stuart at Mackinac. Kittson became the chief trader in the Red River Valley in a business based as much on supplying the Selkirk settlements as it was on the fur trade. Kittson in time turned to transportation on the Red River and moved from it to an extremely profitable association with the young James Jerome Hill. Then, near the end of his trading career, Sibley engaged Martin McLeod, an avid reader who customarily asked for books with his trade goods, and who later wrote the legislation creating Minnesota's common school system.

Like Astor before them, Crooks, Sibley, and Dousman recognized that the fur trade was nearing an end, but they were not prepared for the suddenness of its decline. The American Fur Company, like most businesses in the nation, was seriously affected by the Panic of 1837; and when one of its major stockholders went bankrupt, Crooks's fortunes plunged. The panic was followed by a lengthy depression in which the outside capital was drawn off into new enterprises such as canals and railroads. As Crooks struggled to save his company, the great fur markets in London and Leipzig were slowed by other business failures. Then, five years after the panic, the Chinese market was lost because of war between China and Great Britain. All these difficulties coincided with the increasing European reliance on Australian felt and South American nutria pelts. Crooks tried valiantly to cut his losses by reducing operations, but finally, in 1842, his American Fur Company went bankrupt.

Other factors contributed to the decline of the fur trade. Pressure from land speculators and Wisconsin territorial officials brought about the Dakota and Ojibwe treaties of 1837, by which those tribes gave up most of their lands east of the Mississippi. These treaties were a significant turning point in Minnesota's history, for the ceding of the Dakota lands meant that the fur trade would be replaced by farming, and the Indians, who had previously been so dependent upon the traders, now would become dependent upon the government.

The traders clung to the old business as long as they could, but gradually they turned to other things. Some took up land and became farmers. Others speculated, engaging in land acquisition or townsite planning. Some entered the lumber business. And some, like Sibley and Brown, emerged as leaders in Minnesota's transition from an unorganized territory to statehood.

4

—

MINNESOTA'S QUEST FOR EMPIRE

IN HER REMINISCENT *Three Score Years and Ten*, the aged Charlotte Ouisconsin Van Cleve recalled vividly episodes of Indian and garrison life during her childhood at Fort Snelling. She was awed at the changes that had taken place during her life span—changes that had dramatically transformed Minnesota from an area unoccupied by whites into a modern, populous state.

Every section of the American frontier had Charlotte Ouisconsin Van Cleves—people who marveled at the pace of life, and who proudly claimed that their generation had been witness to the progression from savagery to civilization. The Charlotte Van Cleves never saw themselves as expansionists in a derogatory sense. In pushing aside the Indians, breaking land, and building cities, they were only fulfilling their destiny. But they were expansionists—philosophically as well as physically, for by every thought and action America's frontier people flung themselves against the challenges of foreign powers, against the untamed land, and against the Indians.

A distinct sense of place was a natural outgrowth of frontier expansion. For a host of geographic, economic, political, and cultural reasons, portions of the frontier came to be identified as Ohio, Texas, Kansas, and Minnesota. Such identity was an overriding concern for an area's first settlers. They felt the isolation of the frontier, so their first loyalty was to

Charlotte Ouisconsin Van Cleve, Minnesota pioneer and author.
Courtesy of the Minnesota Historical Society

themselves. In moving to the frontier, they had been inspired by the desire to reject the old and try the new, and their zeal was fired by the belief that in a new land they could form their own territories and states. They had little patience with the thought of government by remote power, and so states' rights, a philosophy as old as the federal union, was an important concept to frontier people.

From the ratification of the Dakota and Ojibwe treaties to the formation of the state of Minnesota, between 1838 and 1858 national expansionism was at a fever pitch—and Minnesotans as a politically identifiable people came into being. Wisconsin Territory was created in 1836, and its leaders assumed that when Wisconsin became a state, it would

have the Mississippi River as its western boundary: the Northwest
Ordinance of 1787 had specified that not more than five states could be
formed out of the Old Northwest, and four states had already been created. When Henry Dodge, territorial governor of Wisconsin, negotiated a
treaty with the Ojibwe at Fort Snelling in 1837, he envisioned those rich
pine forests of the upper St. Croix Valley and all the lands bordering the
west side of St. Anthony Falls as Wisconsin lands. What he did not fore-
see was the tug of war that would occur before the fate of the St. Croix
Valley was finally determined.

Among those who impatiently awaited the Indian land cessions was
Major Joseph Plympton, commandant of Fort Snelling. Plympton was
interested in claiming land for himself, but he had another interest—he
wanted to expel civilian squatters from the military reservation. Over the
years the land about the fort had become a haven for refugees from Selkirk's
Red River colony and for assorted French Canadian drifters. These civilians
had become an irksome problem; the traffic in liquor was almost impossible to control, and Plympton complained that they used so much timber,
fuel was scarce near the fort, and that their cattle and horses grazed at will
on military ground. In July 1838, as soon as the treaties had been ratified
and public land was available, Plympton banned civilian construction of
buildings and cutting of timber on the military reservation. While the trespassers were not forcibly evicted, some of them interpreted the order as an
expulsion notice and removed themselves some four miles downstream to
public domain well outside the post boundaries. Among those who relo-
cated was Pierre "Pig's Eye" Parrant, who soon became the most notorious
character in the straggling settlement. Parrant, about sixty years old, was a
onetime voyageur who had lived at Sault Ste. Marie, St. Louis, and Prairie
du Chien before moving to Mendota. He had a bad reputation; his conduct
was said to be "intemperate and licentious," and his appearance lent cre-
dence to the reputation, for he was described as a "coarse, ill-looking, low-
browed fellow" who "spoke execrable English."[1] Parrant had only one good
eye. His other was "blind, marble-hued, crooked, with a sinister white ring
glaring around the pupil," which gave "a kind of piggish expression to his
sodden, low features."[2] Application of the name Pig's Eye to the settlement
came about quite accidentally. Inspired by Parrant's crooked eye, a cus-
tomer at his tavern gave "Pig's Eye" as the return address on a letter he
was sending. Everyone in the vicinity knew Parrant, and when the response
addressed to Pig's Eye arrived, it was carried directly to the settlement
around Parrant's establishment.

The Roman Catholic bishop of Dubuque soon saw the need to send a missionary to the Fort Snelling vicinity. Though Father Lucian Galtier, a native of France, was but twenty-nine years old and barely able to speak English when he arrived in the summer of 1840, he was to change the destiny of Pig's Eye. The next year the priest built a small log-cabin church along the waterfront. With an eye to the future commerce of the place, he chose a site near what would be a suitable steamboat landing for the erection of his church—a church so humble, he said, "that it would well remind one of the stable at Bethlehem."[3] Because of the biblical association of the apostles Peter and Paul and the close proximity of his residence at Mendota—which was then called St. Peter's, after the river—Galtier dedicated his chapel to St. Paul.

Galtier's hope that this name, which he believed was recognizable by all Christians, would replace the appalling Pig's Eye came to pass. Because of the chapel the place soon became known as St. Paul's Landing; within a few years after the establishment of a post office in 1846, it was generally known as St. Paul. So the name was changed, but hardly so abruptly as a later wit suggested when he wrote the following:

Pig's Eye, converted thou shalt be, like SAUL;
Arise, and be, henceforth, SAINT PAUL![4]

Under its new name, old Pig's Eye was destined to become a bustling commercial center and the capital of both the territory and state of Minnesota. Parrant, perhaps no longer comfortable in his surroundings, moved several miles downstream to the vicinity of Pig's Eye Lake.

St. Paul developed as a trading center at the practical head of navigation on the Upper Mississippi, but the other early settlements in the ceded area started as lumber towns. St. Anthony Falls had long been eyed for its great waterpower potential, and a number of aspiring claimants fretted through the winter of 1837–38 awaiting word that the treaties had been ratified. At last, on July 15, 1838, the steamboat *Palmyra* docked at Fort Snelling carrying word that the agreements had gone into effect. Major Plympton's hopes of claiming the ceded ground on the east side of the falls were dashed by young Franklin Steele, a storekeeper at Fort Snelling. Steele, a Pennsylvanian who had already claimed the falls of the St. Croix, moved with dispatch after the *Palmyra's* arrival. Plympton's men reached the falls within a day after word of the treaties arrived, only to find that Steele and his men had worked through the night staking a claim to one of the nation's choicest sites. Steele did not gain legal title to the claim until it was sold at public auction ten years later. He then built a dam at the falls and began sawing logs cut from the Rum River area. Largely because of Steele's activities, the town of St. Anthony developed.

In the meantime, other lumber towns had sprung up in the St. Croix Valley, where the first sawmill began operating at Marine on St. Croix in August 1839. Nearby, at the head of Lake St. Croix, the widening of the river, fur trader Joseph Renshaw Brown had claimed a townsite. He named the place Dacotah and had visions of an empire, but fortune had a way of eluding Brown. Other men platted a townsite nearby, and before long the new town, Stillwater, outstripped Dacotah and in time absorbed it.

The settlers on the Upper Mississippi and the St. Croix were far removed from most Wisconsinites, who lived south of a line from Green Bay through Madison to Prairie du Chien, and the gap was more than geographic. The men of the Upper Mississippi were not the "Badgers" of the lead mines or the wheat farmers of Dane County. Many were lumberjacks direct from the forests of New England. Most had moved to the St. Croix area without even passing through the settled portions of Wisconsin Territory and thus had little sense of identity with its miners and farmers. Instead, they struck up an understandable alliance with the scattering of fur traders who were moving out of the declining trade into townsite speculation and lumbering.

To provide a legal framework for the vast domain stretching from Lake Pepin to the international boundary, the Wisconsin territorial legislature created St. Croix County. The beginning of the county in 1840 was a landmark for the isolated lumbermen and traders. It gave the towns a common bond and provided invaluable experience for the politically conscious who vied for such positions as county commissioner, sheriff, and membership in the territorial House and Council. Joseph R. Brown soon emerged as the area's most prominent politician. He was the county's first representative in the territorial legislature and won the friendship of key men in Madison. Brown led the formation of a county Democratic organization through which the separatist beliefs of the residents of St. Croix County were propagated. Their relative isolation and their economic uniqueness caused many of these residents to believe that they should be detached from Wisconsin. Thus liberated, they would become the nucleus of a new territory.

The first separation attempt came with Wisconsin's effort to organize as a state in 1846. Morgan Martin, Wisconsin's territorial delegate to Congress, opened the drive for statehood by introducing an enabling bill in the House of Representatives. Martin, basing his arguments on the Northwest Ordinance, preferred a state with the old territorial limits, but most congressmen were of the opinion that a state whose western border followed the Mississippi to its source would be unmanageably large. Expansionists such at Stephen Douglas of Illinois recognized that by restricting Wisconsin they would create the opportunity for the organization of another state roughly equal to it in size out of the remainder of the Northwest. Consequently, the Wisconsin Enabling Act as passed by Congress provided for the present western boundary of the state—a line that for most of its distance follows the St. Croix and Mississippi Rivers.

Residents of St. Croix County had mixed feelings about the act. They were unhappy with a boundary that split the St. Croix Valley, but they were pleased that Congress had denied Wisconsin a large portion of the Northwest. The congressional action was not necessarily final, however, because traditionally enabling legislation was considered a recommendation, not a binding action. So the boundary question was an issue to be considered during the Wisconsin constitutional convention.

In the apportionment for the convention, St. Croix County was accorded one delegate on the basis of its 1,419 inhabitants. The voters chose William Holcombe, agent for a lumber company who later became the first lieutenant governor of Minnesota. Holcombe proved to be a highly articulate spokesman for those who wanted to withdraw from Wisconsin and take a fair portion of it with them.

He had visions of a new state northwest of Wisconsin—a lumbering and commercial state centered in the St. Croix Valley, most likely with Stillwater as its capital, that would enjoy the benefits of both the Mississippi River and Lake Superior. Therefore, Holcombe proposed that Wisconsin's northwestern boundary be drawn from a point on the Mississippi below present-day Winona to the western edge of Upper Michigan. Such a boundary, he contended, would leave room for another state to be formed out of the Old Northwest. He argued that Wisconsin would otherwise be too large and quite out of proportion to other states; but if a sister state to her northwest was created, sectional interests would be more strongly represented in Congress. Presuming what within a few years came to be called popular sovereignty, Holcombe contended that for government to be effective, it had to be close to the people. A "remote location" more than three hundred miles from Madison, he argued, "will continue to be as it has been a source of vexation and to a great degree destructive of the very end which a good government has in view."[5]

But the delegates overwhelmingly rejected a proposal that would have denied the state access to Lake Superior and cost it one sixth of the area east of the St. Croix. Holcombe managed one small victory. The constitutional convention finally agreed not to divide the St. Croix Valley and accepted a boundary from Lake Superior to the Mississippi that would lie about fifteen miles east of the St. Croix. But because of several other controversial sections, such as liberal women's rights provisions and certain banking stipulations, the document was overwhelmingly rejected in the April 1847 election.

The aspiring secessionists of the St. Croix Valley tried again in the second constitutional convention. George W. Brownell, Holcombe's successor, urged the acceptance of the "Holcombe Amendment"; but the delegates not only rejected it, they instead accepted a resolution advising Congress that Wisconsin preferred a northwestern boundary running from near the mouth of the St. Louis River (present Duluth) to a point on the Mississippi only about fifteen miles upstream from St. Anthony Falls. Such a line would have placed Stillwater, St. Paul, and St. Anthony and half of St. Anthony Falls in Wisconsin and would certainly have fulfilled the St. Croix desire that the valley not be divided.

This preference of the second constitutional convention created a crisis for those who wanted to be left out of Wisconsin. Their only hope of salvation, they believed, was to win a reprieve for the newly identified area of Minnesota in Washington. The name Minnesota was first used politically in late 1846 when Morgan Martin, at the very time he proposed statehood for Wisconsin, also asked that Minnesota Territory be formed. Martin evidently saw a Minnesota Territory as advantageous in hastening a treaty with the Dakota that would benefit his fur-trade associates. Also, he probably believed that the removal of Indians from Wisconsin's western border would help his new state to attract settlers. Martin's effort and a second attempt were defeated by Congress, which was unimpressed with the Minnesota area's meager population. Significantly, these failures gave the people west of the St. Croix River a common identity and a common cause.

After Wisconsin's second constitutional convention both Brownell and Holcombe urged the Wisconsin territorial delegate to continue to support their cause, and about 350 men described as residents within the

limits of Minnesota Territory (as defined by Martin's proposal) sent a petition to Washington. They asked for a Wisconsin northwestern boundary
that was not much less ambitious than Holcombe's original proposal. If
it was denied, they prophesied, "the prospects of Minnesota would be for-
lorn indeed." Appealing to the sympathies of Congress, the petitioners
wrote that they had

> full confidence that your honorable bodies will consult the wishes of those
> who are most interested in the solution of this question; and will not do so
> much violence to the feelings of the people of this region as to place them
> within the limits of Wisconsin, in utter disregard of their prayers and
> remonstrances.[6]

The petitioners caused a congressional airing of the boundary question.
The long and sharp debate in the House of Representatives jeopardized
the admission of Wisconsin for a troubled time in the spring of 1848.
Rather than take a partisan stance, the representatives compromised by
voting to admit Wisconsin as a state with the northwestern boundary as
specified in the enabling act. Thus, after two years and thousands of
words, the subject had come full circle and the state of Wisconsin, which
came into the union on May 29, 1848, included the eastern portion of the
St. Croix Valley.

After the admission of Wisconsin, Brown, Holcombe, and other politicians lamented the condition of those unfortunates who had been left
"outside of the United States." Because Congress had not created a territory west of Wisconsin when the state was formed, they contended that
because they no longer benefited from the legal guarantees of the
Northwest Ordinance, they had been relegated to the status of an unorganized territory. Minnesota's leaders could have bided their time and
within a few years someone would again have proposed a Minnesota
Territory, but they were believers in today rather than tomorrow. And so
a small group of ambitious young politicians moved. Public demonstrations were organized and Stillwater was the scene of an Independence Day
celebration replete with parade and orations. Public meetings were held
in St. Paul. Then, on August 4, 1848, eighteen recognized leaders met at
Stillwater to plan for the area's future. Among them were Henry H.
Sibley, Franklin Steele (who was Sibley's brother-in-law), Joseph Brown,
and William Holcombe. The group issued a call for a convention to be held
at Stillwater on August 26 "to secure an early Territorial organization."[7]

The Stillwater Convention "delegates," whose estimated number ranged from thirty-eight to about one hundred, amounted to Minnesota's founding fathers. Although they came by invitation, they were not averse to leaving the impression that they had been elected by their constituencies. All political and personal differences were sacrificed in the interests of securing a territorial organization. In their one-day meeting, dominated by Joseph R. Brown, they drafted petitions to Congress and President James Polk calling for early territorial organization as a matter of justice and pointing out the difficulties of civil administration in an unorganized territory. In order to represent their case effectively they decided to send a "delegate" to Washington at his own expense. Their choice was Sibley, the most popular Democrat in an area dominated by Democrats. It was generally supposed that if Minnesota Territory was organized while the Democrats controlled the White House, Sibley would be named governor. Furthermore, because of his congenial personality he was expected to win support to Minnesota's cause.

The Stillwater Convention delegates entertained no illusions. They knew that Sibley was not an official delegate from any sort of territory, but merely a spokesman for the area that had come to be known as Minnesota. Would Congress receive such an ambassador without portfolio? The delegates could only hope that Congress would, and they adjourned with the expectation that Sibley would soon make his way to Washington to advance Minnesota's cause.

The politically ambitious Sibley, who was obviously pleased with the outcome of the Stillwater Convention, was soon threatened by postconvention politicking. Weeks before the convention the ingenious William Holcombe, who coveted the delegacy, noted that Congress had not repealed the Wisconsin territorial act when that state had been formed. He wondered if that part of Wisconsin Territory left outside the state did not still exist as Wisconsin Territory. Holcombe's novel premise attracted the attention of John Catlin, the last secretary of Wisconsin Territory. Catlin, who aspired for the governorship of the supposed still existent territory, naturally endorsed Holcombe's view. However, his supportive letter did not reach Holcombe until shortly after the Stillwater Convention. With the Catlin missive in hand, Holcombe easily convinced the key delegates to the Stillwater Convention that to be seated in Congress the territorial delegate would have to be elected by the voters of a legal territory.

The plot thickened when Catlin, as self-proclaimed acting governor of Wisconsin Territory, moved to Stillwater and issued an election proclamation. While Sibley suspected a Catlin-Holcombe scheme to deny him the delegacy, his greatest challenge came from Henry M. Rice, who at various times had been both his partner and his rival in the fur trade. Rice, who deliberately skipped the Stillwater Convention, vied for the delegacy at the urging of some anti-Sibley men. Although Sibley's supporters were worried about Rice, who was very popular among many of the old traders, Sibley easily won the late October election by a vote of 236 to 122 and was soon on his way to Washington as the elected delegate of the alleged Wisconsin Territory.

Despite his election, Sibley was advised by some congressional acquaintances not to introduce himself as the delegate from Wisconsin Territory but merely to act as a lobbyist. But Sibley chose the bolder course and asked to be seated in the House of Representatives, where bona fide territorial delegates could participate in all matters except voting. As expected, there was some discussion in the House over the existence or nonexistence of Wisconsin Territory, but that body, by a two-to-one margin, agreed to seat Sibley. Sibley's greatest support came from the West and Northeast and his strongest opposition from Southerners, who were not anxious to facilitate the creation of another free territory.

It soon became apparent that the representatives did not really believe that Wisconsin Territory still existed. One of Sibley's opponents slyly proposed appropriations for the officers of Wisconsin Territory, anticipating that his motion would touch off a lively controversy. It did. Some representatives insisted that the Wisconsin Territory was real, but eleven others took the floor to contend that it had ceased to exist with the creation of the state. Finally, the House ended the charade by defeating the motion. The meaning of the discussion and rejection was clear: Sibley had been seated as a courtesy. The House was willing to give him a podium from which he could work for the organization of Minnesota Territory, but he would have to move with dispatch, for even his strongest supporters did not care to be saddled with the embarrassment of "Wisconsin Territory" for long.

Stephen Douglas, then in the Senate and the emerging champion of westward expansion, again led the move to organize Minnesota Territory. Douglas's support, while beneficial to Sibley's cause, made the Minnesota bill appear like a Democratic Party aim, contrary to Sibley's desire that it be nonpartisan. The Democrats controlled the Senate, but the Whigs had a bare majority in the House, and their man, Zachary Taylor, had been elected president in 1848. Since Taylor would not be inaugurated until

March 5, 1849, the Whigs naturally chose not to expedite the formation of a Minnesota Territory for which the outgoing Democratic President James Polk could appoint territorial officials.

The Whigs, however, were vulnerable. They wanted the passage of the bill calling for the creation of the Interior Department, which was then pending before Congress. Such a department, they believed, was necessary for the administration of the vast public domain in the Southwest that had been added to the Union as a result of the Mexican War. The creation of this new department would also provide the incoming president with many new positions with which he could reward some of his supporters. Well aware of Whig desires, Douglas authorized Sibley to leak the word that he had enough power in the Senate to block the Interior measure unless the Whigs relented in their opposition to the Minnesota bill. The ploy worked, and in the last hours of the Polk administration the law creating Minnesota Territory was passed.

Since the Minnesota bill was caught up in a political trade-off, no one was particularly concerned about whether the area had the requisite population of 5,000 to be made a territory. Douglas said the region had 8,000 to 10,000 inhabitants, but a sheriff's census taken the following summer showed that the actual number was only about 4,300. The territory included those parts of the Dakotas east of the Missouri and White Earth Rivers. The white inhabitants, who were probably outnumbered by Indians four or five to one, were concentrated in the area from St. Anthony Falls to Stillwater and about Pembina in the Red River Valley.

Although they had their territory, some Minnesotans continued to fret about losing the area east of the St. Croix to Wisconsin. Nearly a year after the formation of Minnesota Territory, the *Minnesota Pioneer* reported that Wisconsinites just east of the St. Croix "are all anxious to be annexed to Minnesota."[8] Despairing of ever changing the boundary, puckish editor James Madison Goodhue suggested that Minnesotans "who have been carried up into Father Abraham's bosom . . . look down with compassion upon our neighbors across the great gulf of the Saint Croix and pray for their safe deliverance."[9]

The organization of Minnesota Territory was part of the national expansionist urge. Under the gospel of Manifest Destiny, the United States had annexed Texas and acquired California and the Southwest as a result of the Mexican War and had won a favorable boundary settlement with Great Britain in the Pacific Northwest. Following the war the mania of Manifest Destiny still persisted. It seemed that the destiny of

Americans was only partially fulfilled. The Whig administration of Zachary Taylor could not emulate Polk by warring against some foreign power on the continent, but it could stimulate internal expansion. So the government, responding to popular demands, encouraged the California gold rush, the exodus of settlers to Oregon, the opening of Kansas and Nebraska, and further Indian land cessions in Minnesota. The Indian was to the expansionists nothing more than a deterrent to progress.

Frontier Minnesotans, like their champion Stephen Douglas, extolled popular sovereignty; they insisted, just as the Puritans of Massachusetts and the Wataugans of Tennessee had believed, that the people in a locality should control their own destiny. They demonstrated their dedication to this creed in heated contention over the Wisconsin boundary, and after territorial organization popular will clamored again—this time for the opening of the lands of the Dakota west of the Mississippi.

The Suland, as it was called in frontier newspapers, was coveted for its agricultural potential. Demands for its cession came from farmers, speculators, townsite promoters, fur traders, mixed-bloods, and the federal government. The young Pennsylvanian Alexander Ramsey, whom President Taylor appointed as the first governor of Minnesota Territory, understood that one of his first tasks was to acquire the Suland. Since Ramsey was a Whig in an area dominated by Democrats, and since political suicide was not one of his aims, he quickly emerged as a champion of expansion. Ramsey's plans dovetailed perfectly with those of the territorial legislature and Henry Sibley, Minnesota's first territorial delegate to Congress. As the leader of the old traders, Sibley had a deep personal stake in a Dakota treaty. Many Dakota were indebted to Sibley's traders, whose only chance of collecting was for the Indians to sell their land.

Despite the general clamor for the Suland and the seeming urgency in negotiating a treaty, the Dakota were not brought to the bargaining table until 1851. Some of the delay was caused by dallying on the part of the Indians, but most of it resulted from behind-the-scenes maneuvering in naming treaty commissioners. Sibley and his associates realized that their claims stood little chance of being honored without sympathetic commissioners. Not only did the Dakota leaders have to be convinced that the tribes must assume responsibility for numerous individual debts, but the claims of rival traders had to be negated.

Finally the government named as cocommissioners Ramsey and Luke Lea, who was commissioner of Indian Affairs in Washington, D.C., and the younger brother of army explorer Albert Lea. Sibley had every reason to be satisfied with these appointees. Lea was sympathetic to Sibley's group and Ramsey and Sibley had become good friends. Anticipating Dakota land cessions, Ramsey and Sibley cooperated in depicting the advance of whites in Minnesota. With the assistance of artists in Washington, they designed a seal portraying a farmer with a plow on the east side of the Mississippi at St. Anthony Falls, and across the river a mounted Indian riding into the setting sun. The Latin motto, which translated as "I fain would see what lies beyond," expressed the expansionist mood. Although the symbolism was clear and the territorial seal with some modifications was later adopted as the Minnesota state seal, the original design had one striking error—the sun was shown setting in the east.

Alexander Ramsey (shown about 1851) was the first governor of Minnesota Territory and the second governor of the state of Minnesota.
Courtesy of the Minnesota Historical Society

Following the advice of Sibley's traders, Ramsey and Lea decided to make two treaties with the Dakota: one with the Sisseton and Wahpeton and the other with the Mdewakanton and Wahpekute. It was generally anticipated that there would be some Dakota resistance, so common sense dictated that the groups be divided. There was no point in meeting the assembled Dakota and letting some leaders think they were a mighty nation. The commissioners chose to meet with the Sisseton and Wahpeton first because they were believed to be the more acquiescent. After they had signed, the resistance expected from some of the Mdewakanton and Wahpekute would be compromised.

Although some of the Sisseton and Wahpeton did not care to surrender their lands, they thought resistance was futile. Some of the older leaders who had been at Prairie du Chien in 1825 and had been taken to Washington in 1837 realized the vast numerical superiority of whites, and they also thought they had learned something from the Black Hawk War, in which the army had crushed the last Indian resistance in Wisconsin. The chiefs could not seriously consider refusing to negotiate. Such an action, they believed, would be desperately reckless and could lead to war and the virtual annihilation of their people. They thought it better to negotiate for adequate compensation and decent reservations. Their stance was understandable in 1851, but before many years had passed some of them regretted their decision.

When Ramsey and Lea met with the Sisseton and Wahpeton leaders at Traverse des Sioux near present-day St. Peter in July 1851, the place had a festive atmosphere. The commissioners came well supplied with provisions and liquor. During the week and a half that the commissioners spent at Traverse des Sioux, editor James Goodhue regularly informed his St. Paul readers of progress. The treaty was also of great interest to a young Baltimore artist, Frank Blackwell Mayer, who traveled from his home to distant Minnesota to witness what he believed would be one of history's greatest moments. Mayer made numerous sketches of the treaty scenes and participants and later produced a large, colorful canvas that captured the pageantry and drama of the treaty-signing.

Ramsey and Lea struck a good bargain for the government. The Sisseton and Wahpeton ceded all their claims south of the 1825 Dakota-Ojibwe boundary for only pennies an acre. At the time the chiefs were satisfied, but they soon realized they had been duped into signing another document in addition to the treaty. When the assembled chiefs were lined up to place their mark on duplicate copies of the treaty, some of them

Signing the Treaty of Traverse des Sioux in July, 1851. Photo of an oil painting
by Frank Blackwell Mayer.
Courtesy of the Minnesota Historical Society

happened to notice Joseph R. Brown, an old acquaintance, standing off to
the side with a document on an upright barrel. Since they were steered to
Brown the Indians dutifully marked the paper, probably thinking it was
nothing more than a third copy of the treaty. It was not. Brown had before
him what came to be known as the traders' paper, under which the chiefs
agreed to use tribal funds to reimburse the fur traders for debts accrued
by various individual Indians. Despite vigorous Indian objections, the
traders were finally paid from government monies that should have gone
to the tribes in payment for the ceded lands. Understandably, Indians
resented the despicable trick of the traders' paper, and this resentment
smoldered for years until it was fired by other causes into the volatile
Dakota Conflict of 1862.

After completing the Traverse des Sioux agreement, Ramsey and Lea
moved down the Minnesota River to meeting grounds near Mendota to
deal with the Mdewakanton and Wahpekute. Although some of the
Lower Dakota wanted to resist the commissioners, their chiefs signed an
agreement very similar to the Treaty of Traverse des Sioux. In the Treaty
of Mendota the Mdewakanton and Wahpekute leaders agreed to cede all
tribal claims to the same tract surrendered by the Sisseton and Wahpeton,
and in a separate agreement some of them acknowledged the traders'
claims. The traders could hardly surprise the Mdewakanton and

Wahpekute with their claims, but they convinced some leaders that acknowledgment of the claims was required before they could be paid for their land.

The Dakota treaties of 1851 have been controversial since their inception. Indian resentment against the government's pressure tactics, the low purchase price, and the traders' papers were important background causes of the Dakota Conflict. Modern critics, ignoring the frontier context of the treaties, offer alternatives ranging from the suggestion that the Dakota should have been left on the land to the idea that they should have at least been paid a fair market price for it. It would have been extremely difficult for the commissioners to have determined a fair market price, and even if they had, they could not have made such an offer because the Senate would never have approved a document so out of keeping with other Indian treaties of the time. The Dakota chiefs realized far better than later observers that they really had no choice, for the expansionist government was determined to oust them and it had the power to do so either politically or militarily. Unfortunately, there is much truth in the comment of interpreter William L. Quinn that the treaties of Traverse des Sioux and Mendota "were as fair as any Indian treaties."[10] Expansionists looked upon all Indian treaties as nothing more than legal devices that would open the land. Though Ramsey and Lea lived long before social Darwinism was developed conceptually, they believed it. And the Dakota treaties are not bygones in Minnesota. Since the 1920s Minnesota's scholars have regularly criticized the connivance and duplicity of the negotiations, and the presence of a well-organized, vocal American Indian Movement in the Twin Cities has served as a constant reminder of the treaties, which many Indians regard as the root of later problems of the Dakota.

The Dakota treaties were not approved by the Senate until June 1852, and because there was some question about the location of the reservations, they were not proclaimed by President Millard Fillmore until February 24, 1853. These delays did not deter speculators and settlers from invading the Suland. During 1852 promoters platted townsites including Winona, Belle Plaine, and Mankato, and there were said to be about five thousand trespassers in the region between the Lower Minnesota and the Mississippi.

Locating the Dakota reservations was a contentious process. The federal government initially favored removing the Dakota to a reservation along the Missouri River in present-day central South Dakota, but this plan was challenged by Minnesota's frontier politicians. In territorial politics, there was a class of men who thrived on the Indian question—"Moccasinites," as they were called by the frontier press. The Minnesota Moccasinites stood for the cession of Indian land, but they did not want the Indians removed from Minnesota. A Missouri River reservation would have meant that St. Louis would have controlled the trade with the Dakota, while a location on the Minnesota River would assure the trade for St. Paul. The significance of the Indian trade can be appreciated more fully when one considers that the residents of Minnesota Territory were not greatly different from the early colonial planters of Virginia, who talked grandly of money but had very little. There was plenty of land in Minnesota after the Dakota treaties, but there were no exports and the best opportunity to acquire money was from federal payments to the Indians. The Moccasinites, who included many of the old fur traders, realized far better than anyone else that federal payments to the Dakota would soon pass into the hands of local traders.

If the Moccasinites had a high priest, it was Henry Mower Rice, the former trader who had challenged Sibley after the Stillwater Convention. Rice had considerable real estate interests in St. Paul and he fancied himself a man who could deal with the Indians, so he was strongly committed to the goal of keeping them within the St. Paul trade area. Rice and his cohorts thought of putting the Dakota on the Upper Minnesota, and it was probably Rice who as territorial delegate maneuvered the movement of the Ho-Chunk (Winnebago) from Long Prairie to Blue Earth County rather than to the Missouri River in 1855. The creation of a Ho-Chunk reservation within the Dakota cession and the removal of the white squatters in order to do it can be explained only in light of the determination that the Indians should be supplied from St. Paul.

Keeping the Dakota within the St. Paul trade area was the most important determinant in locating their reservations, but there were other considerations. Rice and the other traders who had a voice in the selection of reservation sites may even have believed that it was more humane to leave the Dakota on reservations within the ceded area than to remove them from their native soil entirely. The final selection of an area along the Upper Minnesota was probably influenced by the belief that the land along that part of the river was not worth much and would not be in immediate demand. This, however, was a miscalculation, for the rush of settlers into the Suland was so staggering that the Dakota were forced to relinquish the northern half of their reservations in 1858.

During the fall of 1853 the last of the Dakota were moved onto their reservations. Although the Indians had only one government agent to administer to them, physically there were two reservations. Both were long and but ten miles wide on each side of the river. The Upper Sioux Reservation extended from the head of Big Stone Lake to the Yellow Medicine River (several miles southeast of present Granite Falls), and the Lower Sioux ran from the Yellow Medicine to Little Rock Creek (north of Sleepy Eye). Although the army located Fort Ridgely near the eastern end of the Lower Sioux Reservation, the troops made little effort to keep the Indians within its bounds. This policy, along with the great length of the reservation, gave the Dakota an important tactical advantage in the Dakota Conflict of 1862 because they could sweep out upon white settlers along a broad front.

The Dakota treaties did not satisfy the appetite of the Minnesota expansionists who wanted access to the forest lands of northern Minnesota as well as the farmlands of the south, and within two years of ratification the federal government persuaded the Ojibwe to cede vast tracts stretching from Lake Superior to the upper part of the Red River. By the end of the territorial period, more than four fifths of the future state had been sold by the Dakota and Ojibwe. Only the northwest and a north central area remained in tribal hands.

The attainment of statehood accentuated demands for further cessions, especially of the northwest, including much of the fertile Red River Valley, which was also the commercial artery connecting St. Paul and Fort Garry (i.e., Winnipeg). Minnesota, however, was interested not only in liquidating Indian land claims but also in expanding yet farther, into Canada.

Manifest Destiny abated nationally after the Gadsden Purchase from Mexico in 1853, but in its lingering days it had a particular impact in Minnesota, where expansionists overtly strived to annex much of Canada. Annexationist sentiment, which peaked in the late 1860s, was a natural outgrowth of Minnesota's ties with the Selkirk settlements on the lower Red River—ties that were encouraged by the laxity of the international boundary.

Since World War I both Canada and the United States have taken pride in the "unguarded boundary" separating their countries. It is ironic that the term is a fairly recent one, since much of the boundary (including that in the Red River Valley) was much freer in the years after its establishment than it has been in recent times. Although the forty-ninth parallel boundary was agreed upon diplomatically in 1818, Great Britain and the United States made no effort to survey and mark it until the 1870s. The astronomer for Stephen H. Long's 1823 expedition did determine the point where the line touched the west bank of the Red River, but the single wooden post that was left behind was looked upon as nothing more than a road marker by Canadians and Americans who crossed the boundary with impunity. Without question, the natural unity of the Red River Valley prevailed over the artificiality of a boundary that was not even marked upon the ground.

Because of this, when several hundred Selkirkers abandoned their settlements about Winnipeg in the 1820s, they found it far easier to enter the United States by way of the Red River than to move to eastern Canada or return to Europe. American fur traders located near Fort Snelling also recognized that they were in a much better position to supply the settlers in the lower Red River area than Canadian or European competitors whose two possible trade routes—one by river from Hudson Bay and the other by the traditional canoe route through the Great Lakes and the border waterways west of Lake Superior—were both slower and more hazardous than routes from Minnesota through the Red River Valley.

American trade to the Red River settlements increased sharply after Norman W. Kittson became associated with Henry H. Sibley in 1843. Although he was ostensibly a fur trader, the enterprising Kittson, from his post at Pembina on the North Dakota side of the Red River just south of the border, based much of his lucrative business on transporting merchandise across Hudson's Bay Company territory to Canadian customers in the vicinity of Fort Garry. Kittson and other American traders moved their goods by Red River carts—contraptions developed by Métis in the Red River Valley. The two-wheel carts were usually made entirely without metal. Pulled by a single ox and driven by one person, they usually traveled in caravans over the various Red River trails connecting St. Paul and Fort Garry. These rough-hewn, squeaky carts symbolized Minnesota's northern movement just as surely as the covered wagon symbolized westward movement in the United States.

Kittson's successful defiance of the Hudson's Bay Company tightened the bonds between Fort Garry and St. Paul and caused the isolated Red River settlers to become increasingly dependent on St. Paul and the United States. Because of this trade orientation, some people on both sides of the border thought American acquisition of Rupert's Land, as the holdings of the Hudson's Bay Company in central and western Canada were called, would be desirable. The Hudson's Bay Company did not know how to deal with Kittson's challenge and was slow to react. Consequently, Kittson's free trade during the 1840s led Minnesota expansionists to believe that the company's days were numbered and that its vast territory would fall like a ripe plum into American hands rather than become part of Canada.

Annexationist dreams were first expressed in the early days of Minnesota Territory, but they were vague and unfocused. Father Georges-Antoine Belcourt, an American Catholic missionary at Pembina, suggested just months after Minnesota Territory was formed that a part of Rupert's Land could easily become part of the United States if the federal government would only support its acquisition. Belcourt's sentiments were shared by Rice and Sibley as well as Alexander Ramsey. As Sibley and Ramsey were planning the Dakota cession of southern Minnesota, they also strove to develop northwestern Minnesota. Ramsey unsuccessfully sought federal aid to improve the Red River trails and to build an army post at Pembina, but Sibley secured a congressional appropriation to negotiate a treaty with the Ojibwe.

The ink was barely dry on the Dakota treaties of 1851 when Ramsey journeyed to the Red River Valley to treat with the Ojibwe. Ramsey persuaded their leaders to sell a block of land abutting the international boundary for only a few cents an acre. The agreement promised to open yet another portion of Minnesota to settlement and to put the added pressure of American land seekers on Canada's doorstep. However, the grand scheme to open both southern and northwestern Minnesota was aborted in the Senate. Southerners who viewed the rapid settlement of Minnesota as a threat to the delicate sectional balance in the Senate opposed all three Minnesota treaties, and to save the Dakota treaties Sibley had to sacrifice the Ojibwe agreement.

This setback and more determined resistance to American traders by the Hudson's Bay Company cooled expansionist ardor somewhat, but Minnesota's dream of expanding across the border was revived and intensified by the writings and speeches of the persuasive James Wickes Taylor. Taylor, who emerged as the chief propagandist of Minnesota's Manifest Destiny, was convinced that interior Canada was destined to become part of the United States even before he moved from his native Ohio to St. Paul in 1857. Taylor and his followers believed that Rupert's Land would be another Oregon. It was destined to become part of the American nation because it lay within the commercial sphere of St. Paul, and Taylor assumed its straggling settlers would be anxious to become part of the United States. With an eye to Rupert's Land, Taylor during prestatehood days was one of the principal advocates of shaping Minnesota so that it bordered on Canada. Much of the support for this idea seems to have been based on the belief that it would give Minnesota a tactical advantage in the future quest for Rupert's Land.

Minnesota's expansionists seized on the Fraser River gold rush to promote their cause. St. Paul newspapers in 1858 likened the discoveries in present British Columbia to those in Australia and glorified to gold seekers the advantages of a route from St. Paul across Canada to Fraser River. For Minnesotans, Fraser River was more important than the concurrent Pike's Peak gold rush, because it held not only the promise of individual gains but the opening of a road to an empire that might prove to be for Minnesota and the Northwest what the Santa Fe Trail had been for the American Southwest. Taylor and his principal associates, Ramsey and Kittson, organized meetings of a Fraser River Congress to promote their road plans. Although some gold seekers trekked from St. Paul to Fraser River, the road was never built, but the Fraser River excitement spurred Minnesota's reach for Rupert's Land to new heights.

Taylor and his cohorts were greatly frustrated during the Civil War years, when the promises of expansion and economic growth were checked by the Dakota Conflict. The war's end was welcomed by these would-be expansionists as an opportunity to build railroads, settle the land, and pressure Canada for the cession of Rupert's Land. Soon after the war, Minnesota's interest emerged as undisguised imperialism. Before 1865, despite some talk of annexation, Minnesotans (and St. Paulites especially) seemed to be much more interested in a commercial alliance than in annexation, but after the war the expansionists would settle for nothing less than American ownership of much of Canada. Taylor, buoyed by his own enthusiasm, called for a union of the United States and Canada. Under his 1866 proposal, the eastern Canadian provinces would have entered the United States as states and the remainder of Canada would have become American territories or public domain.

Although Taylor's scheme received much publicity in Canada and the United States, there was scant Canadian support and not a great deal more south of the border. Nathaniel Banks of Massachusetts, who was sympathetic to the goals of Irish nationalism and an ardent Anglophobe, proposed Taylor's plan in the House of Representatives, but there was only a scattering of support. Then Alexander Ramsey, who had become a

United States senator, adopted the cause in Congress. Ramsey twice proposed annexation of Rupert's Land, but, like Taylor, he soon realized that time and circumstances were against him. Great Britain effectively undercut any Canadian desire to defect to the United States with the Dominion Act of 1867, which gave the Canadians an unprecedented degree of self-government. Then, during the same year, the United States purchased Alaska from Russia, which seemed to indicate to disheartened Minnesotans that the federal government was much more interested in that seemingly worthless region than in Canada. During the congressional debate over funding the Alaska Purchase, Minnesota expansionists rallied to its support, for they saw it as an effective way of squeezing Canada between American scissors. Frustrated by lack of congressional enthusiasm, Ramsey and Taylor sought to pressure Congress with a resolution from the Minnesota legislature, and Taylor wrote the resolution, which the legislature passed on March 6, 1868. The measure supported the funding of the Alaska Purchase, expressed its regret that there had been no plebiscite of the settlers in Rupert's Land over the British decision to make it part of Canada, and added that the "cession of northwest British America to the United States, accompanied by the construction of a northern Pacific railroad" would satisfactorily "remove all grounds of controversy between the respective countries."[11]

Congress remained unimpressed. Despite some oratory by Ramsey in the Senate and Ignatius Donnelly in the House, Congress simply could not accept the idea that Minnesota had a natural destiny to control much of Canada. The rejection was a question not so much of philosophy as of time. The utterances of Ramsey and Donnelly would have been well received during the fervor of the Mexican War, but they were strangely out of place with the mood of the Reconstruction era. Their ideas were old, not new, and had been heard many times before in the halls of Congress. American interest in Canada had been evident in both the Revolutionary War and the War of 1812, and Manifest Destiny was as logically applied to Rupert's Land as it had been to Oregon earlier. But Minnesota's Manifest Destiny was just that—it was Minnesota-inspired, Minnesota-promoted, and Minnesota-supported, but it was the beat of a lonely drummer.

Taylor and Ramsey did not give up easily. Without congressional backing they turned to the Grant administration, from which they elicited private assurances of support, but there was no desire to confront Great Britain over the issue. Finally, in 1870, the expansionists were undone when Canada signaled its determination to govern its own national destiny by organizing the province of Manitoba and sending troops to Winnipeg.

Canada's decisive actions marked an end to Minnesota's long quest for territory. The futile march for empire had run its course, but Ramsey, Taylor, and the other expansionists were proven right in one sense at least. Though they were forced to recognize that Minnesota's physical border had been fixed by its 1858 boundaries, they lived to see a vast economic hinterland added to Minneapolis and St. Paul's sphere of influence as Twin Cities–based railroads edged their way across the northern plains in the 1870s and 1880s

5

―

TRIALS OF STATEHOOD

POPULATION GAINS DURING the territorial years exceeded the wildest dreams of Minnesota's boosters. The steady influx following the approval of the Dakota treaties led the territory's official statistician to estimate the 1855 population at 40,000. The following year there were a reported 100,000, and an official census taken in 1857 preparatory to statehood showed 150,037 inhabitants. In percentages this was the sharpest period of growth in Minnesota's entire history.

The population boom caused territorial officials to launch a statehood drive in 1856—a campaign nearly two years long, and one plagued by party politics. Although Minnesota Democrats and Republicans have had many differences over the years, they were never further apart than during the transition into statehood. Leading Democrats, including Sibley and Rice, like their party nationally, seemed oblivious to the emotional aspects of the slavery issue that shattered political harmony during the 1850s. As staunch supporters of Stephen Douglas's popular sovereignty, Minnesota Democrats were not at all prepared for the spontaneous, angry reaction to the Douglas-sponsored Kansas-Nebraska Act of 1854.

This act, which left the question of slavery in Kansas and Nebraska to be settled by the vote of their inhabitants, was challenged vigorously by opponents of slavery and led to the formation of the Republican Party. When the Minnesota Republican Party was formed during the spring and summer of 1855, its primary aim was opposition to the extension of slavery. Although the only slaves in the territory were those like Dred Scott, who were brought into the area as servants, slavery was an issue in all Minnesota political campaigns and legislative sessions until its abolition.

Minnesota's newly formed Republican Party unsuccessfully challenged Rice's reelection bid, then bided its time. Most of the native-born who were moving into the territory were antislavery Northerners who also supported the Republican call for homestead, or free land, legislation, and most immigrants too had little sympathy for slavery. By the late territorial period it was just a matter of time until the Republicans would gain political control.

As Republican numbers swelled, political rivalry took on a sectional complexion. The Democrats had their greatest strength in the old commercial and lumbering towns—St. Paul, St. Anthony, and Stillwater—while the Republicans dominated the agricultural southeast. Republicans generally believed that they could control an agricultural state, particularly one that was long and narrow, running from the Mississippi to the Missouri with a northern boundary that would leave St. Paul and Stillwater barely within it. Democrats generally favored a state whose economy would be based on both agriculture and lumbering and would stretch from Iowa to the international boundary.

With the future shaping of Minnesota in mind, promoters of southern Minnesota schemed to move the capital from St. Paul to St. Peter in the Minnesota River Valley. A St. Peter capital, they thought, might stimulate the construction of a railroad through southern Minnesota and might also lead to the creation of that long, narrow state in which St. Peter would be the approximate center of population. Though Republicans may have been the prime movers in the scheme, capital removal was not strictly a party issue: some Democrats outside the larger towns resented St. Paul's eminence, and some were members of the St. Peter Company, which stood to gain from capital removal.

The St. Peter Company, which had been chartered by the territorial legislature and authorized to construct buildings in Le Sueur and Nicollet Counties, included Democratic Governor Willis A. Gorman among its prominent members. Whether the chartering of the company was part of the plot is not clear, but within months the interests of the land company and other boosters of southern Minnesota joined in a common cause. In February 1857, when statehood appeared imminent, St. Peter advocates proposed a capital removal bill, which passed both houses of the territorial legislature. St. Paulites were alarmed over the threatened loss of the capital and took action. Joe Rolette, councilman from Pembina and chairman of the committee on engrossed bills, disappeared with the engrossed removal bill—all the way to a hotel room in St. Paul, where he stayed in hiding for a week. The council's sergeant at arms, another St. Paul supporter, conducted a systematic search of all of the wrong places and could not find Rolette. Tradition has it that Rolette dramatically reappeared in the council chambers as the presiding officer brought the session to its close.

Rolette, who was the mixed-blood son of Old Joe Rolette, captured the popular imagination as the man who saved the capital for St. Paul. His prank was actually all in vain, for during his absence another copy of the capital removal bill was passed on to Governor Gorman, who signed it. The act was duly printed as a territorial law, and the St. Peter Company, anticipating that the capital would be moved by May 1, 1857, as required by the act, constructed a modest frame capitol in St. Peter. But Gorman was replaced as territorial governor and territorial officials made no effort to move to the new capital. Supporters of the St. Peter Company had only one recourse—they went to court. Finally, in July 1857, federal district judge Rensselaer R. Nelson ruled that the territorial legislature had exhausted its power of locating when it had named St. Paul the capital, and also that the act signed by Gorman was not a law since it had not been acted on properly. As a result of Judge Nelson's ruling, St. Paul kept the capital and St. Peter's frame building later served for some years as the Nicollet County courthouse.

While much public attention was focused on the capital removal sideshow, Minnesota's main act was playing in the halls of Congress, where Henry Rice had proposed the formation of the state. Rice's motion of December 24, 1856, which was prompted by the year's unprecedented population growth, caused no debate in the House of Representatives although many Southerners voted against it. However, its introduction in the Senate by Stephen Douglas touched off a fiery contest between sectional protagonists. Northerners saw the admission of Minnesota as an opportunity to add two more free senators, and Southerners saw it as a move that would shatter the delicate sectional balance in the Senate. Although most of the criticism was based on the polite arguments that statehood was premature and the population was too sparse, there was some blunt talk. Senator John B. Thompson of Kentucky argued that new states cost the federal government too much for roads, canals, forts, and lighthouses; and he candidly stated that he did not want two Minnesota

Commonly regarded as one of Minnesota's greatest politicians, Henry Mower Rice,
while serving as territorial delegate, proposed Minnesota statehood in 1856.
Courtesy of the Minnesota Historical Society

senators who would be "arrogant" toward the South. Holding that
Congress was not obligated to form a state simply because it had a certain
population, Thompson proposed a solution:

> instead of taking into partnership and full fellowship all these outside
> Territories and lost people of God's earth, I would say let us take them, if

we must do it, and rule them as Great Britain rules Affghanistan, Hindostan, and all through the Punjaub, making them work for you as you would work a negro on a cotton or sugar plantation.[1]

When Thompson voted against statehood for Minnesota, he was joined by twenty-one other senators, all from the South. Despite this opposition, the Minnesota Enabling Act was passed on February 26, 1857. The act closely followed Rice's preference for a state encompassing both prairie and forest, bounded on the south by Iowa, on the east by Wisconsin, on the north by Canada, and on the west by a line from the international boundary south through the main channel of the Red and Bois des Sioux Rivers, then through Lakes Traverse and Big Stone, and from the foot of Big Stone Lake by a line due south to the Iowa border.

After the passage of the Enabling Act, Minnesota's road to statehood was very rough. The election of delegates to the constitutional convention was hotly contested, with slavery as the burning issue. Through their newspapers and from the stump, Democratic candidates lashed out at the "Black Republicans" and decried racial equality. On June 1, 1857, only days before the election, the *St. Paul Pioneer and Democrat* proclaimed the real issue to be "White Supremacy against Negro Equality!"

Both parties claimed victory in the election, and because of a monumental error there was no way to determine who had actually won. In implementing the Enabling Act, the territorial legislature misinterpreted, perhaps deliberately, the section pertaining to election districts. As a result, the voters chose 108 constitutional delegates, or 30 more than was intended under the Enabling Act. Republicans and Democrats alike did not believe that the territorial government could rule on the legality of particular elections, so the matter of 30 disputed seats was left to the constitutional convention.

Shortly after assembling in July 1857 in St. Paul, the convention delegates found that the venomous campaign still divided them. Democrats and Republicans could not agree on the seating of delegates or even on the choice of a presiding officer. The disagreement was so deep-seated that delegates of each party formed their own constitutional convention—each referred to as "the" Minnesota Constitutional Convention. The two conventions met separately for more than a month with little thought of reconciliation. If anything, antagonism deepened. The Democratic territorial treasurer even refused to process expense claims of the Republicans.

Each convention kept its own records of proceedings and drafted its own constitution. Both Democrats and Republicans used the constitutions of other states as models and in some cases copied provisions from them, but the delegates in both conventions also debated issues unique to Minnesota. There was strong minority support for the east-west state, but the majority in both groups favored the Enabling Act provision, in part out of fear that any change would jeopardize statehood. Within the Republican convention there was considerable debate over the question of extending suffrage to blacks. Advocates of black suffrage saw it as a way of protesting the Dred Scott decision, which had been handed down by the Supreme Court only a few months before; but the Republican delegates finally concluded that a black suffrage provision might cause the defeat of the constitution, so they settled for a provision in their draft that the question would be decided by referring it to the voters.

Realizing that the charade had to end sometime, leaders of both conventions formed a compromise committee to reconcile differences between their documents. Considering the volatile background, the committee worked reasonably well, although harmony was somewhat disturbed when ex-governor Gorman broke his cane over the head of Republican Thomas Wilson, who Gorman alleged had provoked the act by swearing at Democratic committee members. The compromise committee agreed that a single document was needed; but rather than write a new draft, they wrote the hundreds of little agreements on words and phrases into the Democratic version of the constitution and then did the same with the Republican constitution. The net result was two documents, both marred by numerous minor errors.

The bitter legacy of the dichotomous constitutional convention carried over into the election of state officers. In October 1857, when Henry Sibley narrowly defeated Alexander Ramsey for the governorship and the Democrats gained control of the legislature, charges of deception and fraud were freely exchanged. Relishing their victory, the Democrats sent their version of the constitution with the Republican changes incorporated into it to Congress, which had yet to act on the admission of Minnesota.

Congressional approval of Minnesota's statehood hung in the balance for four long months before the state was added to the Union as its thirty-second member on May 11, 1858. Opposition came from both North and South. As the Minnesota question was being considered it was caught up in the Kansas problem, which had plagued Congress intermittently since the Kansas-Nebraska Act. When the proslave Lecompton Constitution was sent to Congress from Kansas, Southerners, arguing that the next admitted state should be proslave, delayed action on the Minnesota bill until Kansas could be considered. Then Northerners expressed reservations about admitting Minnesota to the Union because they feared that Minnesota's Democratic congressional delegation would support slavery in Kansas. After weeks of debate the Kansas issue was compromised, but there were other roadblocks to Minnesota statehood. Senator John Sherman of Ohio, probably acting at the urging of Minnesota Republicans, charged fraud in the delegate election and suggested that it be rerun. Sherman's actions were probably prompted by his belief that the Republicans (who were on the upswing in Minnesota) would win a second election, but his suggestion was rejected.

A last obstacle to statehood was of Minnesota's own creation. Both the Republican and Democratic conventions had overestimated the state's population by about a hundred thousand people. Therefore, they provided for three representatives, and three were duly elected and sent to Washington to await seating when the statehood act was approved. Minnesota's critics said there should be only one; other congressmen favored three. They compromised on two, which left the awkward dilemma of the need to eliminate the extra man. The aspirants agreed to settle the question by drawing lots; William W. Phelps and James M. Cavanaugh won, and twenty-nine-year-old George L. Becker was sent home.

By the time statehood was attained, the vibrant optimism of territorial boom days had been shattered by the Panic of 1857 and the ruinous depression that followed in its wake. Plunging real estate values and countless bankruptcies and foreclosures devastated the frontier economy, which had been based on the promise of future growth rather than on sound money and business. In a desperate effort to counteract the depression, the young state guaranteed a $5 million loan to railroads so that construction could begin.

The railroad loan failed to stem the depression, which continued into the Civil War years. Governor Ramsey was in Washington, D.C., seeking aid for the stricken state when news arrived that Fort Sumter had fallen to South Carolina's troops. Ramsey promptly called on Secretary of War Simon Cameron, an old Pennsylvania acquaintance, and offered one thousand Minnesota troops for the Union cause—an action that gave the state the distinction of volunteering the first soldiers for the Civil War.

Thousands of Minnesotans followed those first men who were induct-
ed in the spring of 1861, and during the course of the war about twenty-
two thousand Minnesotans served in Union forces against the
Confederacy and Dakota Indians. They were represented in all major
campaigns and played a decisive part in the war's turning point, the
Battle of Gettysburg.

During the Civil War, Minnesota's economy and prospects improved
even though they were obviously affected by the Dakota Conflict and the
severe drought of 1862–63. The state's 1860 population of 172,022
increased by 50 percent during the next five years, mainly because the
farming area east of the Dakota Conflict front filled in. As thousands of
acres of virgin farmland were brought under cultivation, wheat production nearly doubled. Lumbering, greatly affected by the drought and by
adverse market conditions, revived sharply in 1865, and even the struggling railroad companies finally emerged from the long shadow of the
depression. St. Paul and Minneapolis were connected by a ten-mile track
in 1862, and by 1865 the state had two hundred miles of rail and St. Paul
was but two years away from being linked to Chicago and points east.

During much of the Civil War Minnesota's attention was focused on
the Dakota Conflict of 1862, one of the bloodiest Indian wars in United
States history. The panic began in August when Minnesotans learned that
some reservation Dakota were on the rampage. Stories of Indian atrocities
spread like a prairie fire and were matched by calls for vengeance. To most
frontiersmen the conflict was without cause, instigated by conscienceless
savages. Some of those who were religiously minded might have agreed
with missionary Stephen Return Riggs that the Dakota "were instigated
by the devil."[2] Before the war, Minnesota pioneers were preoccupied with
the daily concerns of living—planting crops, laying by provisions for
winter, building houses, putting up fences. If they thought about the
Indians at all, it seemed to them that treaties and reservations had taken
care of the Indian "problem." Once the Dakota had been placed on their
Minnesota River reservations, they became the forgotten people of
Minnesota. There were a few whites, among them Episcopal Bishop
Henry Whipple, who sympathized with the Dakota and complained
about government policies—the very policies that later came to be
regarded as the underlying causes of the Dakota Conflict.

Smoldering Dakota resentment over the treaties of Traverse des Sioux
and Mendota was inflamed in 1858 when the federal government, using
a reserve clause in those treaties, forced the Dakota to sell the half of their

reservations that lay on the north side of the Minnesota River. Many Indians saw this move, which was made to satisfy an encroaching finger of speculators and farmers, as a prelude to the loss of the entire reservation and final expulsion from their homeland. Many Dakota were also angered by the government's assimilation policy. Its philosophy was bad enough in itself, but its administration by bureaucrats whose primary qualification was political party service complicated matters. Indians could not really believe that the government cared for their welfare when new political appointees paraded onto the reservations every time a presidential administration changed.

The Dakota Indians were not of one mind regarding government policy. Some, reasoning that resistance was futile, donned white people's clothing, cut their hair short, learned English, converted to Christianity, and began to learn to farm. These "progressives" were derisively labeled "cut-hairs" by the "blanket" faction, who clung to the old ways and longed for the time before whites came. The persistent antagonism between cut-hair and blanket soon undermined tribal unity, and in desperation the militants began to believe that their only salvation was to expel the whites— something that could not be accomplished at the conference table.

Tribal discontent was further inflamed by several crises of the early 1860s. On one occasion the Dakota charged that they were shortchanged when some questionable traders' claims were deducted from their annuities. Crop failures on reservation land caused severe food shortages; and then, during the summer of 1862, government officials in Washington debated over whether to pay the Dakota with gold or paper money, and the Indians' agent refused to issue food until the money arrived. When some of the starving Indians angrily demanded rations, trader Andrew Myrick, according to Chief Little Crow, responded that "they would eat grass or their own dung."[3]

The hungry Dakota wandered the countryside in search of food. On a hot, dry day in August, four young men found some hens' eggs along a fence row near an Acton farmhouse. One of them took the eggs, but a companion warned him that they belonged to a white man. Angered, the first young man threw the eggs on the ground and then dared his comrades to go with him to the white man's farm. Once there, the Indians supposedly asked for liquor. The farmer gave them none and then left, going to a neighbor's place. The Indians followed him there and, after some friendly bantering with the white men, challenged them to a shooting contest. A target was set up, and both sides had discharged their weapons when, without warning, the Indians, who had already reloaded, fired upon the whites. Three men and one woman were killed, and then, while fleeing, the young men killed a fifteen-year-old girl.

There had been a time when tribal leaders would have turned these miscreants over to white authorities, but no more. This time, hotheads led by Chief Shakopee called for war. Somehow they persuaded Little Crow to lead them, although he seemed to have recognized that the Dakota stood no chance of winning. One of his companions years later claimed that Little Crow had a plan to sweep the Minnesota River Valley clean of settlers all the way to St. Paul. Whether or not this was the case, the conflict began with a lashing out against the nearest whites. On August 18, the day after the Acton killings, some Dakota struck the Lower Sioux Agency like warriors of old. With the element of surprise on their side, the Dakota war element (whose hard core probably comprised only about one tenth of the nearly seven thousand Dakota) seized control of the Lower Sioux Agency and nearly annihilated a forty-man relief party from Fort Ridgely in the first day's battle. During a week-long offensive, they also devastated many isolated farms and killed dozens of settlers who could offer only feeble resistance, but they failed to take either Fort Ridgely or New Ulm despite sustained attacks on both places.

Governor Alexander Ramsey responded to the crisis by naming his old friend Henry H. Sibley to lead a fourteen-hundred-man relief expedition from Fort Snelling. Sibley took nine days to make the trip, days that must have seemed interminable to those who cried for help, and then he delayed further at Fort Ridgely, trying to marshal his forces. Impatient frontier editors who wanted swift and harsh punishment of the Dakota pilloried Sibley. Jane Grey Swisshelm, the St. Cloud firebrand, cried out in her paper: "For God's sake put some *live* man in command of the force against the Sioux & let Sibley have 100 men or thereabout for his under-taker's corpse."[4] What Sibley's critics did not recognize was that his fourteen hundred men were the rawest of recruits, most with no military experience at all, and that they did not have enough guns or ammunition or even provisions for all the troops. Sibley had so few horses, he had to impress draft animals from farmers during his march from Fort Snelling.

While Sibley at Fort Ridgely tried desperately to make an army out of his ragtag troops, a military burial party was ambushed by Dakota under Mankato, a Mdewakanton leader, at Birch Coulee near present-day Morton. This skirmish proved to be one of the conflict's major engagements. Sibley finally moved up the Minnesota Valley on September 18, still hop-

Henry H. Sibley commanded Minnesota's military force during the Dakota Conflict
of 1862.
Courtesy of the Minnesota Historical Society

ing to negotiate a settlement. After Little Crow refused to surrender
because Sibley could not guarantee amnesty, the opposing sides fought in the
Battle of Wood Lake, the last engagement of the war, on September 23.

The "battle," an awkward standoff punctuated by intermittent gunfire, caused Little Crow to retreat out of Minnesota.

Most of the Dakota who had fought against the whites fled into Dakota Territory or Canada, but Sibley's men rounded up some two thousand Indians and then set to work trying to separate participants and non-

Little Crow in 1861. After the Dakota Conflict this photograph was liberally sold and circulated on picture postcards and in other forms.

Courtesy of the Minnesota Historical Society

This Dakota woman and hundreds of others were confined in the Fort Snelling
prison compound during the winter of 1862–63.
Courtesy of the Minnesota Historical Society

participants. Over a five-week period in the fall, a military board tried
425 Indians and mixed-bloods for their alleged participation in the war.
The trials were a farce—as many as forty men were tried in a single day
with individual trials lasting only a few minutes. Many of the accused

were sentenced on the testimony of an informer who had bargained for his own safety. Finally the court convicted 321 men, sentencing all but 18 of them to death. However, Bishop Whipple interceded for the Dakota, and because of his plea, President Abraham Lincoln ordered that all death sentences except those of accused and convicted murderers or rapists be reduced to jail terms. On December 26, 1862, 38 Dakota were hanged in Mankato.

Even though the Dakota were either imprisoned or dispersed, Minnesotans who lived on the edge of the frontier, with the prairies stretching endlessly westward, did not really believe that Sibley had vanquished the Indians. There was such widespread fear that hostile Dakota would return that forts were built and manned by settlers for several years along a rough line from St. Cloud to Hutchinson to Blue Earth. Little Crow did return; but when he did, he was accompanied only by his sixteen-year-old son. On July 3, 1863, the Indian leader was ambushed and killed while picking berries in a swamp near Hutchinson, not many miles from Acton, where the war began.

There are those who believe that Little Crow met a kinder fate than many of the peaceful Indians who had raised no hand against the government. Hundreds of Dakota, mostly women and children, were confined in unbelievably crowded quarters at Fort Snelling over the winter of 1862–63, with much illness and many deaths. In the spring the survivors were herded like cattle onto steamboats and carried more than two thousand miles to the desolate Crow Creek reservation on the Missouri River in Dakota Territory. Their living conditions at Crow Creek were so unbearable that missionary Samuel Hinman bitterly concluded that they would have been better off if they had fought the whites. "Bishop," he tersely wrote to his superior, Henry Whipple, "if I were an Ind[ian] I would never lay down the war-club while I lived."[5]

This was just the beginning of the dispersal of the Dakota. After several years of subhuman existence, the survivors of Crow Creek were moved to yet another reservation, this one near Niobrara, Nebraska. Some who fled from Niobrara established a community at Flandreau, South Dakota. Most of the Dakota had not been apprehended in 1862, and many—both hostile and peaceful—fled into the Dakotas, where reservations were later formed for them in northeastern South Dakota and at Devils Lake in North Dakota. Other Dakota escaped into Canada, where their descendants remain on small reservations in the prairie provinces. Some Dakota joined their western brethren and lived out their days on the plains of the western Dakotas, Montana, and Wyoming. Some, such as those who benefited from the hospitality of the half-Dakota Alexander Faribault, remained in Minnesota after the Dakota Conflict, while others straggled back from the Dakotas and established small communities in the 1880s near Granite Falls, Morton, Prior Lake, and Red Wing, where some of their descendants still live.

The effects of the war on the Dakota were calamitous. Though there were few deaths in battle, many died in captivity, and the Indians were so scattered that all hope of tribal unity was gone. Then, with congressional abrogation of the Dakota treaties and the abolition of the Minnesota River reservations, they lost the last of their homeland.

The sudden beginning of the conflict and the initial high loss of life made sensational news both in area newspapers and in the East. A tremendous amount of war literature was generated both contemporarily and later. Atrocity stories abounded, and during the harried opening days of the war, panic-stricken settlers charged that 800 to 1,000 whites had been slaughtered. These figures are still sometimes cited, but in reality, casualties included 413 white civilians, 77 soldiers, and 71 Indians, including the 38 who were executed in Mankato. It is no wonder that many Minnesotans believe the Dakota Conflict was the greatest Indian war in the history of the nation. It was not, but it certainly is a classic example of the failure of United States Indian policy.

In the fury of the first few days of the Dakota Conflict, the western fringes of Minnesota's frontier were virtually abandoned. Many settlers closeted themselves in homemade stockades and others fled to St. Paul or to Wisconsin. Some of them never returned. Even though the Dakota offensive lasted barely more than a week, fear that the warriors would return lingered through the remainder of the Civil War. The mass execution at Mankato marked the height of the Dakota phobia. Since only those identified as murderers and rapists were to be hanged, the execution should have been a solemn administration of justice, essentially no different from the handling of white criminals in a frontier society. But it was instead an act of vengeance carried out in a gaudy, almost carnival atmosphere. A massive single scaffold was erected and its rope was cut by William Duley, who had lost most of his family in the Dakota raid on Lake Shetek settlement. Hundreds of spectators came from miles around, and when the men dropped to their deaths, the crowd burst into cheers.

The Dakota Conflict was to the Minnesota frontiersmen the end of a barbarous era. The presence of even peaceful Indians had troubled white settlers, for as long as Indians roamed the land, there was the potential for war, and as long as reservations remained, there was land that could not be claimed. When the war came it was sudden and shocking, but it should not have been a surprise. The clash between the two civilizations was as inevitable as the outcome, and the removal of the Indians and the abolition of their reservations, in the minds of the settlers, freed Minnesota at last from the final vestiges of savagery.

Time has cooled emotions, and over several generations the interpretation of the conflict has changed. To pioneers it was the "Sioux Uprising," a label in keeping with their view that the Indians were solely to blame. The first historians of the war emphasized atrocities perpetrated by some of the Dakota and overlooked the causes of the Indian discontent. Gradually, however, there has been more and more acceptance of Bishop Whipple's view that the Indians—even though some of them were the aggressors—were driven to war. Consequently, recent histories, beginning with William Watts Folwell's *History of Minnesota,* have included more dispassionate coverage of the war and its causes.

Some thirty years after the war, the state of Minnesota erected four impressive granite obelisks to mark conflict sites. Two were placed near the site of the Birch Coulee skirmish and the others were built at the Wood Lake battlefield and Camp Release, where Sibley effected the release of nearly three hundred white captives several days after the Battle of Wood Lake. Within the next decade a private historical organization placed numerous small markers at selected sites, including the spot where the first white casualty occurred. Partially restored Fort Ridgely is located in Fort Ridgely State Park, which was established in 1911. Additional sites have been marked by county historical societies. These markers and sites, along with the Minnesota Historical Society's interpretive center at the site of the old Lower Sioux Agency near Morton, help place the Dakota Conflict in perspective.

6

PEOPLING THE LAND

AFTER THE CIVIL WAR, Minnesota's agricultural frontier closed
with a great rush. The state's population, 439,000 in 1870, tripled during the next two decades. This movement of people, unprecedented in
terms of raw numbers, hastened the breaking of the prairie as claimants
spilled out of the woods into the less hospitable regions in the southwestern and western parts of the state. By the mid-1880s the choicest
farmlands had been claimed, and would-be farmers who entered
Minnesota after that time usually moved into the cutover areas left in the
wake of the advancing lumbermen.

It was the cheap, fertile land that drew settlers to Minnesota's frontier—land controlled either by federal or state government or by railroad
companies and speculators. After the ratification of the Dakota treaties,
the richest portion of Minnesota became part of the federal government's
public domain. Until the passage of the Homestead Act in 1862, the
United States General Land Office disposed of most of its lands under the
Pre-Emption Act, which provided for the cash sale of surveyed government land through district land offices at a minimum price of $1.25 an
acre. This 1841 act was designed to protect the preemptor or squatter by
giving him first option to purchase, but the law worked poorly in frontier regions because it applied only to surveyed land. Very little of the
Suland was surveyed prior to the settlers' rush in the 1850s, so thousands

of squatters faced the possibility of eviction when the land was sold. The plight of these preemptors caused Minnesota's territorial politicians to lobby hard to change the Pre-Emption Act, and in 1854 Congress did amend the 1841 law so that squatters on unsurveyed land also were assured of the option to buy. This was a major victory for frontiersmen, but agitation for free land was still widespread. After the Republican Party nationally endorsed the homestead principle, Minnesota Republicans in the late 1850s and early 1860s became particularly vociferous. Even Minnesota Democrats, although Southerners in their own party were deeply opposed to the free-land goal, joined the chorus. Southern opposition during the antebellum period caused a number of proposals to fail either in Congress or because of presidential veto, but during the Civil War the secession of the Southern states made it possible for a Union Congress in 1862 to pass the Homestead Act at last.

When the act went into effect in Minnesota there was very little settlement west of a line from Blue Earth through New Ulm and Hutchinson to St. Cloud. Minnesota promoters were quick to point out the advantages of the law: any man or woman at least twenty-one years of age who was an American citizen or had begun the naturalization process could obtain 160 acres of land simply by building a suitable dwelling, living on the claim for five years, and paying nominal closing costs. Although homesteads could be claimed only in designated areas because previous land acts remained in effect, the act proved to be very popular in Minnesota. By 1880 more than sixty-two thousand claims had been made and nearly one seventh of the state had been homesteaded.

Although the government of Minnesota never had free land to dispose of as the federal government did, it nonetheless had a generous land policy. The state was given federal land to support the common schools, the state university, and railroad construction, and it obtained thousands of additional acres as a result of federal swampland acts. Much of that public land was sold during the frontier period at prices even lower than those of the federal government.

Minnesota's prairie homesteaders, like other settlers on the sod-house frontier, had difficulty coping with the treeless environment. Usually the only fuels available were buffalo or cow chips or dried grass. Planting and cultivating trees seemed to be the only answer; so the federal government in 1873 supplemented the Homestead Act with the Timber Culture Act, which required claimants to cultivate 40 acres of trees on their 160-acre claims for five years before they could obtain the land free.

Initial response to the new act was poor, but after an 1874 amendment reduced the requirement to only 10 acres of trees, many settlers filed "tree claims." By the end of 1880 more than a million acres of Minnesota land had been claimed under some 8,000 timber claims. Also in 1873, the Minnesota legislature created a bounty system under which farmers were paid two dollars a year for as long as ten years for each acre of saplings they cultivated. Eight million saplings were planted in 1873; within seven years Minnesotans had planted more than 25,000 acres of trees and more than 900 miles of tree rows along public thoroughfares and between farms. Usually the settlers planted thousands of seedlings, so tiny that they were still very small trees when claims were proved. Many of these trees did not survive, and other stands were cut out after the land became privately owned; nonetheless, many farms in western Minnesota are still sheltered from the sweeping prairie winds by groves planted by those first settlers.

Frontier areas always attract speculators, and in Minnesota their greatest opportunities were created because of the existence of military and Indian scrip. The United States had paid bounties to veterans of the Revolutionary War, the War of 1812, and the Mexican War in the form of certificates that entitled the holder to claim 40 to 160 acres of specified public domain. In some instances scrip was also used to pay off government obligations to Indians and mixed-bloods. By a congressional act in 1852, scrip was made negotiable; since many of the veterans had no intention of moving to the frontier, and since many Indians had no interest in becoming landowners, large amounts of the scrip were sold to merchants, bankers, and speculators, often for next to nothing. The scrip frequently changed hands two or three times before the land was actually claimed, but even then farmers often found it possible to obtain land more cheaply by buying scrip than by paying the government price. Sometimes speculators were able to amass large amounts of scrip and redeem it for parcels of land running to thousands of acres.

Despite Minnesota's bountiful land, the region was regarded as an American Siberia. Though steamboats plied the Mississippi to St. Paul, they were slow and unreliable, and when the river froze, Minnesota was virtually isolated. Understandably, the completion of a railroad to Rock Island, Illinois, about 350 miles downstream from St. Paul, in 1854 was welcomed. The railroad contractors sponsored "The Great Railroad Excursion," in which hundreds of guests (including ex-president Millard Fillmore) were taken by rail to Rock Island and then by steamboat to

The 230-foot long sidewheel steamboat *Dubuque* was operated in the
Mississippi River trade, 1867–79.
Courtesy of the Minnesota Historical Society

St. Paul. The excursion dramatized the end of Minnesota's extreme
remoteness, because St. Paul was at best but thirty hours from Chicago
and four days from major eastern cities. The Rock Island connection's
impact was very apparent the next year when a single packet company
transported thirty thousand passengers from the railroad terminus to St.
Paul and other Minnesota ports.

The generation after the Civil War was the age of the railroad in
Minnesota. The line to Rock Island inspired territorial politicians led by
delegate Henry M. Rice to work hard for their own railways, and their
efforts were rewarded by a congressional land grant in 1856. The grant
was to help finance four major railroads radiating from St. Paul, but the
railroad companies were barely organized when the Panic of 1857 hit.
Even the state's $5 million loan was not enough to stimulate rapid con-
struction of the lines. Not until late in the Civil War, after the companies
were reorganized and refinanced, did the tempo of construction pick up.
Finally, in 1867, St. Paul and Chicago were connected by rail.

Minnesota prospered as settlers rode the lines, goods began to flow, and
the railroads continued to expand. Then, in 1873, another frontier panic

struck, but its impact was not as disastrous as that of the Panic of 1857. The railroad companies recouped rapidly: by 1880 there were more than three thousand miles of track in the state and all the main lines had been laid.

The railroad companies were interested in settling the frontier—not just because they stood to profit from transporting passengers and produce, but because they had to sell their federal grants of land to help defray construction costs. Major companies such as the Northern Pacific and James J. Hill's St. Paul and Pacific had immigrants' guides written and printed in English, German, and the Scandinavian languages. These guides were distributed by the hundreds. What immigrant would not have been attracted to a Minnesota described in the following manner?

> The whole surface of the State is literally begemmed with innumerable lakes. . . . Their picturesque beauty and loveliness, with their pebbly bottoms, transparent waters, wooded shores and sylvan associations, must be seen to be fully appreciated.
>
> There is no Western State better supplied with forests. . . . The assertion that the climate of Minnesota is one of the healthiest in the world, may be broadly and confidently made.[1]

Reception houses, such as this one of the Northern Pacific Railroad at Brainerd in 1872, provided free temporary housing for land seekers.
Courtesy of the Minnesota Historical Society

The railroads had agents in principal European cities and American and Canadian ports of entry. They made cooperative arrangements with steamship lines to offer group rates to colonists, they helped immigrants make transfers at railroad centers like Chicago and Milwaukee, and they established reception houses in Minnesota. Railroad cooperation in moving whole colonies led to the establishment of communities such as Ghent, Adrian, and Mountain Lake. Sometimes the companies even platted their own towns along the tracks and carried settlers to them—towns such as Willmar, Litchfield, and DeGraff.

Railroad lands, given companies by the federal government to encourage and fund construction, had to compete with the federal government's free land. To be competitive, the railroads sold land in Minnesota's prime farming belt for three to five dollars an acre, and often a buyer needed only to make a down payment and several annual installment payments with no interest charges. The generosity of the railroads' land policies won them much goodwill among settlers, but this was soon lost when the farmers became victims of the companies' freight practices.

The railroads were not Minnesota's only promoters. Everyone who had something to gain joined the chorus—mercantile firms and land companies, religious organizations, municipal and state agents, and the newspapers. Perhaps Minnesota's most ardent booster was James Madison Goodhue, founder of the *Minnesota Pioneer,* the area's first newspaper. Goodhue came to St. Paul when the territory was only a few weeks old and with his first issue dedicated himself to promoting Minnesota's image. He answered questions from readers outside of Minnesota in his columns, he carried articles designed to encourage further settlement, he eulogized, he editorialized. And, most important, he sent his papers to the major newspapers in the East so that his comments were copied and widely circulated

A common frontier promotional gambit was to compare a new area to other sections of the country, and so Goodhue extolled the "salubrity" of Minnesota's climate and lambasted the "bilious" regions south of Minnesota:

Although we have in Minnesota, immense tracts of land as rich as the best soils in which the victims of agues and bilious fevers find sure and early graves along the sluggish streams of Iowa and Illinois, we have, universally, a pure, bracing, wholesome atmosphere, and *Health* standing up manfully under the burden of daily toil—sound livers and firm muscles. In

Minnesota, honest Toil is not compelled to hobble about through harvest time upon such miserable crutches as calomel and quinine. . . . Never has a case of fever and ague originated here; and except for the use of invalids who come up, pale as a procession of the ghost of Banquo and its attendants, from the damp plains of the South, which like cemeteries open their black jaws and swallow, in their very youth, the generations of livid wretches who have been lured there by the *one idea* of fertility; except for these invalids, who fly from those charnel-houses to recruit their health in this land of cataracts and pine forests, and dry, wholesome atmosphere, there is no use for quinine, or Morrison's pills, or Rowand's Tonic mixture, or any of the anti-bilious nostrums of our times, the sale of which, in some of the towns south of us, constitutes a large share of their commerce.[2]

There were even full-length books written extolling Minnesota, such as the many editions of John Wesley Bond's *Minnesota and Its Resources,* Ephraim S. Seymour's *Minnesota, the New England of the West,* and William G. LeDuc's *Minnesota Year Books,* but Minnesota's government did not consider all of these private efforts enough, so it too joined in the boosterism.

In 1853, the territory sent LeDuc to New York City to display Minnesota products at the Crystal Palace World's Fair. LeDuc was not permitted to display the buffalo he had brought, but his exhibit of crops and vegetables attracted much attention. LeDuc returned from New York convinced that the territory's best hope for rapid settlement lay in attracting foreign immigrants, and he urged official action toward this end. Governor Willis A. Gorman listened to LeDuc, and at Gorman's suggestion the territorial legislature in 1855 passed an act providing for a commissioner of emigration. Gorman named Eugene Burnand, who was well educated and fluent in several languages, to the position. Burnand set up a New York office from which he met immigrant ships, distributed literature, and advertised Minnesota in newspapers and publications of immigrant groups. Burnand emphasized and was especially successful in the recruitment of Germans. Official promotion was discontinued for lack of funds, but in 1867 the Minnesota legislature revived its activity by creating a Board of Immigration. By then state officials believed that the most fertile ground for attracting settlers was the Scandinavian countries, and appropriately they named Hans Mattson, a Swedish immigrant, as commissioner. Mattson had settled at the village of Vasa in the early years of Minnesota Territory and then had served as an officer in a Minnesota unit during the Civil War. "Colonel" Mattson wrote dozens of immigrant tracts and had them translated into the languages of northern Europe. He also made recruitment trips to Sweden and other European countries, and years later, in his book *Reminiscences: The Story of an Emigrant,* wrote that on his first trip he found himself "besieged by people who wished to accompany me back to America in the spring."[3]

Despite all the official and commercial boosterism, perhaps Minnesota's best publicity was the thousands of "America letters" sent back to the "old country" by new Minnesotans. These writers were usually not well-to-do proprietors who would profit by attracting more settlers, but ordinary people who had found new hope and prosperity in a far-off land. Some of the immigrant letter writers revealed a resentment of life, customs, and institutions in the old country and a great pride in things American. One Swedish immigrant, for example, wrote home that

> No one need worry about my circumstances in America, because I am living on God's noble and free soil, neither am I a slave of others. On the contrary, I am my own master, like the other creatures of God. I have now been on American soil for two and a half years and I have not been compelled to pay a penny for the privilege of living. Neither is my cap worn out from lifting it in the presence of gentlemen. There is no class distinction here between high and low, rich and poor, no make-believe, no 'title sickness' or artificial ceremonies, but everything is quiet and peaceful and everybody lives in peace and prosperity.[4]

Historian George M. Stephenson observed that in Sweden the

> 'America letters' fell like leaves from the land of Canaan. They were not only read and pondered by the simple and credulous individuals to whom they were addressed, and discussed in larger groups in homes and at markets and fairs and in crowds assembled at parish churches, but they were also broadcast through the newspapers, which, unwittingly or not, infected parish after parish with the 'America fever.' The result was that the most fanciful stories were circulated about the wonderful country across the Atlantic—a land of milk and honey.[5]

Minnesota's publicity featured numerous claims about the salubrity of the climate. These claims, which originated with the first territorial promoters, were meant to counteract the widespread belief that Minnesota was another Siberia. The climate was not only invigorating, Minnesotans asserted, but health-giving as well. Surprisingly, the claim developed into far more than its first advocates could possibly have foreseen, for Minnesota, from the early 1850s to about the mid-1870s, experienced a tremendous influx of settlers attracted by the alleged restorative properties of its climate.

Salubrious Minnesota became the haven for those afflicted with malaria and tuberculosis, or consumption, as it was then called. The belief that a cool climate would help the afflicted was buttressed by testimonials from individuals who came to Minnesota. One visitor in the 1860s said he had been cured of consumption merely by residing in Minnesota for a time, and he reported that "Minnesota all the year round is one vast hospital. All her cities and towns, and many of her farm houses, are crowded with those fleeing from the approach of the dread destroyer."[6] Minnesota's reputation was further enhanced by the publication of two books in the early 1870s. Ledyard Bill, a New York businessman who had spent a winter in Florida and had earlier written about that state's advantages to health seekers, wrote a work titled *Minnesota: Its Character and Climate,* and in it concluded that two types of climate, very hot and very cold, would provide the most relief for consumptives. When he compared the best examples of each—Florida and Minnesota—Bill gave his final endorsement to Minnesota. The other book, by the more partisan Brewer Mattocks, a St. Paul doctor, included an attack on the undesirability of Florida and other southern states as refuges for health seekers. Mattocks's claims for Minnesota's healthfulness were most dramatic. For example, he advised a young consumptive to move to Minnesota because it was

> greatly favored in having a society superior to most of the new States, because many families of wealth and high social position are obliged to live in our State on account of ill health, rather than the necessity of again commencing life. Most of our large business men and professional men in St. Paul sought our climate for health.[7]

Whether or not Minnesotans could prove their climate was restorative, many people did move to the state in the belief that it would improve their health, including such prominent figures as Doctor William W. Mayo, father of the Drs. Mayo of Rochester's Mayo Clinic; journalists Henry A. Castle and Joseph A. Wheelock; politicians James B. Wakefield of Indiana, who became a congressman from Minnesota, and Stephen

Miller, who became governor of Minnesota; minister and novelist Edward Eggleston; and Dr. Mattocks himself.

While most newcomers to Minnesota sought farmland, thousands of others were attracted by lumbering, iron mining, and urban industry. Lumbering was peaking at the very time that the opening of the Mesabi Iron Range provided other opportunities for unskilled workers. Many native-born Americans and European immigrants during the 1870s and 1880s moved directly to the Twin Cities, where the major businesses were flour milling, sawmilling, and transportation. During this twenty-year period the population of Minneapolis swelled from 13,066 to 164,738, and that of St. Paul from 20,030 to 133,156.

The great influx of population into Minnesota was part of two major nineteenth-century movements—westward movement within the United States and an international westward movement of Europeans to the United States. The frontier beckoned to those who were discontented with their lot in life, and improved transportation, particularly by rail-roads and steamships, made movement easier. Many of the native-born Americans moved west because of soil exhaustion; others because of rising land costs, encroaching industry and urbanization, or high property taxes. Many of the Europeans who came were fleeing from poverty, social inequality, political discrimination and persecution, and religious intolerance. Others, fairly well-to-do in their homelands, had dreams of becoming yet wealthier in the United States.

The native-born Americans who moved to Minnesota came principally from New England, New York, and the Great Lakes states. The New Englanders, or Yankees, which included those who moved directly from New England as well as those of Yankee stock from other regions, were an especially important group, wielding much influence in politics, business, and society. The first large movement of New Englanders into Minnesota came with the beginning of lumbering in the St. Croix River Valley. Yankees provided know-how and capital, and their impact on lumbering was visible as long as there were virgin forests. Isaac Staples, lumber baron of the St. Croix Valley, was a Yankee, as was Dorilus Morrison, the first mayor of Minneapolis and a ranking lumber entrepreneur after the Civil War. In the business world there were the Crosbys, the Pillsburys, and the Washburns of flour-milling fame—all of New England stock—as was Franklin Steele, the area's first millionaire. In politics, the Yankee roster of well-known Minnesotans was long: Sibley and Rice were Yankees, and seven of the state's first ten governors were of

New England ancestry. During the period before 1890, about a third of Minnesota's major administrative officers and supreme court justices were natives of New England.

New Englanders were also prominent in the field of education in Minnesota's early years. William Watts Folwell, the first president of the University of Minnesota, was a New Englander, and Carleton College in Northfield was started by Yankees, with its greatest financial boost coming from the Massachusetts benefactor after whom it was named. New Englanders exerted considerable influence in establishing the public school system, and one of them, Harriet Bishop, is recognized as the founder of Minnesota's first school.

The movement of European immigrants into Minnesota roughly parallels the national pattern. The first settlers were primarily from western and northern Europe—principally from Germany and Ireland—and generally moved to rural frontier areas. The Germans and Irish continued to arrive in Minnesota in significant numbers throughout the 1860s and 1870s. Although some Scandinavians came at the same time, their migration generally came later, from about 1870 to 1900. Rural Minnesota also attracted some eastern European settlers, such as Czechs and Poles.

Despite Minnesota's widely accepted Scandinavian image, the state's largest immigrant group was the Germans. On the eve of World War I, slightly more than 70 percent of Minnesota's population was either foreign-born or native-born with at least one foreign-born parent. Of this number more than one fourth were Germans. To this day, Minnesotans of German extraction are the state's ranking ethnic group. The heaviest concentrations of Germans are in the southern and central counties. New Ulm was established by two distinct German groups during the territorial period; from its founding to about World War II it had a marked cohesiveness that can be related to the utopian socialist philosophy of some of its founders, the existence of an active Turner Society, and the presence of a freethinker element. The height of freethinker influence came in the 1890s with the erection of a mighty statue to Hermann, the famed Teutonic warrior. Though "Herman the German" is taken for granted by many of the current residents, his presence atop the high ground overlooking the city is a unique symbol of the community's one-time psyche.

Religious preference of the German immigrants ranged from Lutheranism, Catholicism, and Pietism through freethinking, and generally each area occupied by Germans tended to be predominantly of one faith. Thus New Ulm had its freethinkers, while Catholics were the most populous group in heavily German St. Cloud and Shakopee. Many of the Germans came as fairly well-to-do land seekers, and a common belief developed that they had a particular talent for selecting the best farmlands. Perhaps in some cases they were able to acquire the best land, but it is now generally recognized that they created the best farms through hard work and a passion for neatness and order.

By the sheer weight of their numbers, the Germans have had an impact on all aspects of Minnesota's development. They have had their colonists, like William Pfaender of New Ulm; their missionaries, like Father Francis Pierz of St. Cloud; their business leaders, like lumber magnate Frederick Weyerhaeuser. However, they have made relatively few contributions to Minnesota politics. This may have been in part because of the German phobia of the two world wars, but even before World War I Germans did not produce major political leaders. Interestingly, in 1978, after the impact of ethnicity as a political asset had clearly waned, Minnesotans elected two United States senators who had German backgrounds. Rudolph E. Boschwitz was born in Germany and David F. Durenberger was a descendant of German immigrants.

Minnesota's Scandinavian tradition arises from its large number of Norwegians, Swedes, and Danes. Collectively, these groups far outnumber the Germans. The federal census of 1890 showed slightly more than 100,000 Norwegians of foreign birth in Minnesota and slightly less than 100,000 foreign-born Swedes—an order reversed since 1900—but only 14,000 Danes. Although similar in certain cultural traits and points of origin, the three Scandinavian nationalities are distinctive. Consequently, they have tended to settle not as Scandinavian communities but rather as separate Norwegian, Swedish, and Danish communities. Urbanization and internal migration have altered the pattern of frontier settlement, but there are still identifiable Norwegian, Swedish, and Danish areas. The heaviest concentrations of Norwegians are in the southeastern counties, the upper Minnesota River Valley adjacent to South Dakota, and the Red River Valley, while the Swedes are most prevalent in the area between the St. Croix and the Mississippi and the region west of Minneapolis. The Danish immigrants settled primarily in Freeborn County near Albert Lea and in Lincoln County on the South Dakota border.

As numbers of Scandinavians were naturalized, they soon replaced New Englanders as the foremost political group. Initially they tended to be drawn into the dominant Republican Party and did not participate in the protest movements. When Knute Nelson, the first of the Scandinavian governors, was inaugurated in 1893, Minnesota's period of Yankee governors came to an end and Scandinavians usually captured the governorship after that time. Of the twenty-four governors since Nelson, all but five have been of Scandinavian extraction. Rudy Perpich, who followed Wendell Anderson as governor in late 1976 when the latter resigned so that he could be appointed to the United States Senate, was the first non-Scandinavian governor since Harold Stassen resigned in 1943. Scandinavians have also been heavily represented in the state legislature and in Minnesota's congressional membership. Since so many of Minnesota's politicians bear Scandinavian names, it is no wonder that the national impression is that Minnesota is almost completely Scandinavian, although other ethnic groups combined outnumber them.

Although Scandinavians were generally well assimilated by the third generation, they have tended to perpetuate their customs and, to a lesser degree, their languages. Lutheranism is the dominant religion among the Norwegians and Swedes, and Lutherans were often leaders in establishing educational institutions in Minnesota—institutions such as Augsburg College in Minneapolis, Concordia in Moorhead, St. Olaf in Northfield, and Gustavus Adolphus in St. Peter.

The Irish follow the Germans, Swedes, and Norwegians as Minnesota's fourth largest immigrant group. The first Irish influx into Minnesota Territory was caused by the disastrous potato famine, which drove millions from the Emerald Isle. Some of the Irish movement into Minnesota Territory was encouraged by James Shields, an individual who later earned the unique distinction of having served as a United States senator from three states (including Minnesota). Before becoming a major figure in Minnesota politics, Shields persuaded numerous Irish land seekers to take up claims in Rice County, near the community of Shieldsville.

After the Civil War, Irish immigration to Minnesota was encouraged by various colonization efforts. Particularly notable in this endeavor was the Catholic Colonization Bureau, whose guiding spirit was Bishop John Ireland of St. Paul. Ireland led the way in starting ten Catholic colonies during the period 1876–81 on railroad lands in western Minnesota, among them the Irish communities of DeGraff, Clontarf, Graceville, Currie, Avoca, and Adrian. Although the Irish were well represented in the rural areas of southern and western Minnesota, their heaviest concentration was in St. Paul, which came to be known as an Irish town even though the Germans there outnumbered the Irish.

Canadians were in Minnesota even before the area had a political identity. During the time that the Upper Mississippi region was within the trade area of Montreal, hundreds of Canadian fur traders worked in the area that is now Minnesota. Such noteworthies as William Morrison, Joseph Renville, and Norman Kittson had both Minnesota and Canadian careers. Some of the earliest squatters about Fort Snelling were French Canadians. Pierre Parrant was notorious, but there were more reputable citizens, such as Louis Robert, who became one of the most important community leaders in the early history of St. Paul. Without doubt, Canada's foremost contribution to Minnesota's citizenry was James J. Hill, who came to St. Paul as an eighteen-year-old in 1856 and then went on to earn his reputation as the "Empire Builder" for his part in organizing the Great Northern Railroad. In the age of railroad giants Hill was the only one who resided in Minnesota. His mansion still stands on Summit Avenue in St. Paul, a symbol of the Gilded Age.

James J. Hill, on October 5, 1911, spoke at Bend, Oregon, during the celebration of the completion of a Great Northern Railroad line to that community.
Courtesy of the Minnesota Historical Society

In Minnesota, Canadian immigrants are usually believed to be French Canadian or English Canadian, but actually, since the Canadians are a national rather than an ethnic group, their numbers include Icelanders, Ukrainians, Scottish, Scotch-Irish, and many other European nationalities. The greatest number of Canadians can be found in the Mesabi Range towns and in the Twin Cities, and there are still identifiable French Canadian communities, such as Gentilly in the Red River Valley.

Southern Minnesota's farming frontier might be considered a melting pot within the Minnesota melting pot, for virtually every ethnic group from western Europe was represented, as were some groups of eastern Europeans. There were English, such as those who started a colony at Fairmont in the 1870s; Belgians who moved to Ghent, one of the communities started by Bishop Ireland; Dutch who settled most heavily in the southwestern part of the state about Edgerton and Worthington and at Hollandale, south of Owatonna. The Welsh who moved on from Ohio and Pennsylvania into Minnesota Territory took up farmland around Lake Crystal, Judson, and Cambria. There were a number of Swiss and Austrians who moved to the southern Minnesota frontier. The eastern Europeans, though relatively few in numbers in southern Minnesota, included Poles, who first moved to Winona to work in its sawmills; German Mennonites, who moved as a group from southern Russia to Mountain Lake; and Czechs, who peopled the Silver Lake, New Prague, and Montgomery areas.

By the time the heaviest wave of immigration from southern and eastern Europe reached the United States, Minnesota's agricultural frontier was nearly closed, and so for those latecomers the greatest opportunities were in the Twin Cities, Duluth, and the towns of the Mesabi Iron Range. The Mesabi Range especially became a mosaic of eastern Europeans. Every small group that was within the old Holy Roman Empire or the kingdom of Austria-Hungary, which was formed in 1867, was represented on the Mesabi. The Mesabi hungered for thousands of unskilled workers to extract the ore from the open pits, so during the 1890s and early twentieth century the streets of places like Virginia, Hibbing, and Chisholm were filled with Finns, Ukrainians, Yugoslavs, Ruthenians, Italians, Bulgarians, Hungarians, and many others. At the turn of the century nearly half of the Mesabi's people were foreign-born; ten years later, at the height of the Mesabi boom, there were thirty-five identifiable ethnic groups on the Range.

Ethnic rivalry on the Range, with its inevitable social stratification and discrimination, led to street fights and knifings. The Range had an unsavory political reputation too, because of the socialist leanings of many of the "Red" Finns, who had fled from the Russian Empire. Gradually, however, mechanization reduced the size of the work force, dispersing some of the ethnic groups and thus hastening the process of assimilation. However, the ethnic diversity remains—people of the Range are still conscious of their Italian or Yugoslav or Finnish origins, but more in the sense of a distinction that identifies but does not divide them.

Of the 4,375,099 Minnesotans reported in the 1990 census, 93.7 percent, excluding white Hispanics, were white. The principal minorities were blacks, Asians, Hispanics, and American Indians. The 94,944 blacks comprised 2.2 percent of the state's total population. Blacks are heavily concentrated in the metropolitan areas; slightly more than half of all blacks in the state live in Minneapolis, followed by St. Paul, which has more than one fifth of all black Minnesotans. Although most Minnesota blacks historically have been urbanites, the state's first blacks (including the famous George Bonga) were fur traders. During the Civil War other blacks came to St. Paul as steamboat laborers, but the major movement occurring after World War I was part of the northern shift of blacks that led to huge black populations in Chicago and Detroit.

In the 1990 census the 77,886 Minnesotans classified as Asian or Pacific Islander were 1.8 percent of the population. Within this category the largest ethnic groups were Hmong, Korean, Chinese, and Vietnamese. St. Paul was the ranking Hmong center, with 11,499 of the 16,833 in the entire state. The migration of Hmong and Vietnamese to Minnesota, and the United States in general, was caused by the collapse of the pro-American governments in Southeast Asia in the spring of 1975. With the American evacuation at the end of the lost Vietnam War, many of the people who had supported the American war effort became refugees. Various refugee organizations, including a student group at the University of Minnesota, which had first attracted Vietnamese students in the 1950s, encouraged and coordinated the Hmong and Vietnamese refugee movement to Minnesota.

In 1990 1.2 percent of Minnesota's population was of Hispanic origin. Nearly two thirds of them were Mexican. The Mexican migration to Minnesota started before the turn of the century because of the need for seasonal labor in sugar-beet fields. The World War I labor shortage intensified the hiring of Mexicans not only to toil in beet fields but also to harvest potatoes and vegetables such as peas and asparagus, and to work in vegetable canneries. The largest Mexican population is in St. Paul, but Mexicans are also well represented in agricultural processing centers in southern Minnesota and the Red River Valley, including Albert Lea, Fairmont, Madelia, St. James, and Moorhead.

In recent times the number of American Indians in Minnesota has increased dramatically, and their culture has been transformed from primarily rural to primarily urban. In 1950 Minneapolis and St. Paul respectively had only 426 and 163 Indians of the 12,528 in the state. However, in 1990 about 60 percent of the 49,392 Indians in Minnesota lived in urban settings. The largest concentrations were in Minneapolis, with 12,335; St. Paul, with 3,697; and Duluth, with 1,837. To a degree the movement of American Indians to the Twin Cities is part of the broader societal shift nationally from rural areas to cities, but lack of opportunity in isolated rural reservations has also been a significant contributing factor. Urbanization coincided with a renewed Indian emphasis on their traditional culture and a rejection of the longheld white assimilationist doctrine. In 1968 the American Indian Movement (AIM) was formed in Minneapolis to combat discrimination against Indians. The organization subsequently championed Indian causes through confrontational tactics.

Urbanization has unavoidably altered the original patterns of Minnesota settlement, so much so that the largest representation of any given ethnic group is likely to be in the metropolitan areas. Nonetheless, the ethnic heritage remains. Minnesota's calendar abounds with ethnic observations—Kolacky Days in Montgomery, Oktoberfest in New Ulm, Robert Burns Day in Mapleton, and St. Patrick's Day in St. Paul. The Swedes across the state observe Svenskarnes Dag ("The Swedes' Day"), a midsummer festival held near the longest day of the year. The special day for Norwegians is *Syttende Mai* (seventeenth of May), Norwegian Constitution Day. It is possible, of course, to single out particular ethnic contributions—the Germans, the art of brewing; the Danes, the development of dairy cooperatives; the Scandinavians, generally education. But the greatest impact Minnesota's broad ethnic base has had may simply be that Minnesotans have a heightened awareness of the diversity that has created both Minnesota as a state and the nation as a whole.

7

THREE FRONTIERS

MINNESOTA WAS BLESSED with three frontiers that attracted distinct types of pioneers: lumbermen, who reaped the waiting harvest in the vast coniferous forests; farmers, who claimed the fertile soil of the west and south; and miners, both big businessmen and common laborers, who extracted the iron from the northern ranges. Although geography molded the economic diversity of the land, to a large degree time and circumstance governed the rapidity with which these frontiers developed.

In the second half of the nineteenth century, great changes were wrought by the Industrial Revolution. These changes, especially improved transportation, major advances in technology, and the restructuring of the old economic and social orders, all contributed to Minnesota's headlong rush from frontier to modern state. Because of the vast undeveloped resources at their command, Minnesotans were able to apply technological advances and make significant contributions to the new order. Huge quantities of Minnesota's high-grade lumber were used to build cities and railroads, enough ore was extracted from the ranges to make Minnesota the ranking iron-ore producer in the nation, and Minnesota revolutionized the flour-milling industry. (See map on page 314.)

The pioneer farmers who moved into Minnesota Territory knew of railroads, since many of them had moved by rail at least part of the way to the frontier, and they knew that eventually they would come to rely on railroads to transport their produce. But they also knew that it took time to break the virgin land and produce paying crops, and they were prepared for those lean subsistence years. Most pioneer farmers realized too that it took time to learn the land's vagaries. The elements were immutable; people were powerless to lengthen the growing season, and so they had to adapt their crops, their animals, and themselves to the conditions imposed by nature.

Thousands of those first pioneers had been inspired by visions of Minnesota as a veritable wilderness garden, and initially they did harvest wild fruits, berries, and nuts, and hunted, trapped, and fished to fill their larders. But these people had come to farm, and as soon as they could break a bit of ground, they planted. Because they did not know what Minnesota's soil and growing season would produce, they tried a little of everything. At first the farm products were used by the farmers themselves or else bartered at the local markets, but all the while they were searching for a fast-growing, profitable cash crop that could be exported.

In 1859 nearly a third of the total grain produced was corn, followed closely by potatoes, wheat, and oats. That same year, Minnesotans also harvested orchard products, hops, flax fiber, hemp, nearly forty thousand pounds of tobacco, and more than three thousand pounds of rice. Even silk cocoons and wine from cultured grapes were reported in the agricultural census. Ironically, most farmers who had money during that depression year earned it by digging and selling the wild ginseng root, which abounded throughout the Big Woods and the adjacent deciduous forest areas. The root, much in demand in China, where it was prized for its purported medicinal properties, remained an important Minnesota export during the early Civil War years and was lauded by many as Minnesota's salvation during those lean times.

In the late 1850s wheat was produced in sufficient quantities so that some was exported, and more and more farmers became convinced that wheat was where prosperity lay. By 1860, production more than doubled, and for the first time wheat became the state's ranking crop. Production accelerated throughout the Civil War and afterward, until by 1870 Minnesota was the twelfth-ranking wheat producer in the United States. Within another decade, it had moved into fifth place. In 1868 a writer for *Harper's Magazine,* ignoring both other states and other crops in Minnesota, declared that "Minnesota is preeminently the wheat growing State of the Union. . . . Owing to the peculiarity of her climate and soil, she is the best adapted of any of the States to the raising of this staple.

Wheat is in fact almost her exclusive object of production. None farm here except for this."[1]

Wheat was never Minnesota's only crop, but it was clearly king during the 1860s and 1870s. The high point in its relative importance was reached in 1878, when nearly 70 percent of all the state's tilled land was planted with wheat. Production continued to rise until 1902, and the censuses of both 1890 and 1900 showed Minnesota to be the nation's leading wheat producer. But millions of acres of the state's frontier land were then opened, and the percentage of wheat in relation to other crops declined. The record year in terms of bushels of wheat harvested was 1902, but by that time only 30 percent of the state's cultivated land was in wheat.

Today pictures of vast fields of golden wheat are associated with the Great Plains, and it is difficult to envision southeastern Minnesota, with its timbered areas, dairy farms, and cornfields, as a wheat belt; but throughout the frontier era in the northern United States, wheat was the traditional staple crop because in comparison to other crops it demanded less soil preparation and cultivation. It usually could be planted profitably the first year after the tough prairie sod was broken.

Ripe wheat and farmstead in Aitkin County, about 1910.
Courtesy of the Minnesota Historical Society

Many Minnesota farmers tried corn at first, but they soon found that the heavy, root-packed prairie ground required repeated workings before the soil was mellow enough for corn's deep roots. The farmers who sowed wheat rather than corn, having come from milder climates, tended at first to plant the varieties of winter wheat that they were accustomed to raising. Hard experiences with winter kill, however, very rapidly caused them to shift to spring wheat that could be planted in April and harvested in late July to mid-August. Although the land was not being used intensively, it did not matter to farmers because frontier land was plentiful and cheap; besides, there was a cash market for wheat, which there was not for other Minnesota grains in the 1860s and 1870s. Minnesota's wheat boom also coincided with advances in farm mechanization, which made it possible for farmers to handle larger and larger acreages during the short harvest season.

Though vast acres of fertile, cheap land lay waiting to be cultivated, frontier farmers were inhibited by a limited capacity to work the land. Many of Minnesota's first wheat farmers cut grain with a cradle scythe. A good man working long days with such a scythe could cut only two to two

Hand-cutting wheat with cradle scythes was replaced by machine harvesting during the Industrial Revolution.
Courtesy of the Minnesota Historical Society

and a half acres a day, and then there remained the laborious work of raking the grain, tying it into bundles, shocking it, and, finally, threshing it. Needless to say, the fields of the man who harvested in this manner were very small. There were mechanical reapers in existence; the first was invented by Cyrus McCormick in 1831, and during the 1850s it was improved with the addition of a self-rake. Some of these improved reapers were in use in Minnesota by the early 1860s, but what farmers really wanted was a machine that would tie the grain into bundles as well as cut and rake it.

The development of such a binder was a real challenge. First it was necessary to invent a mechanical device that could tie knots, and then to find a suitable material to use for binding. A wire binder was perfected and patented in 1874 and immediately put to wide use, but just as immediately problems developed. Cattle and other animals were injured or killed by bits of wire buried in straw stacks, and wire in the harvested grain so damaged millstones that wheat containing wire particles was docked on the market. The twine binder, which was first mass-marketed in 1880, remained the principal machine for cutting wheat and other small grains until the popularization of the combine. With a twine binder pulled by three or four horses, an operator could cut from ten to fifteen acres a day. At last the agonizingly slow task of raking loose grain and tying it by hand was eliminated.

While binding technology was being improved, so were threshing machines. In the 1860s, the most used thresher was a small machine powered by horses that walked on a treadmill, but during the 1870s steam threshers became a common sight. The first steam-powered machines were turned by small stationary steam engines whose furnaces burned wood, coal, or sometimes even straw, but a glimpse of better things to come was provided with the exhibiting of a steam tractor at the Minnesota State Fair in 1879.

These manifestations of the Industrial Revolution were the leavening in the rapid growth of Minnesota's three frontiers. After more than a decade of experimentation, wheat emerged as the sought-after cash crop, and its rise coincided with improved methods of harvesting and with expanding railroad networks so that the tremendous yields could be marketed widely. Then, as the lumber frontier and the iron ranges boomed after the Civil War, they provided huge markets for wheat and other produce from the southern Minnesota agricultural frontier. The wheat farmer, the flour miller, and the lumberman had a common meeting place in Minneapolis, which, because it lay just south of the great coniferous

Wheat and other small grains were cut and tied into bundles by the twine binder,
whose movable platform dropped the bundles on the ground.
Courtesy of the Minnesota Historical Society

forest and just north of the principal wheat area, was both a sawmilling
and a flour-milling city. Minneapolis was, in the 1870s, as the metropolitan area is today, the meeting place of east and west, of urban and rural,
of industry and agriculture.

Until the early 1870s Minneapolis was just one of Minnesota's many
flour-milling centers. During the 1860s the number of mills in
Minnesota leaped from 81 to 507, most of them small-capacity mills that
ground flour in return for a share. Most were water-powered, like the
famous Archibald Mill at Dundas on the Cannon River, but some were
steam-powered and there were even some of the Dutch windmill type,
including the Seppman Mill near Mankato. Although the mills were
found throughout the wheat area in the southern part of the state, the
greatest concentration was in the Cannon River towns—Faribault,
Dundas, and Northfield. But there were also 13 mills clustered around
the Falls of St. Anthony by 1870; and Minneapolis had the advantages of

not only bountiful waterpower but a growing home market because of its increasing urban population. These advantages were sufficient to attract Cadwallader Washburn, a New Englander who had made a fortune in Wisconsin lumber and had served as governor of that state. Washburn brought capital and business acumen into flour milling, along with the ambition that was necessary to make it more than a local concern, and he led the way in the development of the new technology that revolutionized flour milling.

Like all Minnesota millers, Washburn was confronted with the problem of satisfactorily grinding spring wheat. Traditionally winter wheat had commanded higher prices than spring wheat because it was softer and yielded white flour, much preferred by consumers, with much less processing than spring wheat. But Minnesota was a spring-wheat area, so millers had to work with a very hard grain that had a brittle bran coat.

Cadwallader Washburn, a former governor of Wisconsin, pioneered modern flour milling in Minneapolis.
Courtesy of the Minnesota Historical Society

When ground between the grist stones, all four parts of the wheat kernel—the outer, or bran, coat; the thin layer of gluten cells; the starchy interior, which comprised most of the kernel; and the embryo—were crushed together. Spring wheat mashed in this fashion yielded an undesirable product. The bran flecks made the flour dark and speckled, hence unappetizing to most consumers, and the oily embryos caused the flour to turn rancid rather quickly, which greatly inhibited storing and marketing. With winter wheat, even though the soft gluten layer was usually ground fine, the bran coats tended to stay whole and could be sifted out, but with spring wheat the hard gluten layer often broke into coarse particles that tended to separate from the flour along with the bran. This was particularly distressing since the gluten was not only the most nutritious part of the kernel but also that element in the flour that enabled the baked product to rise. Because spring wheat was richer in gluten, millers realized that it had the potential to produce better flour than winter wheat, but they had to find some way of grinding the gluten and the starch together and eliminating the bran. Hence, by the late 1860s there was considerable talk about the need for a "middlings purifier"—middlings being the name given to the gluten and bran waste, which was sometimes ground into a course, dark, but very rich flour.

Some millers at Winona, Hastings, and Dundas discovered that they could produce superior flour by cracking the kernels instead of crushing them and then grinding the middlings after laboriously sifting out the bran, but this method was slow and not adaptable to large-scale production. Alexander Faribault, in the town of Faribault, pursued the idea of purifying the middlings by machine. Faribault brought a young French engineer, Edmund La Croix, to his mill to experiment with a purifier. La Croix and his brother were familiar with purifiers that had been used experimentally in France as early as 1860, and they built one for Faribault's mill in 1868 and used it for two years before the mill was destroyed by a flood.

Word of La Croix's device leaked out, and George Christian, who formed a partnership with Washburn in 1870, hired La Croix to perfect a purifier for Washburn's Minneapolis mill. La Croix and Christian worked on their project in secret. The Frenchman spent most of his time locked in a room at the mill, and by the spring of 1871 his completed machine was installed. Although inspired by earlier French models, La Croix developed a unique device with moving sieves that were covered by an air blast that separated the bran coats from the middlings. The middlings, which at that point had only been cracked, not crushed, were then ground again, resulting in a fine, white flour rich in protein.

Flour milling changed dramatically with the advent of the "New Process" flour from Washburn's mills in 1871. For the first time it was possible to mass-produce high-grade white flour from spring-wheat, and for the first time in history spring wheat was more in demand than winter wheat. Not only was spring-wheat flour more nutritious, but about 12 1/2 percent more bread could be made from any given quantity of the New Process flour; and the demand for Minneapolis flour soared.

The ability to produce New Process flour, also known as Patent flour because it was advertised as having resulted from a patented process, quickly spread to all Minneapolis millers. La Croix left Washburn and Christian and installed a purifier for a rival, and then the company's head miller, who had worked with La Croix, joined the Pillsbury Company. Millers reaped unprecedented returns from the New Process flour. Christian noted that "our profits the first year of the 'New Process' . . . were fifty cents a barrel, the second year they averaged a dollar a barrel, the third year two dollars, and the fourth year anywhere from four to four and [one] half dollars a barrel."[2] Washburn and Christian netted profits of $650,000 from a single mill over a three-year period. Because of the New Process, flour milling became Minnesota's first big business, and the demand for Minneapolis flour stimulated great expansion in the 1870s and 1880s.

Although the middlings purifier was an essential first step in modernizing flour milling, millers were still plagued by the shortcomings of the sandstone millstones. Not only was it costly and time-consuming to replace the stones, but as they wore down a fine grit was mixed with the flour, so Minneapolis millers looked about for some way of eliminating the stones. Because of their experience with the middlings purifier they looked to Europe for inspiration, and they found that many millers were replacing stones with rollers. Christian experimented with rollers as early as 1873, and within a few years many mills were using a combination of stones and rollers—stones to crack the wheat and rollers to refine it. But there were problems in arranging the rollers and questions as to whether porcelain or corrugated iron or steel was the best roller material. When Washburn and his new partner, John Crosby, learned that Hungarian millers who worked with wheat similar to Minnesota's were the leading developers of roller mills, they decided to send an agent to Budapest to learn Hungarian trade secrets. William de la Barre, a young Austrian engineer, found that when the Budapest "mill owners learned that I was from the United States, and particularly from Minneapolis, the doors of the mills were closed against me."[3] The enterprising de la Barre finally made arrangements with a Hungarian miller to visit a mill for a number of nights so that he could study the practical application of its roller mills.

Upon de la Barre's return, Washburn and Crosby completely equipped one of their mills with the Hungarian method of interspaced steel rollers that ground wheat into as many as eleven different grades of flour. The gradual-reduction method (as it came to be called) soon completely replaced grist stones because the rollers could do more work with less power; they lasted much longer than the stones and were said to have increased flour yields.

The new technology exemplified by the middlings purifier and the gradual-reduction process caused Minneapolis to emerge rapidly as the country's leading milling center. The genius of Washburn and the men he gathered around him did not lie in invention, but rather in the capacity of men like the La Croix brothers, Christian, and de la Barre to learn from others.

New Process flour was Minneapolis's best advertisement, but the city

Horse-drawn wagons were used in Minneapolis by Washburn-Crosby Company to deliver Gold Medal flour.

Courtesy of the Minnesota Historical Society

and Washburn-Crosby was given another great boost in 1880 when the company's flour won the gold medal for spring wheat at the Millers' International Exhibition in Cincinnati. Within a few months the company began marketing its flour under the Gold Medal brand and the trademark has been internationally famous since.

At the time of his death in 1881, Cadwallader Washburn was lauded as the man who had "found milling a trade and left it a science."[4] During the last eleven years of his life he did more than any other individual to promote the revolutionary shift to modern flour milling and in elevating the importance of Minneapolis. Within a year of his death the city took its place as the nation's leading flour producer, a position it held for almost half a century. Flour milling was so identified with Minneapolis that it became internationally known as the Mill City and its professional baseball team in the American Association was called the Millers.

From 1870 to 1890 Minneapolis flour production rose from about two hundred thousand barrels annually to seven million. Most of the capital and business experience behind flour milling came from former lumbermen such as Cadwallader Washburn and his brother William D., Governor John S. Pillsbury, and Dorilus Morrison. Without the nearby lumbering frontier, it is unlikely that Minneapolis would have had the capital to finance the new flour mills. As flour milling expanded, the millers promoted railroads westward, not only to market flour but also to tap the wheat lands of the distant Dakota and Montana prairies. With the extension of the Northern Pacific and the Great Northern through western Minnesota and North Dakota and the construction of the Milwaukee Road into South Dakota, Minneapolis was able to draw on a vast wheat frontier at the very time that the importance of wheat as a crop in Minnesota was declining. Looking eastward, millers led by William D. Washburn promoted a shorter route to the markets in the United States and Europe through the construction of a railroad to Sault Ste. Marie in Upper Michigan. When the line was completed in 1887 it not only reduced shipping costs but freed the millers from the dominance of Chicago-based railroads. Largely because of the combined interests of millers and lumbermen, Minneapolis emerged as the most important railroad center northwest of Chicago.

By 1890 Minneapolis was the world's leading wheat market, and its buyers were exporting wheat as well as selling it to local millers. In its marketing role Minneapolis became the center for great grain storage facilities and the headquarters for companies that operated railroad line

The Engesser Brewery of St. Peter was typical of the many small breweries in turn-of-the-century Minnesota.
Courtesy of the Minnesota Historical Society

elevators. Flour milling also stimulated banking in Minneapolis. Millers had to buy wheat for cash during the short harvest season and then store it until it was needed. This holding operation demanded great amounts of capital; as the leading millers became active in organizing banks, the city became a major financial center. All this activity contributed to the city's growth and made a very broad hinterland dependent upon it: thousands of farmers or their suppliers who ultimately sold wheat in Minneapolis tended to look to the Mill City as the source of farm machinery and other manufactured products and capital.

Flour milling also spurred related manufacturing in Minneapolis. In the early years flour was generally marketed in barrels, so numerous cooperage firms sprang into being. Later, when cloth and paper bags replaced the barrels, the city became an important manufacturing center for these products, and by the mid-1920s only St. Louis surpassed Minneapolis in the production of bags. Flour milling also ultimately stimulated allied food businesses. During the early twentieth century the increasing popularity of durum wheat flour, which was better suited for macaroni and spaghetti products than for bread, caused these businesses to develop in Minneapolis; during the 1890s various cereal manufacturers were attracted because of the availability of the needed raw materials.

By the 1870s much of the Minnesota land that had been planted to wheat year after year was nearly exhausted, and crop rotation seemed the most feasible way to improve it. At the same time, wheat farmers found land values rising simply because the country was becoming settled. Increased occupancy drove the original frontier prices of a few dollars an acre to forty dollars or more in just a few years. The wheat farmer could afford to cultivate a staple crop on cheap land, but increasingly expensive land accompanied by rising property taxes forced him to look for ways to use his ground during more of the year in order to realize larger returns.

There were other problems too—stem rust, discriminatory railroad rates, questionable elevator practices, and insects. Wheat farmers, or anyone who raised crops to sell, had to sell immediately after the harvest and so were especially vulnerable to railroad rate fixing. To meet increased costs, many farmers tried to produce more, which only forced many to

The large St. Paul brewery of Theo. Hamm Company, shown in about 1900, developed into one of the nation's largest distributors.

Courtesy of the Minnesota Historical Society

mortgage their farms to buy more machinery. Wheat farmers complained that they were also bilked by the grading and weighing done by the elevator companies controlled by railroads and millers.

In the midst of these concerns Minnesota farmers were ravaged by the great Grasshopper Plague. For five successive summers waves of hoppers (actually Rocky Mountain locusts) swept over most of western and southern Minnesota. They chewed wheat to ground level, sometimes denuded trees, and even ate the paint from buildings. Stories of the Grasshopper Plague contain a certain grim humor. One often repeated tale was about the farmer who abandoned his horses to an advancing horde only to return later to find two of the gargantuan hoppers pitching horseshoes to decide which one got to eat the farmer. In desperation farmers devised tar traps, which were pulled through the fields, but they were more a gesture of defiance than an effective destroyer. In 1877 the state of Minnesota offered bounties for the insects and their eggs and Governor John S. Pillsbury finally proclaimed April 26, 1877, a day of prayer and fasting in the hope that it would help lift the plague from the land. At last, by 1878, the locust cycle had run its course, but many people believed they would return, and in part because of that belief wheat farmers looked to new ventures such as dairying, which seemed to promise more insurance than a staple crop.

Although wheat persisted after 1880 in much of southwestern Minnesota and in the Red River Valley, where it was well suited to the Valley's bonanza farms, there was a decided shift to diversification in the older farming sections of southeastern Minnesota. Finally, over a period of about thirty years, nearly all of the old wheat lands were diversified. This trend, hailed by its advocates as Minnesota's road to economic salvation, was characterized by an increasing emphasis on scientific agriculture. The old crossbreeds were replaced with purebred livestock, farmers engaged in systematic crop rotation, and crops and animals suited to Minnesota's rigorous climate were developed. Dairying in particular emerged during the diversification movement, and during the 1880s and 1890s Minnesota became one of the leading dairy states, a status it has enjoyed ever since. Minnesota's pioneer dairymen exhibited their products throughout the United States, and their prize-winning displays, along with those of Minnesota wheat and flour, at the Pan-American Exposition in Buffalo, New York, in 1901 earned the Gopher State yet another nickname—"the Bread and Butter State."

Dairying during the late nineteenth century was aided by a number of advances, including the round silo, the introduction of the cream separator from Europe, and the Babcock milk-fat test. This test, developed by Stephen Moulton Babcock, a University of Wisconsin agricultural chemist, provided a simple method of measuring the richness of milk, and it encouraged improved feeding practices and the search for better milk producers. The growing concept of year-round dairying, however, necessitated changing the habits of the farmers. Traditional spring calving caused the market for dairy products to be depressed during the summer and fall because of the milk surplus and to be almost inactive during the winter, when cows were dry. The solution, said Oren C. Gregg, of Marshall, Minnesota, was to breed some of the cows to calve in the fall. Gregg, as superintendent of the University of Minnesota's Farmers' Institutes, traveled throughout the farming sections of the state urging farmers to accept his advice. His zeal caused some local wits to suggest that his middle initial stood for "cow," but Gregg is remembered in Minnesota history as the "Father of Winter Dairying."

Winter dairying was only part of the answer. Dairymen still had much to learn about cattle breeds and feeding, and Theophilus L. Haecker, who came to the University of Minnesota Agriculture School in 1891, did more than any other individual to make Minnesota dairying scientific. He determined the most effective diets for milk cows, and he developed judging standards for the selection and breeding of cows. He also wrestled with the problem of the best type of animal for Minnesota's climate and finally concluded that the Holstein (now the commonest breed by far in Minnesota) was the most productive. Haecker also strove to improve the marketing of dairy products. After visiting the dairy co-ops organized by Danish immigrants at Clark's Grove near Albert Lea, Haecker concluded that this form of business, owned and managed by its own members, was very efficient, and his advocacy helped popularize the movement. By the 1930s the idea of participant-owned businesses had spread from dairying to elevator companies and other aspects of farm marketing and to such ventures as rural electrification projects. The co-op movement in Minnesota grew beyond Haecker's greatest expectations. In 1921 hundreds of co-ops united to form the Minnesota Cooperative Creameries Association, which began marketing its products under the Land O Lakes label in 1924. The immediate popularity of the brand name caused it also to be made the company's name in 1926. As one of Minnesota's largest agribusinesses, Land O Lakes became nationally famous.

Although the influence of scientists such as Haecker advanced dairying, one of its greatest boosts was given by the private experimentation of Wendelin Grimm, a farmer. When Grimm moved to Carver County to farm in the late 1850s he carried with him some "everlasting clover" seed from his native Germany. He planted the seed and then carefully saved seeds from the plants that survived the winters, developing a hardy variety of alfalfa, which proved to be a superlative cattle feed. Grimm did not brag about his accomplishment. Instead, he fed his own animals and said nothing. One of his neighbors recalled that Grimm's cattle were fat during the summer of 1863, a notorious drought year when corn was scarce. When the neighbor asked where Grimm had obtained his corn, the response was: "*'Kein Körnchen, nur ewiger Klee'*—not one kernel, only everlasting clover."[5] Grimm's close neighbors imitated him, but as late as 1900 alfalfa was virtually nonexistent in Minnesota outside Carver County. Then some of Grimm's seed was called to the attention of the University of Minnesota Agriculture School. During the decade from 1910 to 1920, Grimm Alfalfa finally emerged as a ranking forage crop, with a more than twenty-fold increase from the roughly two thousand acres planted in 1910.

Adaptation was also the key in developing other Minnesota crops.

Cooperative creamery in Madison, Lac Qui Parle County, 1923.
Courtesy of the Minnesota Historical Society

Peter M. Gideon did for apples what Grimm did for alfalfa. After moving to a farm on Lake Minnetonka in 1853, Gideon spent more than forty years experimenting with fruit that would thrive in spite of Minnesota's winters. His greatest accomplishment was the "Wealthy" apple, named after his wife, the former Wealthy Hall. Although apples grow fairly well throughout most of southern Minnesota, the area about La Crescent in the southeastern corner of the state has emerged as the state's apple center.

While Minnesota's farmers were struggling to adapt their crops to the land, its lumbermen were harvesting a crop that nature had planted centuries before. The common frontier references to the coniferous forest zone as the "pineries" belied the region's complexity, for most of that forest was actually made up of spruce, balsam fir, tamarack, white cedar, and jack pine intermingled with large stands of deciduous trees such as scrub oak, maple, birch, and aspen. Some of the coveted white pine was found in every county east of the Mississippi, but the richest stands were in an arc that swung southwestward from Duluth through the Snake River area and then westward across the Rum River south of Mille Lacs before turning north and following the Mississippi to about

Cooperative creamery in Milaca, Mille Lacs County, about 1915.
Courtesy of the Minnesota Historical Society

Leech Lake. Within this arc, the best white pine lands were in Carlton County near present-day Cloquet.

Even within its favorite habitat the white pine did not exist as a continuous forest. Stands of it were usually scattered among other trees, a circumstance that hindered cutting operations, for as long as there was white pine the lumbermen wanted nothing else. As they ferreted out the prized pine they destroyed thousands of other trees and, more seriously, increased the dangers of forest fires by abandoning their waste among the trees they bypassed in their unrelenting pursuit.

In the eyes of the lumberman, the white pine was without fault. It was a large tree, oftentimes 100 feet tall with a diameter of $2\frac{1}{2}$ to 3 feet at its base, with some specimens reaching 150 feet or more. Its wood was strong, odorless, and so soft and straight-grained that usable boards could be split off with a broadax. Its lightness gave it a buoyancy in streams where hardwoods would have sunk, and its lumber was comparatively long-lasting. Because of these virtues, the tree had been prized since colonial times, when it was cut in New England for ships' masts for the Royal Navy and for merchant vessels. Later generations of lumbermen followed the trail of the white pine, felling it along Michigan and Wisconsin streams before they reached Minnesota.

Although the lumbering frontier generally moved from New England westward, it did so rather haphazardly. Before railroads, lumbermen were almost completely dependent on river transportation for their logs. As long as there was white pine to the west they found it much easier to leapfrog to virgin forests along a navigable stream than to haul logs from the interior to the rivers. Thus New England lumbermen became interested in the forests of the upper St. Croix even though millions of acres of white pine remained in Michigan and Wisconsin.

The desire to open the pinelands on the upper St. Croix was one of the reasons for the Dakota and Ojibwe treaties of 1837. Even before the treaties were ratified, eager Yankee lumbermen had staked claims along the St. Croix. The first sawmilling town was Marine on St. Croix, but it was soon surpassed by Stillwater. The lumber that supplied Stillwater's mills generally came from the Snake River, a Minnesota tributary of the St. Croix. The town's first market was downstream to St. Louis and to intervening points such as Hannibal, Missouri, and Clinton and other river towns in Iowa. In the beginning, Marine on St. Croix and Stillwater lumbermen marketed only cut lumber; but as the pace of harvesting picked up and as demand increased, they began selling rafts of whole logs, which were sawed after they reached their destinations. Before 1851 Stillwater's market was small and almost entirely downriver, but after the Dakota treaties the territorial population boom created an immediate and heavy home demand for Minnesota pine lumber.

Stillwater dominated antebellum lumbering, but it had its rivals. St. Anthony became a booming lumber center, drawing on the pineries along the Rum River, and both Stillwater and St. Anthony were challenged by Winona, which lay farther from the pine forests but closer to the ready market in the rich farm belt of southern Minnesota. Winona, on the banks of the Mississippi, deserved its title as the gateway to the West, for the nearest stream navigable by steamboats to the west of Winona was the Minnesota River, with its elbow at Mankato 120 miles distant. Much of that intervening space could easily be supplied by wagon from Winona; but Stillwater, upstream from Winona and with no easy access to the Minnesota River, could not touch the southern Minnesota market, and St. Anthony lumbermen who traded up the Minnesota to St. Peter and Mankato were severely hampered by the seasonal nature of steamboating. Because of this, Winona controlled the sale of lumber in well over half of the area between the Mississippi and Minnesota Rivers.

Winona's first sawmill was started in 1855, the same year that John Laird and his brothers began marketing lumber bought from mills along the St. Croix and Chippewa Rivers in Wisconsin. Two years later the Lairds, who had been joined by their cousins, James and Matthew Norton, opened their own mill at Winona and began processing logs floated down from Minnesota and Wisconsin streams. The cousins later organized the business as Laird, Norton Company and it ultimately became one of the largest lumbering companies in the entire Upper Mississippi region, though Winona was never quite able to overcome the lead of Stillwater and St. Anthony.

Logs and lumber were the major exports of territorial Minnesota; until about 1860 lumbering surpassed agriculture as Minnesota's most lucrative business. The 1860 census showed commercial lumbering in three Minnesota counties—Hennepin, where St. Anthony Falls was located; Washington, with mills at Stillwater and Marine on St. Croix; and Winona. Washington County produced an estimated $400,000 worth of lumber, while Hennepin and Winona Counties had about one half and one fourth of that, respectively. While lumbering was the state's foremost economic activity, even after two decades of harvesting it was still a fairly small business. In terms of cutting, the forests had barely been touched. Coupled with sparse population and the fallacious belief that the white pine belt stretched all the way from the Snake and Rum Rivers to Canada, the slow pace of development helped to create the myth of the inexhaustible forests.

Cutting large white pine, such as this one in southern Koochiching County (1916), required a three-man crew—two sawyers and an axeman.
Collection of William E. Lass.

James Madison Goodhue promoted Minnesota Territory by prophesying that "centuries will hardly exhaust the pineries above us,"[6] and an early St. Anthony mill manager was convinced that the Rum River pineries alone would supply seventy mills for seventy years. These men would not have believed that nearly all of Minnesota's white pine would be gone in seventy years. In 1871 Hans Mattson, trying to attract immigrants, proclaimed that "the great forests will for hundreds of years furnish work for loggers at the same time that sawmills and other factories using lumber will need large numbers of workers."[7] Nine years later a Twin Cities journalist oblivious to the rampant cutting in the pine belt during the 1870s predicted that "Not one-hundredth part of it ever has or will be required by the lumbermen who annually infest the region."[8] Those who tried to stimulate lumbering did not seem to realize that even when pines of all types were counted—including the lowly jack pine—less than one fifth of Minnesota's total forest area was pine.

During the quarter-century following the Civil War, Minnesota lumbering truly became a big business. In 1857, the last year of territorial status, the log cut was about 100 million board feet; the yield of 1869 was more than double that amount, and production again doubled during both the 1870s and the 1880s. In 1889 more than 1 billion board feet were harvested and Minnesota had risen from fourteenth to fourth in rank as a lumber state.

Postwar expansion was spurred by the rapid settlement of the treeless Great Plains states, which looked to Minnesota for building materials; by the construction of a railroad network; and by the sharp population rise in Minnesota. As Minnesota's prairies were being occupied by wheat farmers in the 1870s and 1880s, so also were much of the enormous grasslands of Kansas, Nebraska, the Dakotas, and Montana. Most of the prairie homesteaders first lived in sod shanties or tar-paper shacks, but these were conditions they tolerated only until they had the wherewithal to buy pine lumber and build more substantial dwellings. Minnesota became both the supplier of the pine and the recipient of the wheat produced by the prairie settlers. Not only was Minnesota's pine used for the construction of thousands of farm buildings on the plains but it also built hundreds of towns and cities that sprang up on America's last frontier—cities such as Miles City, Bismarck, Sioux Falls, Omaha, Wichita. Even the railroads that carried the pine to the settlers depended on lumbermen for ties and other construction materials to extend their lines west.

Despite the advent of Minnesota railroads, much of the state's lumber and some of its logs were floated down the Mississippi—mainly to St. Louis—until the early twentieth century. In 1882, a record year, St. Louis received more than 160 million board feet of white pine lumber from the Upper Mississippi. Much of this was used locally, but the city was also the chief emporium for a broad trade area that stretched to distant New Mexico.

Increased demand after the Civil War turned Minneapolis into the greatest sawmilling center in Minnesota and, in time, in the nation and the world. Minneapolis on the west bank of the Mississippi and St. Anthony on the east merged in 1872, so the story of lumbering in Minneapolis was really a continuation of the St. Anthony saga. As lumbermen moved beyond the Rum River and farther up the Mississippi, Minneapolis remained the natural destination for logs floated downstream.

Because of its railroads, Minneapolis developed outlets in all directions. The completion of the St. Paul and Sioux City line in 1872 through the Minnesota River Valley to Mankato and then by way of St. James and Worthington through southwestern Minnesota opened parts of

During the winter cutting season lumber gangs lived in camps such as this one in Pine County, about 1870.

Collection of William E. Lass

Minnesota and northwestern Iowa and gave Minneapolis vital connections with Sioux City, Omaha, Kansas City, and points west. In most
years well over half of the line's tonnage consisted of westbound lumber
and eastbound wheat. Other sections of southern Minnesota fell within
Minneapolis's sphere with the construction of the Iowa and Minnesota
Railroad and the Minneapolis and St. Louis line, which was completed
through Waseca and Albert Lea to connections at the Iowa boundary in
1877. Minneapolis reached out into the Red River Valley, North Dakota,
and parts of Montana by way of the St. Paul and Pacific, the line later
called the Great Northern, which was finally extended to the West Coast
in 1893 by James J. Hill.

In the 1880s Minneapolis businessmen led by William D. Washburn
constructed yet another important railroad—the Minneapolis, St. Paul and
Sault Ste. Marie. Washburn's primary goal was to bypass Chicago and give
Minneapolis flour a direct market to the eastern states, but Washburn was
a lumberman as well as a miller and clearly recognized the interdepen-
dence of the two industries in Minneapolis. He knew that the Soo Line
would open new markets for Minneapolis flour and would give the city
direct access to some of the finest forests in Minnesota and Wisconsin—
forests that Minneapolis could not have tapped by river transportation.

During the twenty years from 1870 to 1890, Minnesota's population
shot from 438,000 to nearly 1.3 million, and Minneapolis became the
undisputed metropolitan center. Most of the towns and cities in western
Minnesota were started during this time, most were built with
Minneapolis lumber, and it was to Minneapolis mills that those prairie
farmers sent their wheat. As the city was earning an international reputation as the "Mill City" because of flour manufacturing, many of its residents called it the "Sawdust Town." In 1870 there were 207 sawmills in
Minnesota, but Minneapolis alone had 13 clustered about St. Anthony
Falls. Minneapolis sawmills increased in number as well as in size, but
they still had difficulty meeting the demands of both the Twin Cities and
the prairie hinterlands, so Minneapolis distributors imported lumber by
river and by rail from other Minnesota and Wisconsin mills.

The city fed upon itself—the flour milling, the railroads, and the lumbering swelled the city's population of nearly 47,000 in 1880 to more
than triple that during the next decade, when Minneapolis and St. Paul
combined had more than 250,000. To the immense housing needs of
these people was added industrial construction—more flour mills, huge
grain terminals, warehouses, and more sawmills. While Minneapolis had

plenty of sawdust, it also had miles of muddy walkways much of the year, which were improved by laying boardwalks. During 1887 the city used 6 million feet of lumber to construct sixty-seven miles of boardwalk. Because the mills handled white pine almost exclusively, these boardwalks were probably made with some of the world's finest lumber.

There was still enough lumbering business left for Minneapolis's principal rivals, and both Stillwater and Winona grew during the 1870s and 1880s. Stillwater continued to be a main supplier of both logs and lumber for points on the Mississippi, and through rail connections supplied some of the western market, while Winona sawmillers cemented their hold on their trade area to the west by the extension of the Winona and St. Peter Railroad through Rochester, Owatonna, and Waseca and extended their business yet farther when the line was pushed across Minnesota and eastern South Dakota to the Missouri River in the early 1880s.

Duluth became a lumber town when it was liberated from its isolation by the completion of a railroad to St. Paul in 1870. But even more impor-

Stillwater's growth created a need for hotels such as the Sawyer House, shown about 1872.
Courtesy of the Minnesota Historical Society

By the late nineteenth century horses had generally replaced oxen to haul logs
from an assembly point in the forest to a river or rail destination.
Collection of William E. Lass

tant to the development of the quiet village on the shores of Lake Superior
was its selection by Jay Cooke as the starting point for his great transcon-
tinental railroad. As the Northern Pacific pushed westward, lumber from
thousands of white pine was shipped from the Duluth area for its ties,
trestles, and bridges. In 1871 the line was completed to Moorhead on the
Red River, and the next year it reached the Missouri River, where the
town of Bismarck sprang up. The Panic of 1873 halted the line at
Bismarck for six years, but when construction resumed, new markets for
Duluth and Minneapolis lumber were opened along its route through
western North Dakota and the Yellowstone River Valley of Montana.

The railroad, which was so important in the marketing of Minnesota's
lumber, was the most conspicuous symbol of the state's abrupt entry into
the new world of technology, but the actual process of lumbering was also
affected by the Industrial Revolution. Lumbering, however, was not revolutionized overnight like flour milling through the development of a

"River pigs" were photographed (about 1870) sorting logs on the St. Croix River.
Collection of William E. Lass

spectacular new process. Increased demand following the Civil War stimulated a series of technological innovations, and those in turn helped
bring production to a peak, which caused the rapid denuding of the pine
forests and the abrupt decline of frontier lumbering in Minnesota.

Lumbermen, like farmers and millers, looked for new devices and
methods that would increase their speed, efficiency, and production. The
urge to move faster became more pressing as the trees along navigable
streams were cut away and the length of the haul from lumber camps to
assembly points on a river or railroad became longer. The Yankees who
made up Minnesota's first generation of lumberjacks called upon their
New England experience, and they cut trees during the winter months,
when frozen ground and snow facilitated dragging them to a river bank.
Then, with the opening of navigation, the logs were guided by teams of
men called "river pigs" to places like Stillwater or Minneapolis, where
they were either milled or formed into rafts for downstream markets.

Later lumbermen continued this pattern of cutting during the winter and moving logs to market during the navigation season, but their nearly frenetic efforts to keep apace of the burgeoning market led to important changes. During the 1870s and 1880s lumbermen turned to the peavey and the cant hook, and they used spar lines to load log sleighs and railroad cars. The yoke-shaped go-devil, which could carry but a single log, was replaced by the dray, a heavy sleigh capable of hauling thousands of board feet of logs in a single load. Lumbermen also began using horses instead of the plodding oxen and they learned to ice their roads. During the 1890s ice roads became yet more sophisticated as a special rutting device was developed which cut tracks for the sleigh runners in the haul roads and made it necessary to ice only the ruts rather than the entire surface of the road. The use of steam tractors on farms led lumbermen to believe that some type of machine could be developed for use in the forest, and by the late 1880s there was some experimentation in the logging areas with steam traction engines. Though these steam loggers (which had both sled runners and caterpillarlike tracks) were used to some extent, they were never very popular because of their high price and operating costs. Then, as the movement away from the rivers accelerated, narrow-gauge lumbering railroads came into widespread use in the 1890s and early twentieth century. All of these advances in the practical aspects

This sawmill at Bemidji in 1922 featured the typical mill pond, conveyor ramp that carried the logs from the pond to the saws, and silo-shaped incinerator with a screened top to burn waste.
Courtesy of the Minnesota Historical Society

of cutting occurred at a most auspicious time. Traditionally, sawmilling had been a navigation season business because the logs had to be moved through mill ponds, but the development of the "warm water pond," in which an agitator kept the water from freezing, enabled mills to saw year-round, and the cutting of timber proceeded at a yet more rapacious rate.

The high point came in 1900, when Minnesota's production of slightly more than 2 billion board feet made it the third-ranking lumber state, the highest position it ever attained. This output, which was roughly double that of ten years earlier, declined gradually until about 1905, and Minnesota dropped to fifth position. Then lumbering plummeted quickly as dozens of Minnesota mills closed and entrepreneurs shifted to the Pacific Northwest. By the early 1920s Minnesota lumber yards depended primarily on Pacific Northwest imports. Finally the large white pine mill at Virginia closed in 1929, and the last major log drive on Rainy Lake, the scene of some of the last extensive cutting of virgin timber in Minnesota, took place five years later.

The leveling of the forests was far more sudden and ultimately more calamitous than most of the participants anticipated. Lumbermen knew that the virgin forests were going to disappear, but they simply went on doing what they had always done. Lumber was the stuff out of which cities and fortunes were made, and when technological improvements enabled men to cut and mill faster, they did. Most lumbermen were spurred by increased competition, especially after Michigan lumberers swarmed into Minnesota in the 1890s following the depletion of Michigan's white pine. As they battled each other for a larger share of the white pine market, they also feared competition from the yellow pine of the South and the Douglas fir and western pine of the Pacific Northwest, so they increased production merely to retain their relative share of the market. They were also influenced by Minnesota's sorry record of disastrous forest fires, such as the awful Hinckley fire of 1894 and the Chisholm fire of 1908. These and hundreds of lesser fires meant the loss of thousands of acres of Minnesota's coniferous forests. It has been estimated that more of Minnesota's forest was lost to fire than was cut by lumbermen, and the ruinous conflagrations were seized upon as an excuse to cut faster before more timber was lost to the flames.

An unusual marketing situation stimulated cutting too. The opening of the Vermilion and Mesabi iron ranges created heavy local demand for white pine as thousands of buildings were flung up during the iron-ore boom. As this was occurring there was an increased market for

Minnesota's pine in the East because Michigan and Wisconsin production had slackened. Lumbermen also cut rapidly in order to lower their property-tax liability because the taxes were lower on cutover land than on timbered land. Lumbermen justified the denuding of the forest too by telling themselves that they were the cutting edge of another farmers' frontier—that they were helping to pave the way for cultivation of the land. This sentiment was so strong in lumbering areas during the 1890s and early 1900s that conservation efforts were usually criticized as nothing more than deterrents to agricultural development. As one looks at the rocky, rugged terrain in much of northern Minnesota today, it is difficult to see how they could have so deluded themselves.

Frontier lumbering was of brief duration, but it affected Minnesota in a multitude of ways. Lumbering helped populate Minnesota by providing employment for thousands of men; it provided inexpensive building materials for farms, and for towns and cities. Pioneer lumbermen lent their considerable influence to the formation of Minnesota Territory, and they participated in the drive for Dakota land cessions in southern Minnesota, which expanded agricultural development, which in turn provided foodstuffs for the lumber camps. A number of virgin areas in central, eastern, and northern Minnesota were opened up because of lumbering. Sawmilling was the first industry of Stillwater, St. Cloud, Little Falls, Brainerd, Duluth, Virginia, and many other places. Lumbering and sawmilling were the most important businesses of frontier Bemidji and International Falls, and lumbering ranked next to flour milling as the major industry in Minneapolis for almost forty years.

Lumbering provided the first major accumulation of capital in Minnesota—capital that was used to start or encourage other businesses. Lumbering capital promoted banking, railroad construction, and flour milling. Virtually all of the early important banks in Stillwater, Minneapolis, and Duluth were organized by lumbermen. Some lumbermen (such as Dorilus Morrison, who was also a banker) lent capital to railroads, and the millions of dollars needed to modernize flour milling came from such former lumber barons as John Pillsbury and Cadwallader Washburn.

Lumbermen actively supported charitable, educational, and cultural institutions. William H. Laird assisted Carleton College, the Pillsburys generously donated funds to the University of Minnesota during the 1800s when state support was niggardly, and the Weyerhaeuser family assisted Macalester College in St. Paul, the Forestry School of Yale

University, and many other institutions. Amherst H. Wilder of St. Paul, who had investments in lumbering, provided for a charitable foundation that is very active yet today, and Thomas B. Walker, using his personal collection of paintings and sculpture as a base, established the Walker Art Gallery in Minneapolis.

Minnesota politics and government were conditioned by lumbering. The state, through the office of the surveyor general, provided a registra-

This massive statue of Paul Bunyan (about 1937) on the shore of Lake Bemidji helps perpetuate his place in American folklore.
Courtesy of the Minnesota Historical Society

tion service for log brands, and in its efforts to stimulate frontier expansion sold quantities of state lands to lumbermen at minimum prices. Liberal, permissive state legislation also facilitated the construction of numerous dams, which were needed to raise water levels for moving logs. Some individuals associated with lumbering were politically active. Franklin Steele was a power behind the throne in the early Democratic Party in Minnesota; William Holcombe, the Stillwater lumberman active in the formation of Minnesota, served as the state's first lieutenant governor; Dorilus Morrison was the first mayor of Minneapolis; and David Marston Clough served as state governor from 1893 to 1899.

The entrepreneurs of lumbering left a Minnesota legacy, but so too did the lumberjacks who labored in the rough and rugged camps and by night regaled themselves with tall tales traditional to the lumbering industry. They told stories about strange forest creatures, like the monkeylike agropelter that killed unwary lumberjacks by flinging hefty branches down on them; the hugag, a mooselike animal with jointless legs who slept by leaning on trees; and the sidehill gouger, a fascinating gopherlike beast that had shorter legs on its uphill side and so was committed to a life of moving around hills in the same direction. Interestingly, the lumberjacks talked little and perhaps not at all about the best-known folk hero of lumbering—Paul Bunyan. Paul is, to a large degree, the creation of various twentieth-century imaginations.

Extensive interviewing by Minnesota's foremost historian of lumbering, Agnes M. Larson, failed to uncover a single person who during the time he had worked in the Minnesota lumber camps had heard of Paul. The plethora of Bunyan literature began with the publication of an article in the Detroit, Michigan, *News-Tribune* of July 24, 1910. This first story, written by James McGillivray, contained some of the larger-than-life aspects of a genuine American folk hero; but such embellishments as Paul's blue ox, Babe, whose footsteps formed lakes and who could drink a river dry in one gulp, were added later and say far more about the American fascination with gargantuanism than about frontier knowledge of Paul Bunyan. During the twenty years following the appearance of McGillivray's story, dozens of Bunyan tales and books were published, and the impression left was that they were tales directly from lumber camps.

Nonetheless, Paul has captured the American imagination and has a particular place in Minnesota lore because many of the Bunyan tales have Minnesota settings. The legend is further fed by the large statue of Paul that stands on the lakeshore at Bemidji and by the Paul Bunyan Center at Brainerd, which features a massive concrete Paul who greets thousands of children by name every year.

During the early 1880s, despite age-old rumors of mineral wealth and confirmed findings of iron ore, there was little speculation about the potential for large-scale iron mining in Minnesota. Yet barely more than a quarter-century after the first ore was taken from the Soudan Mine near Lake Vermilion in 1884, the Vermilion Range was fully developed, the Mesabi Range had become the largest iron-ore producer in the nation, and the Cuyuna Range was opened. The discovery of the Vermilion Range in the 1880s and the Mesabi in the 1890s caused a boom unprecedented in the history of Minnesota's frontier. As thousands of iron seekers and attendant businesses were drawn to the newfound riches, towns sprang up on the Vermilion and Mesabi with a spontaneity common to gold rushes. In just a few years Tower, Ely, Virginia, Hibbing, Mountain Iron, Chisholm, and other places mushroomed from straggling camps to small cities, and Duluth, the emporium of a vast mining and lumbering region, rapidly changed from a small, isolated frontier town to a minor metropolis.

Tales of the valuable minerals of Lake Superior date from the era of the French voyageurs. The French learned about copper in Upper Michigan from Indians who had used it for centuries, and they assumed that the region held vast, unknown mineral wealth. Although the French made no effort to develop Lake Superior mines, their belief that the land was mineral-laden was perpetuated by the British and passed on to the Americans. The United States, through Lewis Cass, governor of Michigan Territory and territorial superintendent of Indian affairs, reserved mineral rights in northern Minnesota in an 1826 treaty with the Ojibwe even though there was no proof of the existence of copper or iron or anything else. The old beliefs were given yet more substance when Daniel Webster, writing under the name of President John Tyler, defended the Webster-Ashburton Treaty on the grounds that the region between the St. Louis and Pigeon Rivers, later known as the Arrowhead Region, had valuable mineral deposits. Although Webster was propagandizing, his message proved to be that of a seer when members of a United States Geological Survey team reported the discovery of iron ore near Gunflint Lake in 1850.

This find caused Governor Alexander Ramsey to urge further investigation of the territory's mineral potential. Later territorial and state governors also encouraged such investigation, and finally, in 1865, the legislature appropriated funds to employ a state geologist who was to reconnoiter the Vermilion Range. Henry H. Eames was hired for the task, and he and his brother Richard brought back far better news than anyone had expected. Eames had not found significant iron deposits, but he had discovered mineral-bearing quartz, which the chief assayer of the federal mint in Philadelphia determined would yield $25.63 in gold and $4.42 in silver to the short ton.

Eames's find created an immediate sensation. Rumors of gold at Oronoco on the Zumbro River in Olmsted County in 1858 had attracted gold seekers who were soon disappointed. Others left the state for the Pike's Peak and Fraser River gold fields. When the news of Eames's discovery was circulated, it reached an audience that wanted to believe, and the Vermilion Lake Gold Rush of 1865–66 was on. As the hopeful beat a path to Vermilion Lake, a wagon road was opened from Duluth, and a

George R. Stuntz, a Duluth pioneer, was an early and enthusiastic promoter of
Vermilion Range iron mining.
Courtesy of the Minnesota Historical Society

town of several hundred with all the trappings of the western gold-rush towns sprang up. All that was lacking was gold. None of the would-be miners found gold-bearing quartz, and the rush ended as suddenly as it had begun. The spot where Eames had found gold was never determined.

Although the Vermilion gold rush was a bust, it had significant implications. The improved road made the area more accessible, and some of the prospectors, including George R. Stuntz of Duluth, came away convinced that valuable iron-ore deposits lay near Vermilion Lake. Stuntz, who had at one time been a United States government surveyor, had started a trading post along the Duluth harbor in 1852. Five years later the town was formed by a union of little settlements, and Stuntz believed that it was destined to become the commercial center of the Northwest. The opening in 1855 of a canal through the troublesome Sault Ste. Marie, connecting Lakes Superior and Huron, brightened Duluth's prospects, and the growth of the city seemed further assured when it became the eastern terminus of the Northern Pacific. But Stuntz and fellow promoter George C. Stone envisioned Duluth as more than a shipper of wheat and lumber. They believed that its development—and, for that matter, the development of the whole of northern Minnesota—depended on mining and marketing iron ore.

The restored first locomotive used by the Duluth & Iron Range Railroad
is on display at Two Harbors.
Courtesy of the Minnesota Historical Society

The transshipment of iron ore on Lake Superior required the construction of
massive ore docks such as these at Two Harbors photographed in 1912.
Collection of William E. Lass

But they were men of little means. They knew that, unlike a gold
prospector with a pan who might strike it rich and be able to walk out
with his find, the aspiring iron miner had to think of sinking shafts, of
managing large crews of experienced miners, of constructing railroads
from mine to lake and then building ore docks to facilitate loading into
Great Lakes ships. Stuntz and Stone were superficially familiar with the
problems of iron mining because the Marquette Range of Upper
Michigan had been producing ore since the 1840s. This Michigan success
stimulated the search for ore west of Lake Superior. With a knowledge of
the existence of ore on the Vermilion Range and some understanding of
the complexity of mining and marketing ore, but without funds, Stuntz
and Stone could only turn to capitalists.

Their selection of Charlemagne Tower was logical. Tower was an
attorney for various Pennsylvania iron-mining companies and the agent

for a number of eastern investors. He was intrigued by the specimens of ore shown to him by Stone, but before committing himself to an investment of several million dollars he needed further proof. So Tower and another sponsor, Samuel A. Munson of Utica, New York, commissioned a private geological reconnaissance of the Vermilion Range. On two occasions, in 1875 and in 1880, Professor Albert Chester of Hamilton College, New York, was guided over the Vermilion by the knowledgeable Stuntz. Chester was impressed by outcroppings of iron-bearing rock and by formations that resembled those of Michigan's Marquette Range, so he strongly recommended to Tower that the range be developed. In the course of his investigations Chester was led over the eastern part of the Mesabi Range, but he saw nothing noteworthy. If Chester had had more time and more curiosity, Tower might have been in a position to exploit what eventually proved to be the richest range of all.

After Chester's second expedition, Tower, along with his son Charlemagne Tower, Jr., and Stone and Stuntz, organized the Minnesota Iron Company. Through Stone, who was then a member of the Minnesota legislature, Tower made it clear that he expected concessions from the state to encourage his venture. The state legislature approved a measure under which the Minnesota Iron Company would be taxed only a penny a ton on all ore mined or shipped. Although this seemed much too generous to later critics who railed about eastern exploitation of Minnesota, it was understandable at a time when the young frontier state hungrily sought any type of industrial development. Once the tax question had been resolved, Tower and his associates opened the Soudan Mine on the south side of Vermilion Lake.

Although the first ore was found near the surface, it soon became apparent that most of the hard ore was in a vertical formation and would have to be mined by underground methods. This necessitated the importation of skilled miners, so Tower hired Cornishmen and Swedes from the Marquette Range and put them to work on the Soudan Mine. To move the ore from the mine to Lake Superior, Tower sought the shortest possible route: from Lake Vermilion to Agate Bay, where the town of Two Harbors was established. Once a seventy-mile track was completed and ore docks had been readied at Two Harbors, the first ore was moved out from the Soudan Mine in July 1884.

Tower's operations were supervised by Charlemagne Tower, Jr., who moved to Minnesota and lived for a time in Tower, the mining town near Vermilion Lake named for his father. The younger Tower was the principal agent in encouraging further exploration and development by the Minnesota Iron Company. His father, who did more than any other single individual to develop Minnesota iron mining, never set foot in the state.

In 1886, during its second full season of mining, the Minnesota Iron Company exported more than three hundred thousand tons of ore. This large quantity and the richness of the hematite (which sometimes ran to about 65 percent iron) attracted hundreds of prospectors who combed the breadth of the Vermilion Range. During 1887 in particular, Duluth was buoyed by excitement as hundreds of professionals and amateurs sought ore deposits. Important finds were made northeast of Vermilion Lake, where Ely was started as a mining town and where the significant Chandler Mine was developed.

The Vermilion Range excitement of 1887 quickened interest in the Mesabi Range, which had been bypassed by Tower and his associates even though their railroad cut into some interesting-looking red earth. Even before iron ore was discovered on the Mesabi it was known as "the Range" because of its hilly eastern portions, which rose hundreds of feet above the adjacent flat terrain. The Ojibwe knew the hills as the Missabe, their name for the sleeping giant who in their tradition had once roamed the

The Merritt Brothers' camp at the Biwabik mines was located in typical forested Mesabi Range terrain before strip mining radically altered the landscape.
Courtesy of the Minnesota Historical Society

area and now reposed in his eternal grave under the hills. The Mesabi Range fooled Chester and others because its formations were not like those of the Marquette and Vermilion Ranges. Trained geologists such as Chester entered the area seeking hard ore-bearing rocks rather than soft iron ore, and their very depth of knowledge caused them to overlook the obvious because it was so unexpected.

However, there were men who believed that iron ore lay in the sleeping giant. Of these men Lewis H. Merritt, one of the pioneer settlers of Duluth, was the best known and the most determined. Merritt was a veteran timber cruiser and his faith was unfettered by professional knowledge. He insisted that the Mesabi held iron ore—an insistence that he passed on to his sons. The Merritts were the first to find Mesabi ore, but they were not alone in the search, for by the late 1880s hundreds of ore prospectors ranged over the Mesabi hills. On November 16, 1890, James A. Nichols, who worked for the Merritts, uncovered soft red ore just under the surface of the ground. The joyous Merritts had the rare opportunity of naming a place in the wilderness that would become world-renowned. The discoverer of the Soudan mine had wishfully named it after the African Soudan after spending his first winter in Minnesota, but the Merritts were not cynical and did not fancy themselves clever. They chose the simple and descriptive name Mountain Iron. In 1891, with the discovery of the Biwabik mines about ten miles east of where Virginia was later established, their stake in the Mesabi seemed assured.

Hoping to duplicate the "luck" of the Merritts, perhaps as many as fifteen thousand prospectors spread over the Range in 1892. Duluth relived the hectic days of the 1887 Vermilion rush. The Mesabi was ballyhooed in the Duluth press, and the outfitting of ore seekers again became a major business. It was soon evident that rich ore did not exist throughout the Mesabi, but rather occurred in comparatively small pockets along the Range. The task was to find the pockets. Although there were thousands who failed, instant success came to some men such as Frank Hibbing, who struck it rich at the place where he started his town. Such successes attracted many knowledgeable and wealthy men who wanted a part of the Mesabi. They included a number of experienced Michigan iron miners such as John Munro Longyear, whose cousin Edmund J. Longyear traveled the length of the Mesabi, taking thousands of core samples with diamond-bit drills. The Longyears were prospecting for the Pillsbury family, who had bought quantities of Range lands for lumber during the great land sale at Duluth in 1882, and for many years managed their

Mesabi interests. Among those drawn to the Mesabi in 1892 was Henry W. Oliver, a Pittsburgh steel magnate. Oliver visited the Mesabi on his way home from the Republican National Convention in Minneapolis and was instantly impressed. Recognizing the vast potential of soft ore that could be taken from the surface, he began buying and leasing land on the Mesabi. He was but the first of the steel barons to become interested in the Mesabi, and it was not long before he and his kind had gained control of the great Mesabi Range.

Flushed by their initial successes in finding ore, the Merritts—with neither capital nor experience in big business—aspired to control Mesabi iron mining. They were able to acquire sizable landholdings inexpensively because the state, in its efforts to stimulate mining, leased the Merritts 141 quarter sections, charging only one hundred dollars each for a fifty-year lease. Encouraged by this easy acquisition, the Merritts began to think about marketing the ore. As experienced lumbermen they knew something about the problems of moving heavy goods long distances, so from the start they thought about a railroad from the Mesabi to Lake Superior and about ore docks on the lake. Their original plan was to build a railroad line that would join the established Duluth and Winnipeg Railroad at Brookston, about twenty-five miles west of Duluth. The Duluth and Winnipeg, in return for the guaranteed ore shipments, agreed to construct a large number of ore cars. The Merritts built their railroad—the Duluth, Missabe and Northern—and shipped ore from Mountain Iron to Superior, Wisconsin, in October 1892. Their hopes were buoyed by this first shipment from the Mesabi, but they were disappointed when the Duluth and Winnipeg Railroad failed to live up to its agreement to construct the ore cars.

Undaunted by this setback, the Merritts decided to construct their own ore cars and to extend their own railroad all the way to Duluth. Perhaps they would have succeeded if the Panic of 1893 had not caught them in a precarious overextension. To meet construction costs and salaries the Merritts had to put stock of the Duluth, Missabe and Iron Range Railroad on the market. John D. Rockefeller bought about half a million dollars' worth. When the Merritts again could not meet their obligations they approached Rockefeller through agents about his possible interest in advancing more credit.

Rockefeller made the loan, but only with some rather unusual stipulations. The Merritts had to agree to form a combination with Rockefeller in which they assumed an interest in some of his Michigan and Caribbean

One of several brothers who discovered iron ore on the Mesabi Range, Leonidas J.
Merritt symbolized pioneer prospectors.
Courtesy of the Minnesota Historical Society

mining ventures, and he in turn acquired a controlling interest in their
Mesabi properties. The Merritts had an option to buy back the Mesabi
interests within a year, but all except one refused to exercise it because by
then they had had problems that led them to charge Rockefeller with
fraud and misrepresentation. Although they won a judgment in a lower
court, the opinion was reversed by the United States Court of Appeals in
St. Louis. Ultimately, Rockefeller made a settlement with the Merritt
family in return for their dropping of charges. Years later, in 1911, a
United States Senate committee, while investigating alleged monopolies,
investigated the Rockefeller-Merritt affair. The investigation did not
show any wrongdoing on Rockefeller's part but revealed instead the
naïveté of the Merritts and the shrewd acumen of Rockefeller.

The Merritts are heroes in Minnesota because they pursued their dream. They found the Mesabi ore when geologists passed over it; and though they lacked capital, experience, and skill, they dared to challenge the nation's industrial giants. When brother Lon (Leonidas J.) died on May 9, 1926, he had a reported worth of only $2,450; but he was a symbol of the free-spirited prospectors of Minnesota's mining frontier, and it was he who was used as the model for the figure of the prospector that is carved into the base of the statue of Governor John A. Johnson that stands on the state capitol grounds.

Rockefeller's venture following the Oliver entry into the Mesabi Range solidified the pattern of control by absentee landlords. At the same time that Rockefeller interested himself in Minnesota iron ore, two of Oliver's Pittsburgh colleagues, Andrew Carnegie and Henry C. Frick, also bought or leased Mesabi lands. When the Oliver-Frick-Carnegie interests were merged in 1901 into United States Steel, a combination engineered by

Some Mesabi Range mines, such as the Fayal Mine at Eveleth (1915), were started as underground mines.

Collection of William E. Lass

The soft and shallow iron ore of the Mesabi Range facilitated strip mining. In 1915 the Oliver Iron Mining Company removed ore from its Union Mine at Virginia with a locomotive and ore cars.

Collection of William E. Lass

John Pierpont Morgan, Minnesota's iron lands passed almost entirely into the Oliver Division of the gigantic corporation.

James J. Hill provided the exception to the rule that Mesabi lands were controlled by major out-of-state businesses. Hill became involved in the Mesabi quite inadvertently. In 1897 he was persuaded to purchase the bankrupt Duluth and Winnipeg Railroad, and the railroad proved to have a land grant that included some ore lands on the Mesabi. Then, somewhat later, he acquired a Mesabi Range logging railroad. In both instances Hill was primarily interested in adding to his railroad network, but he may also have sensed the potential value of the railroad lands even though iron ore had not yet been discovered on them. In 1906, after many ore discoveries on his holdings, Hill formed the Great Northern Iron Ore Properties. This corporation leased its lands to United States Steel and by the end of 1914 had been paid royalties of more than $30 million.

The Mesabi was very different from other Lake Superior iron ranges because its ore was soft like soil, and it lay close to the surface in horizontal beds. There was no need to dig deep underground mines and extract the ore from hard rock; instead, the miners could simply scrape away the topsoil, which in places was only a few feet deep, and scoop out the ore-bearing earth. Strip-mining became the pattern on the Mesabi. There were some small underground mines, but even many of these were converted to open pits when the advantages of that method were proven. Veteran miners like the Cornishmen who first worked the deep Vermilion mines ridiculed the so-called mining of the Mesabi. It may not have been mining in the traditional sense, but there was no scoffing about its effectiveness. The steam shovels, which were first used in 1894, could move thousands of tons each day. Largely because of the introduction of the open-pit process, the Mesabi Range in 1894 assumed first place in production among the Lake Superior ranges. A decade later there were 111 open pit mines on the Mesabi.

Although the soft ore of the Mesabi was plentiful and easy to extract,

The construction of the nearly 600-yard long Duluth ship canal across Minnesota Point in the early 1870s provided easy passage from Lake Superior to the city's harbor and stimulated Duluth's growth as the major Lake Superior port. The aerial lift bridge connecting the city and Minnesota Point was built in 1905.
Courtesy of the Minnesota Historical Society

it did present problems for the steelmakers because it was dusty and did not burn well in the Bessemer furnaces. For these reasons, the ore for its first several years was not so much in demand as was the hard ore from other ranges. However, as improvements in the furnaces were made, the Mesabi ore became easier to use and its softness was no longer an issue.

The Mesabi Range was like many of America's last frontiers. It opened during the Industrial Revolution, and the application of the new technology transformed it almost overnight—the forests were cut or burned over, towns sprang up along the narrow spine of the Mesabi from Babbitt in the east to Grand Rapids in the west, and gaping chasms appeared as the heavy ore was gouged from the face of the land. Within a decade after the Merritts opened Mountain Iron, the uncertainty of exploration and experimentation had been replaced by systematic extraction and marketing of ore by major capitalists. The Mesabi had become the greatest source of iron in the United States and Minnesota had become the ranking iron producer in the nation.

The taming of the Vermilion and Mesabi Ranges coincided with the final days of Minnesota's agricultural frontier and the lumbermen's rapacious assault on the coniferous forests. By the opening of the twentieth century, there was but little undeveloped or unexploited land left in the state, and the patterns had been established that were to dictate Minnesota's future character and prospects.

8

—

A LEGACY OF PROTEST POLITICS

T HE POLITICAL CAREERS of Hubert H. Humphrey and Walter F. Mondale, who both served as vice presidents of the United States and were later unsuccessful Democratic presidential candidates, have called particular attention to Minnesota's Democratic-Farmer-Labor Party. Formed in 1944, the party has some Democratic origins, but it also has a distinctiveness derived principally from its Farmer-Labor traits, the roots of which lie buried deep in Minnesota's long tradition of protest politics.

Henry H. Sibley, the state's first governor, was a Democrat, but after he completed his term in 1859 there was an unbroken reign of Republican governors for the next forty years. Even the election of John Lind in 1898 and John A. Johnson six years later did not seriously erode Republican control. Their election is attributable primarily to their personal qualities and their Scandinavian backgrounds as well as to petty squabbling among the Republican rivals at the time. Republicans still firmly controlled the legislature through the Lind and Johnson years, and Republican presidential candidates carried Minnesota regularly until 1912, when Theodore Roosevelt, the Progressive candidate, swept the state. Franklin D. Roosevelt in 1932 was the first Democratic presidential candidate to win Minnesota's electoral votes. But despite this impressive record, Minnesota's Republicans were not without opposition; almost continually after the mid-1870s they were buffeted from the Left by agrarian reformers who attacked them as the party of big business, hard money, and the protective tariff.

Frontier Minnesota was a natural seedbed for agrarian discontent. The wheat farmers whose hopes had been buoyed by the lure of cheap, productive land and the promise of the good life were soon disillusioned. The Industrial Revolution seemed to promise much, but the railroads that made the markets more accessible charged high and discriminatory rates and the farmers were also at the mercy of elevator companies (often controlled by railroads and flour millers), which cut into farm profits through fraudulent weighing and grading of wheat. The high cost of farm machinery, another of the blessings of the Industrial Revolution, drove many farmers into debt and increasing farm tenancy drove them to the money lenders, who were usually agents of eastern capital. To meet rising costs, the wheat farmers did the only seemingly logical thing—they produced more. Their critics said they overproduced—that that was the root of the "farm problem." Throughout the long era of discontent, farmers refused to accept this reasoning. In their view they were being victimized by the giants of the new industrial world—the railroads, the millers, and the eastern money cartels.

During the heightening of the agrarian revolt in the 1890s, thousands of farmers agreed with the admonishment of Populist Mary Lease of Kansas that they should "raise less corn and more Hell."[1] During the dry years, at least, those were easy things to do. But farmers had groped for solutions long before they organized the Populist Party in the early 1890s.

The first farm spokesman in the troubled period following the Civil War was Minnesota's Oliver H. Kelley. In 1849 Kelley moved from Boston, Massachusetts, to a farm near what became the town of Elk River. In 1864 he was appointed a clerk in the United States Department of Agriculture. Then, early in 1866, he was sent to study the agricultural resources of the war-torn Southern states. Kelley returned to Washington convinced that the depressed conditions of rural America would be improved through cooperative farm associations—associations that might even become national in scope. He and a few associates organized the National Grange of the Patrons of Husbandry in Washington late in 1867, but lack of interest in the new organization caused Kelley to return to Minnesota with the hope of forming Granges in his home state. With the assistance of Daniel A. Robertson, a well-known public figure and former editor of the *Minnesota Democrat,* then the state's best-known newspaper, Kelley organized the North Star Grange at St. Paul in 1868.

Oliver H. Kelley of Elk River founded the National Grange of the Patrons of
Husbandry in 1867.
Courtesy of the Minnesota Historical Society

Patterned along Masonic lines, the Grange emphasized secret rites,
brotherhood, and sisterhood. The association as Kelley envisioned it
would unite the farmers and encourage them to study new farming methods, engage in cooperative buying and selling, and attempt to influence
legislation. Kelley and other Grangers insisted that they were not a political party; Kelley was above politics, believing that highly principled
men acting in unison would somehow prevail.

Agrarian grievances against Minnesota railroads, particularly the Winona and St. Peter line, stimulated the rapid formation of Grange lodges. The Minnesota State Grange was organized in 1869, and by the end of the next year there were nearly fifty active local Granges in the state. The highest Minnesota Grange membership was reached in 1874, just a year after Congress chartered the National Grange.

After the organization of the Minnesota State Grange the reformers concentrated most of their efforts on railroad freight rate regulation. Inspired by Illinois laws, Minnesota Grangers pushed for similar measures. Governor Horace Austin was sympathetic to their demands, as were many legislators, and with strong bipartisan support the first of Minnesota's Granger laws was passed in 1871. It established the office of railroad commissioner and it specified rates that could not be adjusted except by legislative act. As expected, the railroads ignored the law, which caused its supporters not only to file a lawsuit against the Winona and St. Peter Railroad but also to work for yet stronger legislation.

During their efforts to get the railroad act enforced, many Grangers learned that it was not enough to lobby for railroad regulation: they needed their own political arm. Many agreed with the assessment of Ignatius Donnelly that the Grange was like "a gun that will do everything but shoot."[2] Donnelly spearheaded the drive to weld Grangers into a potent political force. He began his long championship of agrarian causes when he helped organize a lodge at Hastings in January 1873, but his conversion to the Grange creed was questioned by many from the start. Throughout his career he was hounded by critics who charged that he was neither a farmer nor a friend of farmers, but instead had associated himself with political dissent simply to further his own ambitions.

By the time he became a Grange organizer, Donnelly was well known in Minnesota. A native of Philadelphia, he had moved to the territory as a townsite speculator during the flush times of the mid-1850s. With glowing optimism he and his partners platted Nininger, another of the countless cities of tomorrow that studded the territory, but Donnelly was much sobered and considerably poorer when the Panic of 1857 sent real estate values tumbling. He had gotten involved in politics too, and, as one of the bright young men in the Republican Party, was nominated for the lieutenant governorship in 1859 on the ticket with Alexander Ramsey. He and Ramsey were swept into office on the Republican tide, and at age twenty-eight he started his elective political career. Donnelly moved from the lieutenant governorship to the House of Representatives in 1863. During three terms in Congress he was a regular Republican, but partially because of personal ambitions he broke with Ramsey, then the boss of the state Republican organization. This move lost him much support in his own party, so after failing in an 1868 reelection bid he turned to lecturing and through this avenue campaigned actively for the Liberal Republican Party in the 1872 presidential campaign.

Donnelly's experience, speaking ability, and facile mind assured his rapid emergence in Granger ranks. During 1873, when the Grangers urged further railroad regulation, they were upstaged by Republican gubernatorial candidate Cushman K. Davis, who was widely known throughout the state for his antirailroad stance, popularized in his speech "Modern Feudalism." With Davis's nomination there was little chance that the Grangers could dominate the Republican Party, so Donnelly schemed to form a political arm of the state Grange. Despite opposition from some Grangers who contended that political organization violated Grange principles, Donnelly and his supporters met at Owatonna in September 1873 and formed the Anti-Monopoly Party, which soon came to be known as the Anti-Monopoly Independent Party. As an advocate of the rights of the little people against giant corporations, the party urged railroad regulation and monetary reform.

Aided by the Panic of 1873, which hurt Republican candidates, Donnelly was elected to the state senate as an Anti-Monopolist. Angry debtor farmers also carried many other Anti-Monopolists into the legislature, and, with Donnelly as the leader of a coalition of Anti-Monopolists and Democrats, the reformers pushed through a second Granger law. This act of 1874 provided for a board of three railroad commissioners with power to hold hearings, establish rates, and force railroads into receivership; railroad cases were to be given priority in the state courts.

The reformists soon realized that they had achieved a hollow victory. Because railroads had been so adversely affected by the panic, the railroad commissioners did not enforce the 1874 law and usually rubber-stamped existing freight rates. In 1875, because it was generally believed that the stringent act was impeding the railroads in particular and the entire economy in general, the 1874 law was repealed and Minnesota was left with a single railroad commissioner whose only real duty was the gathering of information about railroads.

Despite the repeal, the state supreme court upheld the constitutionality of the 1871 law; and in 1876 the United States Supreme Court, acting on an Illinois case, also ruled that states could regulate railroads. Ten

years later, when the Supreme Court reversed itself, Congress was moved
to revive an idea that had first been advanced by United States Senator
William Windom of Minnesota in 1874. Windom, widely recognized as
a financial genius and later secretary of the treasury under Presidents
James A. Garfield and Benjamin Harrison, had suggested some type of
federal railroad regulation. Windom was not a crusader; instead he
seemed to have realized that federal regulation would simply have the
effect of guaranteeing a reasonable profit to the railroads. Whatever
Windom's motives may have been at the time that he suggested federal
regulation, the creation of the Interstate Commerce Commission in 1887
was welcomed by dissident farmers.

The Panic of 1873 marked the eclipse of the Grange. Its vitality was
undermined by public sympathy for the railroads and the 1876 Supreme
Court ruling undercut its basic reason for existing, since the courts henceforth had the power to control the railroads. Although the Grange was
waning, its offspring, the Anti-Monopoly Party, was flourishing. By
1876, the party had turned its attention almost entirely to the money
problem and was becoming increasingly identified with the national
Greenback movement. Next to the railroads, the money question was the
most pressing matter to debtor farmers. They protested vigorously at paying off debts with currency that was increasing in value; they much preferred an inflationary money that permitted them to fulfill their obligations with currency that was worth less on the dollar than at the time they
had borrowed. The period of the 1870s through the 1890s was deflation-
ary, and farmers strongly urged currency reform.

The first reform impulse was to continue printing and circulating
greenbacks, which had been issued during the Civil War to conserve the
Union's gold. But hard-money men dominated by eastern bankers urged
retirement of the paper money and a reliance on gold. The Greenback
movement, known in its early years as the Ohio Idea, was well enough
organized by 1876 to hold a national convention in Indianapolis.
Donnelly attended, and during the next several years was one of the
Greenbackers' chief spokesmen in Minnesota and the nation. In 1878 he
ran as a Greenback candidate for Congress but was defeated by William
D. Washburn, a younger brother of miller Cadwallader Washburn. The
Greenback Party, although it made a respectable showing in the congressional elections of 1878, succumbed, like the Anti-Monopoly Party
before it, to the winds of change. Vast silver discoveries in Colorado in the
mid-1870s assured a surplus of that metal, and when Congress accepted

limited coinage of silver in 1878, the old Greenbackers and the farmers who wanted cheap money became silver advocates.

The silver movement was nurtured through the 1880s by a new farm organization, the Farmers Alliance, which was started in New York in 1877 by Grangers who wanted a political voice. During 1880 Milton George, the Chicago editor of the *Western Rural,* popularized the Alliance movement, and the next year the first state Alliance was organized in Nebraska and local chapters were formed in Minnesota. By 1882, the Alliance, with about a hundred thousand members nationally, had really become two organizations—the Southern Alliance and the Northern Alliance—a division primarily caused by the race issue. In Minnesota as elsewhere, Alliance popularity rose and fell in relation to the farm economy. Good crops and acceptable market prices caused the Alliance to decline in 1883–84, but during the winter of 1884–85 it revived sharply when wheat prices fell. An overall decline in farm incomes in the mid-1880s, however, strengthened the Alliance until Minnesota had 438 local units in 1886, when the first state convention was held.

Nationally, the Alliance stressed the old educational and economic goals of the Grange. The Minnesota Alliance achieved one of its aims in 1885, when the state legislature created the Railroad and Warehouse Commission, which, among other things, was to inspect scales at the terminal elevators in Minneapolis, St. Paul, and Duluth. The law, while welcome, did not go far enough to satisfy the delegates to the 1886 convention, who called for state inspection of local elevator scales as well. The delegates also urged state-imposed reductions of rail rates, regulation of railroad monopolies, and making the use of free railroad passes by state officials a crime.

Alliance delegates clearly saw themselves as representatives of the common people who were being victimized by plutocrats; they maintained in their platform "that there are really but two parties in this State to-day—the people and their plunderers. The only issue is: Shall the people keep the fruits of their own industry, or shall the thieves carry them away?"[3] Believing they were exploited, the farm agitators sought an alliance with organized labor. The labor movement in the Twin Cities was headed by the Knights of Labor, which had grown dramatically with the modernization of flour milling, and the Minnesota Alliance arranged its first state convention as a joint meeting with the Minnesota Knights of Labor. The two groups drew up separate platforms, with labor demanding an income-tax law, a state bureau of labor statistics, and prohibition of child labor. Representatives of agriculture and labor talked about a formal political tie and discussed the creation of a Farm and Labor Party; but the party was never formally organized because farmers and laborers believed their aims could be better accomplished through the Republican Party, which adopted their demands and added them to its platform.

The Alliance and the Knights of Labor were pleased with the prospects of achieving their goals through Minnesota's major party, but Republican betrayal of their interests in 1886 and again in 1888 caused them to think more and more about organizing a third party—a party devoted solely to representing the farmers and laborers. And Ignatius Donnelly again came to the fore. After his Greenback experience Donnelly had embarked on a literary career, in which he wrote knowingly although unconvincingly about a variety of popular subjects. In his first book, *Atlantis: The Antediluvian World* (1882), he insisted that the legendary lost continent had not only really existed but was the fount of civilization, which subsequently spread to other continents. This widely read work was closely followed by *Ragnarok: The Age of Fire and Gravel,* a challenge to the glacial theory. Donnelly's explanation of the earth's surface deposits of gravel and silt was that they resulted from the planet having been in contact with a giant comet. His books made Donnelly a literary figure of note, and, with his newfound reputation as the "Sage of Nininger," he became a popular lecturer. This success turned him to yet another area—Shakespearian literature. His resulting labor, *The Great Cryptogram* (1888), was an ingenious effort to show, through an extremely complicated cipher, that Francis Bacon had actually written many of the works attributed to William Shakespeare. Although this book was not a literary success, it did reveal another aspect of Donnelly's complex and fascinating personality and tended to confirm the popular public impression that he could be counted upon to champion unique, if not bizarre, notions.

Throughout his literary phase Donnelly never abandoned the urge to return to Congress, so in 1889, after twenty years of detachment from the Republican Party, he attempted to win its endorsement for United States senator. Again he was frustrated by the supporters of William D. Washburn, whom Donnelly thought had defeated him by fraudulent means in both the congressional race of 1878 and the senatorial contest. The embittered Donnelly, convinced that Washburn epitomized the evils of politics, wrote *Caesar's Column,* his last major work. Like Edward Bellamy, whose *Looking Backward* had been published only a few years before, Donnelly wrote of a Utopia, but his ideal society was placed a cen-

tury in his future. The story told of a Ugandan who visited New York
City in 1988 only to find that the legacy of corrupt politics had reduced
the once-proud American democracy to a mob-ridden society. In this new
world, one of the crime lords, Caesar Lomellini, had the heads of his

Ignatius Donnelly, politician and writer, was the most famous Minnesotan in the
late nineteenth century.
Courtesy of the Minnesota Historical Society

decapitated victims stacked into columns, from which came the title
Caesar's Column. Fearing that its decadence might spread, the Ugandan
convinced his countrymen to convert their nation into a Utopian Socialist
republic, which within a few years became a blissful earthly paradise on
daylight saving time.

In the real world of politics, Donnelly not only had lost to Washburn
but had estranged many Alliance members who questioned his sincerity
after his trafficking with the Republicans. In 1890, when the Minnesota
Alliance ran its own candidates, Donnelly, who aspired to the gubernatorial nomination, was passed over in favor of Sidney M. Owen, the popular editor of a farm journal. Donnelly survived the rebuke and became one
of the leaders in uniting the Northern and Southern Alliances into the
Populist Party. When the "People's Party" held its national convention at
Omaha in the summer of 1892, it drew up a reformist platform calling
for measures such as a graduated income tax and public ownership of railroads and utilities, and Donnelly wrote a stirring preamble to it.
Appealing to the disillusioned and the disaffected, he urged major
reforms because "from the same prolific womb of governmental injustice
we breed the two great classes—tramps and millionaires."[4]

Whatever aspirations Donnelly had to be the party's presidential nominee were dashed when the Populists turned to the less colorful but less
controversial James B. Weaver of Iowa. Donnelly had to fight hard even
to become the Populist gubernatorial candidate in his home state. During
the ensuing campaign he challenged Republican candidate Knute Nelson
to a debate. As the front-runner, Nelson, a former congressman who was
very popular with farmers and who had been courted earlier by the
Alliance, saw no need for such a debate. Theodore Christianson, a rather
shrewd political observer and a three-term governor of Minnesota from
1925 to 1931, noted later that "the people came to hear and applaud
[Donnelly] . . . but in November they voted for Knute Nelson."[5]
Donnelly finished a weak third in the gubernatorial contest and only two
dozen Populists were elected to the state legislature.

Although the Populists hardly dominated, their interests were served
nonetheless when the legislature provided for state licensing of all grain
elevators on public rights-of-way and appropriated funds for the construction of a state-owned grain terminal elevator in Duluth. The latter
measure, which seemed too socialistic to many conservatives, was declared
unconstitutional by the state supreme court, which held that the state's
constitution forbade the contracting of debts for internal improvements.

Nelson, however, succeeded in enhancing his standing with some of the political dissidents by proposing a public works program to help solve unemployment after the Panic of 1893.

The panic, which seemed to underscore the evils of the old system and the inability or even unwillingness of the major parties to assist the common people, helped the Populists in the 1894 elections. Nationally the party's vote was more than 40 percent higher than it had been in 1892, and in Minnesota the Populists temporarily became the state's second-ranking party. Knute Nelson, the incumbent Republican governor, was more popular than ever and easily won reelection; but Sidney M. Owen, the Populist candidate, finished well ahead of Democrat George L. Becker, who as a former railroad agent was vulnerable to the charge that he represented a special business that was opposed to the interests of farmers.

After the election the Populists anticipated continued success, but they failed to reckon with the free-silver sentiment within the Democratic Party. When William Jennings Bryan led the Democrats on the silver crusade of 1896, the Populists suffered the fate common to third parties—their platform was absorbed by a major party. In 1896 Minnesota Populists accepted the inevitable and, like their counterparts in many other states, agreed to a "Fusionist" ticket composed of Populists, Silver Democrats, and Silver Republicans. John Lind, a Silver Republican and the Fusionist gubernatorial candidate, narrowly lost to the Republican nominee. Lind, a former congressman from New Ulm who was extremely popular with farmers and Scandinavians, won the governorship in 1898, but by that time he was in reality a Democrat and the Populist Party as such was dead.

When compared to a number of western states, including some that were carried by the Populists in the presidential election of 1892, Minnesota's Populist gains were modest. The party never captured the governorship; it sent only two men to the national House of Representatives and it never controlled the legislature. But in Minnesota, as elsewhere, the Populist era paved the way for the progressive movement, a broader and yet more profound criticism of American institutions and practices.

Carl H. Chrislock, in writing about Minnesota progressivism, observed that "the inauguration of Governor John Lind on January 2, 1899, heralded the progressive era in Minnesota."[6] In his opening message Lind suggested a series of sweeping reforms. He called for an increase in railroad taxes and the creation of a state tax commission to study alternatives to the onerously high property taxes. Lind also suggested the creation of a supervisory state board of control to make state institutions more fiscally responsible, and he asked that consideration be given to ideas such as the direct primary, initiative, referendum, and recall. Faced with a hostile legislature, Lind accomplished none of his major goals, but subsequent developments gave him a significance not apparent at the time. During the twelve years after Lind left office, Minnesota was profoundly affected by the tone he set. Minnesota's conversion to progressivism was not so rapid as that of neighboring Wisconsin, which won a national reputation for sweeping reforms under Governor Robert La Follette, a progressive Republican, but in time the reform urge in Minnesota became broadly based and transcended party lines.

The muscle in Minnesota's progressivism came from the small towns, whose citizenry, like the surrounding farmers, resented railroads, big banks, and the Twin Cities. These rural residents saw rampant industrialization and urbanization as threats to traditional agrarian America, so they cried out against the evils of big business. Progressivism's appeal in the Twin Cities was narrower; metropolitan business interests were attracted to tariff reforms, which promised to help them economically, and there was popular support for such ideas as direct primaries, but there was no general reaction against the increasing power of big urban business.

Although the thrust of progressivism finally affected all aspects of corporate business and political reform, the fear of railroad domination was particularly strong in the minds of Minnesotans. In late 1901, when it became publicly known that railroad barons James J. Hill and Edward H. Harriman, with the assistance of John Pierpoint Morgan, had formed the Northern Securities Company, a merger of the Northern Pacific, Great Northern, and Chicago and Burlington Railroads, there was an angry public response. In an age when railroads were the only effective means of transportation, this merger created a virtual transportation monopoly in Minnesota. Hill's participation in the merger did little to assuage the ire of Minnesotans.

Even if he had been otherwise inclined, Governor Samuel R. Van Sant had little choice other than to challenge the Northern Securities Company. Within days after its formation he ordered his attorney general to bring suit in the name of the state against it for violating a Minnesota statute forbidding construction of parallel rail lines by the same company. Van Sant also spearheaded a widely publicized conference of the governors of Minnesota, South Dakota, Montana, Idaho, and Washington at which the merger was condemned. President Theodore Roosevelt instructed the Justice Department to proceed against the company, and as a result of the federal suit the Northern Securities Company was ordered dissolved and Roosevelt had taken his first important step in earning his reputation as the "trustbuster."

The antirailroad crusade was continued during the administration of Van Sant's successor, John A. Johnson, with the passage of a new law forbidding the issuance of free railroad passes. By the time of Johnson's governorship, the public mood for reform had deepened. Most big businesses were under attack and there was a loud demand for more democratic, more responsive government. Johnson, although he was much more conservative than the later common impression, epitomized the type of leadership needed in an age when responsiveness and openness in government were the expectation. The state's first native governor, Johnson was born to Swedish immigrant parents in a St. Peter log cabin and left school when he was thirteen years old. He read widely and worked in a general store and as a supply clerk before buying an interest in the *Saint Peter Herald* when he was twenty-five. His political start was inauspicious: he was defeated in a bid for a seat in the state House of Representatives in 1888 and for the state Senate six years later. He was elected to the Senate in 1898, but was again defeated in 1902. By the time he ran for governor as a Democrat in 1904, he had, in the words of Theodore Christianson, "left no important legislation on the statute books of the state, had done no outstanding committee work and had in no way distinguished himself. But by his affable nature he had won many friends among Republican as well as Democratic members."[7]

By strength of character and personality and also because of a power struggle among rival Republicans, Johnson won the governorship in 1904 even though Theodore Roosevelt swamped his Democratic opponent in the presidential election and all other state elective offices were won by Republicans. The handsome, gentlemanly Johnson appealed to many voters with his characteristic openness. When asked by a reporter what he had to say about reports that his father had been a drunkard, Johnson replied simply: "Nothing—it is true."[8] To answer the taunt that his mother had taken in washing, he responded: "Took in washing? Yes, she did—until I was old enough to go out and earn something. But she never took in any washing after that."[9] Criticized by both Right and Left,

As governor, 1905–09, the extremely popular John A. Johnson was a
moderate progressive-age reformer.
Courtesy of the Minnesota Historical Society

Johnson appealed magnetically to Minnesota's electorate throughout his
administration. He was reelected in 1906 and again in 1908, when he was
the only successful Democratic candidate for state executive office.

As governor, Johnson recommended the nomination and election of
nonpartisan judges, a state income tax, and more stringent railroad regulation, and he was the first governor to suggest a Minnesota worker's
compensation law. However, most of his reform effort was aimed at curb-
ing fraudulent practices of insurance companies operating in the state. At
Johnson's instigation President Theodore Roosevelt called for a conference of the states to adopt uniform insurance regulation. As permanent

chairman of the conference, Johnson attracted national attention when twenty-two states passed laws regulating insurance companies in keeping with the recommendations of one of the conference's committees. As part of the crusade Johnson became active in the International Policyholders' Committee, a reform group based in Boston. Through his association with this group he became a popular banquet speaker, and as early as 1905 the group's leader, Boston multimillionaire Thomas Lawson, heralded Johnson as a presidential possibility.

Johnson's supporters saw him as a viable conservative alternative to the liberal William Jennings Bryan, and he was nominated for the presidency as a favorite-son candidate in 1908 at the Democratic national convention. Although Johnson garnered few votes and Bryan easily captured the nomination, it was obvious that his supporters were thinking ahead to 1912. Some believe that he could have been the Democratic presidential candidate in 1912. His sudden death on September 21, 1909, ended a career of great achievement but yet greater promise.

Johnson himself was a moderate reformer. The real flowering of progressivism in the state came during the administration of Johnson's

Street scene at 5th Street entrance to Minneapolis City Hall, about 1905.
Courtesy of the Minnesota Historical Society

Downtown Minneapolis looking south on Nicollet Avenue from
Washington Avenue, about 1910.
Courtesy of the Minnesota Historical Society

successor, Republican Adolph O. Eberhart, a man of limited vision whose
reform impulse was stimulated late during his administration only by the
political instinct to survive. Many members of Eberhart's own party,
including United States Senator Moses E. Clapp and Congressman
Charles A. Lindbergh, were leaders in the insurgency against the
Republican Old Guard and President William Howard Taft. After
Eberhart witnessed the involvement of Minnesota's Republican congressmen in the overthrow of conservative leadership in the House of
Representatives, the defeat in 1910 of the only Minnesota congressman
who supported Taft's opposition to tariff reform, and the rising progressive tide in Minnesota and the nation, he became very interested in
reform.

By 1912 Eberhart's problem was twofold: he had alienated many liberals in his own party by his lack of reform zeal, and since he had completed Johnson's third term and served a full term of his own, many of his

opponents complained that he was actually seeking a (not unprecedented) third term. So Eberhart convened a short special session to consider a host of reforms in the summer of 1912. In less than two weeks the legislature approved amendments to the federal constitution calling for an income tax and direct election of United States senators, extended the direct primary to state offices, and provided for fair political campaign practices. The *Minneapolis Journal* pronounced the session to be

> in many ways . . . the most memorable in the history of the state. In thirteen days the legislature has completely revolutionized the state's present political system . . . The special session of the legislature has sounded the death knell of the old party convention system. And with the convention system will go, if the supporters of the statewide primary bill and the corrupt practices act are right, the paid political worker, the hanger-on at elections, the perennial follower of the man who seeks office.[10]

Eberhart's conversion (even if for only tactical reasons) and the success of the special session, followed by the victory in Minnesota of Progressive Party presidential candidate Theodore Roosevelt, stimulated yet more reforms. The 1913 legislature extended the nonpartisan principle beyond judgeships to include such local posts as county coroner and surveyor and, with very little deliberation, even forbade party designation for state legislators. The extension of the nonpartisan principle to the legislature was a most curious event in Minnesota history. Some thought it was the epitome of democratic reform, but the law evidently passed primarily because of the influence of liquor lobbyists who believed dry laws could be forestalled by obfuscating party lines. The legislature remained officially nonpartisan for sixty years, thereby adding to Minnesota's independent and even maverick tradition, but, in actuality, the conservative caucus was predominantly Republican and the liberal caucus was composed mostly of opposition groups.

The Progressives' view of themselves as good people who wanted a just, moral society helped stimulate the long-standing drives for prohibition and woman suffrage. By 1908 Minnesota Progressives generally supported the idea of partially controlling the liquor traffic by a county option law, which would empower voters to ban liquor sales within their counties. The county option concept, which was quite popular nationally, was widely thought to be a likely precursor of total prohibition. To its adherents county option not only promised to reduce drinking but also to curb the power of brewers and distillers, who allegedly supported such evils as political machines and bribery of legislators and other government officials.

The controversy over county option enlivened legislative debates for half a dozen years. After county option proposals were defeated in 1909 and 1913, the issue was the paramount one in the 1914 gubernatorial campaign. The Republican candidate William E. Lee ran as a dry, and although Winfield Scott Hammond, the Democratic candidate, did not personally endorse county option, he tactfully avoided being stigmatized as a wet by indicating that he would sign such a bill if approved by the legislature. After Hammond's victory, the predominantly dry legislature quickly enacted county option in February 1915. Flushed with this victory, drys immediately proposed, but failed to achieve, statewide prohibition, which by the end of 1914 had been adopted by fourteen states. County option was eagerly embraced by many Minnesotans. By mid-June 1915 thirty of the state's then eighty-six counties had held elections on the question, and by January 1920, when national prohibition began, forty-six Minnesota counties had banned liquor sales.

The nationwide prohibition crusade, led by such organizations as the Anti-Saloon League and the Women's Christian Temperance Union, was boosted sharply after April 1917, when the United States entered World War I. Arguing that it was unpatriotic to use grain to manufacture liquor when millions of people worldwide were short of bread, the prohibitionists joined a suddenly strong international call to ban the manufacture and sale of intoxicating liquors. During the war Congress responded by endorsing a constitutional prohibition amendment, which had to be approved by the legislatures of three fourths of the states. By the end of 1918, fifteen states had ratified the amendment, and during the frenzied rush of the next several weeks, Nebraska, the thirty-sixth and last required state, ratified the amendment on January 16, 1919. Within a day four additional states, including Minnesota, ratified the prohibition amendment.

Although Minnesota was one of the last states to ratify the Eighteenth Amendment and one of only sixteen states that did not enact state prohibition before the amendment was approved, it wrongfully gained a reputation as a leader in the national prohibition movement. This misunderstanding of Minnesota's role stems from the Volstead Act, named after its author—Congressman Andrew J. Volstead of Granite Falls. Since the Eighteenth Amendment did not define liquor or specify an enforcement process, Congress had to implement it through legislation. Volstead, a conservative Republican lawyer who had first been elected to represent Minnesota's seventh congressional district in 1902, had risen to the chairmanship of the House Judiciary Committee by 1919. In that position he assumed the responsibility for writing an enforcement act. Apparently sensing that he would be forever linked with the prohibition amendment, Volstead emphasized that he had not been an active prohibitionist, but was duty-bound to carry out a legal mandate. The Volstead Act, which went into effect in January 1920, proved to be one of the most unpopular laws in the nation's history and contributed significantly to the repeal of the Eighteenth Amendment in 1933. In legally defining intoxicants as any beverage whose alcohol content was at least one half of 1 percent, the Volstead Act incurred the wrath of beer drinkers, many of whom might have supported a ban on stronger liquors.

As with prohibition, Minnesota lagged behind national trends in the quest for voting rights for women. After woman suffrage was first called for in 1848 at the initial meeting of the Woman Rights Convention in Seneca Falls, New York, the idea languished for a time, but gained strength in the last third of the nineteenth century. Wyoming Territory led the nation in authorizing woman suffrage in 1869, but Minnesota suffrage advocates had to settle for morsels rather than the whole loaf. By the opening of the progressive period, Minnesota women could vote only on school and library questions. Although these gains were modest at best, state suffragists had forged a significant alliance with the Women's Christian Temperance Union after the establishment of its Minnesota chapter in 1877. Linking the prohibition and woman suffrage issues not only helped establish the moral credibility of both, but made them logical stepchildren of the progressive urge to better society.

Progressive impulses, combined with outcomes of the Industrial Revolution such as urbanization and new professional opportunities for women, helped bring the woman suffrage matter to the fore. Suffrage advocates stressed that women should be granted the vote as a matter of justice and also that they were uniquely qualified to champion such progressive measures as child and women's labor laws, women's property rights, vocational training for girls, and beautification of urban environments. Although public perception of woman suffrage in Minnesota became more favorable after 1901, when suffrage activists from twenty-six states held their annual convention in Minneapolis, the legislature could not overcome its traditional opposition to general state suffrage.

However, starting in 1914 the crusade was reinvigorated under the national leadership of Carrie Chapman Catt. Catt, who resumed the presidency of the National American Woman Suffrage Association, developed a strategy for achieving nationwide woman suffrage. Faced with the realization that only eight states had authorized full woman suffrage before 1914, Catt emphasized the need to add a woman suffrage amendment to the federal constitution. In Minnesota the constitutional amendment campaign was led by Clara H. Ueland, who in 1914 became president of the Minnesota Woman Suffrage Association. Ueland, wife of attorney Andreas Ueland, had long been active in educational and social causes. Before assuming the presidency of the state

Clara H. Ueland served as the last president of the Minnesota Woman Suffrage
Association and the first president of the Minnesota League of Women Voters
Courtesy of the Minnesota Historical Society

suffrage organization she had been president of the Equal Suffrage Association of Minneapolis.

Using Catt's New York model of organizing a state by legislative districts and using paid organizers, Ueland forced the Minnesota legislature to face the woman suffrage issue. Ueland's efforts were challenged by the very active woman-dominated Minnesota Association Opposed to Woman Suffrage, whose aim was complemented by kindred organizations in both Minneapolis and St. Paul. After Ueland and her opponents debated before the Minnesota Senate in 1915, the legislature failed by a lone vote to refer to the voters a woman suffrage amendment to the state constitution.

Ueland subsequently concentrated on the federal amendment, because the Minnesota constitution was difficult to amend. Any Minnesota amendment had to be approved by a majority of those voting in a general election rather than a majority voting only on the amendment. Thus, someone who abstained from voting on an amendment in effect voted against it. However, following Catt's approach, Ueland and the Minnesota Woman Suffrage Association saw advantages in seeking state approval of woman suffrage in presidential elections. Despite support from a number of progressive legislators, Ueland failed to achieve this in 1917.

Especially after Democrat Woodrow Wilson was inaugurated president in March 1917, the moderate, consensus-building approach of Catt and Ueland was challenged by the Congressional Union for Woman Suffrage. Formed in 1914 by Alice Paul, who was deeply influenced by radical British suffragettes, the Congressional Union evolved into the National Woman's Party in 1916. Using such tactics as picketing, boisterous demonstrations, hunger strikes, burning Wilson in effigy, and willingly being arrested and imprisoned to advance its cause, the party accelerated the suffrage drive. Although the Minnesota chapter of the party was less strident than the national organization, its leaders nonetheless supported picketing of the White House and Congress.

After the United States entered World War I in April 1917, Catt and Ueland endorsed women's participation in the war effort. This patriotic gesture, combined with the increasing visibility of the thousands of women who worked in war-related industries, caused a groundswell of prosuffrage sentiment. By war's end women were fully enfranchised in fifteen states, and in fourteen others could vote in presidential elections. After a carefully orchestrated lobbying plan by the Minnesota Woman Suffrage Association, the legislature in February 1919 passed a presidential election suffrage measure, which was promptly and enthusiastically signed by Governor Joseph A. A. Burnquist.

The surge in women's political power during the war was not lost on Congress. In 1918 the House of Representatives supported the suffrage amendment by the required two-thirds vote, but the effort was defeated in the Senate. This wartime momentum was carried into the postwar

A famous orator who had championed woman suffrage and prohibition, Anna Dickie Olesen was the Minnesota Democratic candidate for the United States Senate in 1922.

Courtesy of the Minnesota Historical Society

Congress. Within a two-week period in late spring 1919, both houses resolved to refer the amendment to the states. During the fourteen-month ratification campaign, the Minnesota legislature on September 8, 1919, approved the Nineteenth Amendment in a special one-day session. After Tennessee, the thirty-sixth state, approved the amendment, it was proclaimed to be in effect on August 26, 1920.

Anticipating the approval of woman suffrage, the National American Woman Suffrage Association in March 1919 formed its successor organization—the National League of Women Voters. With the subsequent formation of state chapters, Ueland gained the distinction being the last president of the Minnesota Woman Suffrage Association and the first president of the Minnesota League of Women Voters.

The formation of the League of Women Voters clearly indicated that suffragists realized that gaining the franchise was nothing more than an important first step in increasing political participation by women. In 1922, the first year they were eligible to run, four of eight women running were elected to the Minnesota House of Representatives. Before the end of the 1920s three others were elected to that chamber.

The 1922 election also featured a respectable showing by Anna Dickie Olesen, the Democratic nominee for the United States Senate seat held by Frank Billings Kellogg. The thirty-seven-year-old Olesen, famed as an orator, Chautauqua lecturer, and an advocate of both woman suffrage and prohibition, easily captured her party's nomination, but finished well behind the winning Farmer-Laborite, Henrik Shipstead, and Kellogg. However, she garnered nearly 18 percent of the senatorial votes and significantly outpolled Edward Indrehus, the Democratic gubernatorial nominee, by an almost three-to-one margin.

During the late stages of the prohibition and woman suffrage movements, Minnesota and the nation drifted from their progressive preoccupations to concern with European affairs and involvement in World War I. Fears of an uncertain loyalty from many in Minnesota's large German element caused the state legislature to create the Commission of Public Safety, which among other things was to control seditious activity, ensure compliance with the national military draft, and take steps to conserve food, fuel, and other essentials for the war effort. Unfortunately the commission, which was dominated by ultraconservatives, became a virtual government in its own right, employing its own agents and constabulary. Arbitrarily assuming powers and responding vigorously to the worst fears of superpatriots, the commission clashed with officials of New Ulm and

Brown County over alleged draft evasion and attempted to squelch political dissent and union organizing, which the commission thought detracted from the war effort.

Another object of the commission's wrath was the newly formed Nonpartisan League, which had spread into Minnesota from its North Dakota origin. The League was yet another organization intended to represent embattled farmers. Its founder, Arthur C. Townley, was inspired by both Socialists and a radical farm group, the American Society of Equity, that had espoused great political and economic power for farmers after its formation in 1902. Townley, a native of Browns Valley, Minnesota, had taught school before moving to Beach, North Dakota, where he joined his brother in a large flax-farming operation. As the "Flax King of North Dakota," Townley's prospects were promising, but, like many staple-crop farmers, he found himself irretrievably in debt because of one poor crop. After his 1913 disaster Townley began actively planning a new organization that would truly represent farm interests. Townley himself was not a socialist and he personally believed that socialism (at least under that name) would not be acceptable to farmers, but he thought some key socialist ideas were sound and could be achieved under the banner of a major party.

Townley formed the Farmers Nonpartisan League in February 1915, not to create a new party but to dominate an existing one that would have a broader respectability and base. Recognizing that the Republican Party was dominant in North Dakota, Townley and his supporters sought to control it. Through a massive recruitment effort in 1915–16, the Nonpartisan League actually dominated the North Dakota Republican Party and won the governorship and control of the legislature in the 1916 elections. Since some of its aims, such as state-owned and -operated grain terminals, packing plants, and flour mills, were frankly socialistic, the League appeared to be the most radical protest group spawned by the half-century of farm discontent. It officially supported American involvement in World War I, but it called for tight government control of wartime profiteering, and some of its more radical members believed the thesis of Russia's Bolshevik leader Vladimir Lenin—that the war was nothing more than a power struggle between rival imperialists. The League's lukewarm enthusiasm for World War I made it extremely suspect to the Public Safety Commission, which in a fit of zealous patriotism tarred the League's supporters and German-Americans with the same brush, thereby creating a rather strange fellowship.

Arthur C. Townley, founder of the Nonpartisan League, spoke at many rural
outdoor meetings in Minnesota.
Courtesy of the Minnesota Historical Society

After the League moved its national headquarters to St. Paul early in
1917, its Minnesota membership rose sharply. From the start Townley
and his principal aides realized that Minnesota, unlike North Dakota, was
both agrarian and industrial and that the League would have to enlist the
support of both farmers and organized labor. The support for the League
from labor, wheat farmers, and German-Americans was sufficiently
strong to encourage Townley to attempt to dominate the Minnesota
Republican Party, but incumbent Republican Governor Joseph A. A.
Burnquist, a strong supporter of the Public Safety Commission, rejected
all League overtures. The League then challenged Burnquist in the 1918
Republican primary with former congressman Charles A. Lindbergh, a
dedicated opponent of American involvement in the war. After Burnquist
defeated Lindbergh, the League entered an opposition candidate in the
general election. When the Minnesota attorney general ruled that the
candidate had to have a party label, League officials designated him the
candidate of the Farmer-Labor Party.

Although the name was first used in 1918, the party was not officially formed until four years later. Townley himself never abandoned his original notion that the League should be a nonpartisan influence group, but, like other founders in history, he had to recognize that his creation grew beyond his expectations. David H. Evans, the League's gubernatorial candidate in 1918, finished well behind Burnquist but well ahead of the Democratic candidate—meaning that almost overnight the League had become Minnesota's second-ranking political group. This rank was reaffirmed in the 1920 state elections, and the League, even though it was accused of advocating atheism, communism, and free love, continued to gain in strength because of the postwar agricultural depression.

Those who did not take the League seriously enough—and there were many—were rudely awakened in 1922 when League candidate Henrik Shipstead, a Glenwood dentist, upset incumbent United States Senator Frank Billings Kellogg. Kellogg, who had won national stature for prosecuting antimonopoly cases for the federal government, had returned to Minnesota long enough to become in 1916 the first elected senator in the state's history. However, he courted defeat when he failed to detect and respond to the feelings of angry farmers and laborers.

Kellogg went on to be secretary of state in the Coolidge administration and was awarded the Nobel Peace Prize in 1929 for his part in initiating the Kellogg-Briand Peace Pact, while Shipstead came to epitomize midwestern isolationism. After serving three full terms as a Farmer-Laborite senator, Shipstead returned to the Republican fold in 1940 and was elected to a fourth term. He was never converted to the internationalism of World War II; in 1945 he was one of only two American senators who voted against approval of the United Nations charter. Finally, in the Republican primary of 1946, he was defeated smashingly, his isolationism no longer appreciated.

The depth of the Farmer-Labor strength had become very evident with Shipstead's surprising win over Kellogg. In 1923, when Senator Knute Nelson died, Magnus Johnson challenged Republican Governor Jacob A. O. Preus in a special election for the remainder of Nelson's term. The earthy, robust Johnson, who purportedly delighted farm audiences by standing on a manure spreader and proclaiming that that was the first time he had ever stood on a Republican platform, was castigated by the opposition as a "dirt farmer." Although he was short on both manners and syntax and, his enemies said, on intellectual capacity, Johnson—as a friend of the farmers—was victorious. With his win the Farmer-Labor Party controlled both Senate seats.

Although Minnesota, like most of the Midwest, was detrimentally affected by the agricultural depression that persisted throughout the 1920s, the Farmer-Labor Party did not benefit at the state level. The party temporarily held both Senate seats, and two of its members in the House of Representatives contributed significantly to the activities of the farm bloc. But in the struggle for control of the governorship, the party prevailed only after the great crash of 1929.

The stock market plunge and subsequent depression, which embarrassed the old orders in both Washington and St. Paul, opened the way for the emergence of one of the most colorful and controversial figures in Minnesota's history—Floyd B. Olson. As Minnesota's New Deal governor, Olson attracted national attention as a speaker, as an advocate of change, and as a potential vice presidential and even presidential candidate.

Olson is often compared to John A. Johnson: both were Scandinavians, both came from humble backgrounds, both were magnetic speakers, both were men of the people who seemed to have the interests of the common people at heart, and both died during the height of their careers. But Olson was the rougher gem. Sometimes coarse and ribald, he often offended, while Johnson was unfailingly gracious. Johnson typified the age of consensus politics, in which reformist sentiment crossed party lines and political independence was in vogue, but Olson was a product of political partisanship. He represented a new liberal group that urged its reforms with evangelistic fervor. Olson also lived in a harsher age than Johnson: the disaffection of the progressive era was mild compared to the bitterness of the New Deal years, when it seemed to many that the old system had at last failed utterly. Olson, unlike Johnson, continually had to seek a balance between political extremes ranging from those of his ultraliberal supporters to those of his archenemies, who saw him as a homegrown Red.

Olson, whom biographer George H. Mayer portrayed as "more rebel than radical,"[11] was conditioned by his upbringing in the slums of north Minneapolis. Continual contact with the poor and struggling imbued him with a lifelong sympathy for the underdog. As a young man he labored in Alaska and up and down the West Coast before returning to Minnesota and working his way through law school. After serving as county attorney of Hennepin County he became the Farmer-Labor gubernatorial candidate in 1924, only to be defeated by Republican Theodore L. Christianson in a campaign marked by charges that Olson was in

Governor Floyd B. Olson with Walter Bullock, operations manager, Northwest
Airways, before leaving for Washington, D.C., November 1, 1933.
Courtesy of the Minnesota Historical Society

league with the Communists. He learned from his defeat and earned public acceptance through his vigilant prosecution of political graft and his
compassionate attitude toward petty offenders.

With this background he went into the governorship with a commitment to reform, but with strong opposition from conservatives who dominated the legislature during his first term. Although Olson's situation improved with increasing Farmer-Labor strength during his second and third terms, he never enjoyed a truly supportive legislature. Nonetheless, he successfully championed some major changes—the acceptance of a graduated state income tax, the banning of yellow dog contracts and injunctions, and the postponement of farm mortgage foreclosures.

A master of rhetoric with immense crowd appeal, Olson spoke for the poor farmers and laborers. To them he seemed a beacon of hope, but he also polarized opinion he tended to be greatly loved or greatly hated. Through his advocacy of the rights of labor and his efforts to aid the state's farmers he earned a national reputation as the country's most liberal governor, but in an age when people desperately cried for a solution it was beyond the power of any one man to offer one. To the opposition he was too socialistic, and to many in his own party he was not liberal

The Minnesota state capitol (about 1933) was designed by noted architect
Cass Gilbert and completed in 1904.
Courtesy of the Minnesota Historical Society

enough. After he pursued a middle course in the bloody Minneapolis truckers' strike of 1934 and failed to push vigorously the socialistic 1934 platform of his own party, which advocated public ownership of banks, factories, mines, transportation, and utilities, Olson came under increasing attack and was more open than ever before to charges that he was pragmatic but little else. He certainly was not a doctrinaire radical, and he resisted efforts to propagate the third-party faith nationally. Olson's posture was one of cooperation with Franklin Roosevelt and the New Deal, and his disinterest in a national third party in 1936 was dictated by his desire not to undercut Roosevelt's strength in Minnesota.

In 1936 Olson fully expected that he would be elected to the United States Senate and that his party would continue to control the governorship; but during the campaign he died from cancer, an event that deeply affected his party and the immediate political history of the state. His biographer observed that "death enhanced Olson's reputation because he died before public apathy and the increasing threat of war undermined the reforming zeal of the mid-1930s. As the lesser left-wing leaders who succeeded him wasted their energies in futile skirmishes, Olson's faults were forgotten and his achievements took on legendary proportions. Minnesota came to remember him as a fearless and effective crusader for social justice." [12]

Like many protest movements before it, the Farmer-Labor Party rose quickly, peaked during a time of troubles, and then plunged rapidly into public disfavor. Elmer A. Benson earned the distinction in 1936 of winning the governorship by the largest plurality in Minnesota's history, and then two years later lost it by another record margin. Benson fell victim to the patronage excesses of his party, his unswerving dedication to liberal causes, and his unwillingness or inability to dissociate himself from Minnesota's small group of Communist activists. Benson, who in the minds of many was the gravedigger of the Farmer-Labor Party, has naturally been compared to Olson. Carl H. Chrislock observed that:

> the marked difference between Olson and Benson is aptly expressed in an often-repeated tale, possibly apocryphal but nevertheless illuminating. It tells of a businessman discussing militant Farmer-Labor rhetoric shortly after the 1936 election. He complained that 'Floyd Olson used to say these things; but this son of a bitch [Benson] *believes* them.' [13]

Benson's fall was not all of his own doing. The Republicans of 1938 were not the conservatives who had battled Olson; they were led by

Harold E. Stassen, a bright, articulate, progressive young lawyer who preached the gospel of "enlightened capitalism," his answer to the socialism of the Farmer-Laborites. Stassen, only thirty-one when he won the governorship, had risen through the party's ranks on the strength of his leadership in the Young Republican League, which supported many New Deal measures. After Stassen surprised Republicans by winning the primary, he waged an extremely effective campaign in which he pledged to rid Minnesota of Communism and corruption in government.

During his first term, the nation's then youngest governor effected a major reorganization of state government and instituted a state civil service system. He seemed to be an ideal administrator—a moderate reformer in the spirit of the old progressives and perhaps a Republican

Harold E. Stassen, pictured about 1939, became nationally famous as the Boy Governor.
Courtesy of the Minnesota Historical Society

answer to Roosevelt's New Deal. Stassen was put on center stage in 1940 when he delivered the keynote address at the Republican National Convention and then successfully led the floor fight for the nomination of presidential candidate Wendell L. Willkie. After this national exposure he was twice reelected governor of Minnesota, only to resign in 1943 to enlist in the navy. At President Harry S. Truman's invitation he served as a member of the United States delegation to the San Francisco conference in 1945 that drafted the permanent United Nations charter. Then, in 1948, he began his seemingly never-ending quest for the White House. He was undone by Thomas Dewey in the Oregon primary, but from his position as president of the University of Pennsylvania he entered the lists again four years later. Ironically it was the large write-in vote for Dwight D. Eisenhower in Minnesota's primary that ruined Stassen in 1952. He later served as special presidential assistant for disarmament in the Eisenhower administration, and then, following defeats in his bids for governor of Pennsylvania and mayor of Philadelphia, in 1964 he resumed his fruitless quest for the presidency of the United States.

Unfortunately, his lingering presidential ambitions, which in 1976 especially seemed like nothing more than a wistful bid for attention, have beclouded his earlier accomplishments, particularly as governor of Minnesota. Not only did he lead a Republican resurgence in Minnesota that carried into the mid-1950s, but his reforms set the tone for his Republican successors, who accepted and advocated a greater role for state government. Social and welfare legislation of those Republican years helped make Minnesota one of the ranking states in taxes levied and amounts spent for public-assistance programs. In a broader view Stassen's internationalism encouraged thousands of Minnesotans to abandon the isolationism of the 1930s. His view of unprecedented American involvement in world affairs paved the way for a new internationalism in Minnesota politics such as that espoused by Stassen's friend and supporter Senator Joseph H. Ball, a former journalist who was one of the most internationally-minded senators during World War II. The emergence of Harold Stassen is perhaps symbolic of Minnesota's transition from the isolationist vision of Henrik Shipstead and famed aviator Charles Lindbergh, the son of the former congressman and Farmer-Labor leader, who was one of the country's most vocal opponents of American involvement in European affairs before the United States entry into World War II.

Stassen's 1938 victory was the death knell of the Farmer-Labor Party. Although the party ran state candidates in the next two elections, it was but an echo of what it had been in the days of Floyd Olson. More and more Farmer-Laborites thought of affiliation with the Democrats. The folly of the two small groups independently challenging Minnesota's dominant Republicans and the new liberal image of the Democrats heightened interest in a merger. Thomas Gallagher, the 1938 Democratic gubernatorial candidate, first launched a merger campaign early the next year. With the 1940 election in mind, Gallagher, who still wanted to be governor, hoped to challenge Stassen after unifying the two liberal minority parties. Gallagher's overtures were seriously considered, but personal rivalries and ideological factionalism within the ranks of both parties and the unwillingness of numerous Farmer-Laborites to sacrifice their party's unique identity aborted the merger effort. Nonetheless, continuing merger sentiment was stimulated by the realization that only with a unified party could the state's liberals ever wrest control from the immensely popular progressive Republicans.

Finally, in April 1944, through the coalescence of national and state considerations, the Democratic-Farmer-Labor Party was created. President Franklin D. Roosevelt's long-standing desire to unify the parties assumed renewed importance after he announced his intention to run for an unprecedented fourth term. Anticipating a close election, the national Democratic Party saw Minnesota as a swing state, whose vote was critical to Roosevelt. Obviously, a state campaign by a unified party would help the president.

Within Minnesota the merger had been vigorously promoted since early 1943 by Elmer Kelm, chairman of the Minnesota Democratic Party. The failure to merge, Kelm believed, would not only result in Roosevelt losing Minnesota but lead to a Republican sweep of all congressional seats as well. Moderate Farmer-Laborites, typified by Hjalmar Petersen, who had been elected lieutenant governor in 1934 and had briefly served as governor after Olson's death, had been the most receptive to merging from the start. But many within the Benson faction, which included Communists and Communist sympathizers, had sharp foreign policy differences with the Roosevelt administration before World War II. However, after Russia and the United States entered the war in 1941, the radical Farmer-Laborites endorsed America's wartime alliance with Communist Russia. Their support for Roosevelt became yet stronger after Russian dictator Joseph V. Stalin in 1943 abolished the Comintern, the agency responsible for promoting Communism internationally. Stalin's action caused Earl Browder, chairman of the Communist Party in the

United States, to urge cooperation between Communists, who seemingly no longer aimed to foment international revolution, and western democracies. These wartime policy changes gradually led the recalcitrant Benson and his followers to become pro-merger.

Throughout merger negotiations Farmer-Laborites demanded that the unified party's name reflect their heritage. Hubert H. Humphrey, a premerger Democrat who had run unsuccessfully for mayor of Minneapolis in 1943, realized the significance of a party label. In working with the national Democratic Party during the last phases of merger talks, Humphrey emphasized that the retention of the Farmer-Labor name meant thousands of votes for the new party. Thus, the party came to be called the Democratic-Farmer-Labor, or DFL.

Despite winning two congressional seats—the districts of Minneapolis and St. Paul—and Roosevelt's victory in Minnesota and reelection, the party was beset with problems. Veteran Farmer-Laborites, led by ex-governor Elmer Benson, resented the young liberals with their close ties to the academic world and their lack of specific commitment to the old Farmer-Labor ideals. On the other hand, Humphrey and his followers were bothered by the radicalism of the traditional Farmer-Laborites, the strong taint of fiscal mismanagement that continued to haunt the Benson crowd, and the association of Benson and his key supporters with Communists.

The differences were exacerbated by sharp clashes over the foreign policy of the Truman administration and came to a head during the Democratic-Farmer-Labor schism of 1948. Most newcomers to the party were internationalists who supported the Marshall Plan and other foreign-assistance programs, while the Bensonites saw foreign aid as nothing more than an effort to perpetuate Fascist governments abroad. While most of the party rank and file were ardent Truman backers, the Benson element backed Henry A. Wallace, the Progressive Party candidate in 1948. Quarreling was bitter at every level within the party, and ultimately Benson and his supporters were rejected and virtually ridden out of the party. In the spectrum of Minnesota politics the Democratic-Farmer-Labor Party, which nationally is invariably noted for its liberalism, in 1948 actually came under the control of politicians who were considerably more moderate than the hard-core Farmer-Laborites. Some of Benson's supporters, after assessing alternatives, came back within the fold; but others, including Benson himself, had little to do with the party after the schism. To his dedicated followers Benson epitomized Farmer-

Labor ideals, and it seemed very appropriate to James M. Shields, Benson's biographer, to call him "Mr. Progressive."[14]

Gaining control of the Democratic-Farmer-Labor Party was only part of the battle for Humphrey and his supporters. They also had to establish their legitimacy with the voters. Elected mayor of Minneapolis in 1945 as a nonpartisan law-and-order candidate, Humphrey was reelected two years later. As mayor he was lauded for his crime-control policies and also won a national reputation for his advocacy of civil rights, which included leading the call for a strong civil rights plank in the Democratic national platform in 1948. After winning his party's nomination for the United States Senate, he defeated incumbent Joseph Ball in the November election. At the same time three other Democratic-Farmer-Labor candidates, including Eugene J. McCarthy, were elected to the national House of Representatives.

The events of 1948 marked an important transition in Minnesota politics: the formation of the Democratic-Farmer-Labor Party and its emergence as a major political force reestablished the pattern in Minnesota of two major parties, nationally affiliated, vying for political control. The pattern may have been the same, but the parties were different—different primarily because protesters like Oliver H. Kelley, Ignatius Donnelly, Arthur C. Townley, and Floyd B. Olson had insisted over and over that government must be responsive to the needs of its people.

9

THE DIVERSE ECONOMY

MINNESOTA'S HIGHLY DIVERSIFIED economy of the late twentieth century reflects both an extension of the frontier economic pillars of farming, lumbering, and iron mining and the emergence of the Twin Cities as one of the nation's leading metropolitan centers. The traditional manufacturing and financial foundations of Minneapolis and St. Paul eased the passage of both into the present economy, featuring high-technology industries.

Although all three frontier enterprises have been drastically altered, each is still associated with a particular section of the state. Minnesota is one of the most agricultural of the fifty states, ranking seventh in farm cash receipts in 1994. This dependence on the land unavoidably affects the character of Minnesotans. There is a preoccupation with weather, particularly during the growing season, because a whole year's work and investment can depend on the rainfall of but a few days. During dry years, the week-after-week forecasts of nice weekends that so delight suburbanites can spell disaster for rural residents. And Minnesota has a large rural area. The statistical shift of the population from rural to urban did not occur until 1950, and thousands of those who are now classed as urban residents actually have farm or small-town backgrounds. This inherent ruralness has shaped the perception Minnesotans have of themselves. Sinclair Lewis, Sauk Centre's famous son who won the Nobel Prize in literature in 1931, first attracted widespread attention with his novel *Main*

Street, a classic portrayal of small-town parochialism based on his home-town. Others, however, have glorified the small towns: for many years, Northfield has advertised itself by way of a sign at the edge of town as a place of "Cows, Colleges and Contentment."

Diversification that saved Minnesota farmers from the tyranny of "King Wheat" has accelerated in recent decades. Although wheat is still a major crop, its acreage lags far behind corn and soybeans and is slight-ly less than hay. Since shortly after World War I corn has been the rank-ing cereal in both acreage and production. Corn was grown by territorial pioneers in southern Minnesota, but its successful commercial culture has been a story of adaptation. At first farmers turned to oats as the main field crop to replace wheat, partially because of the difficulties in finding strains of corn suited to Minnesota's climate. From the 1890s through World War I, University of Minnesota scientists worked at developing more productive and hardier corn. They did succeed in drawing the corn belt farther north by pioneering several faster-maturing varieties, but

By the late 1940s combines that both cut and threshed small grains had generally
replaced binders. This photo was taken in Marshall County in the Red River
Valley, about 1960.
Courtesy of the Minnesota Historical Society

corn yields even as late as the 1920s were not much better than those of forty or fifty years earlier.

However, Minnesota corn has experienced its own green revolution. The average yield of 30.4 bushels per acre for the period 1922–31 increased to 46.6 for the decade 1947–56. For 1973 it was 91.4 bushels per acre, and the record 142 bushels per acre was set in the exceptionally good growing season of 1994. Improved production was first of all caused by an almost complete shift to hybrid varieties between 1935 and 1946. But by then yields were also stimulated by better cultivation as horse-drawn equipment was replaced with tractor-powered plows and cultivators. Widespread use of commercial fertilizers, herbicides, and pesticides, as well as improved tillage practices, which among other things permitted more concentrated planting, have also helped boost production. In 1995, when about one eighth of Minnesota's total landed area was in corn, the state ranked fourth nationally in its production after Iowa, Illinois, and Nebraska.

Although corn has been a major cash crop, it also became significant as the principal fattening grain for animals. The successful corn culture stimulated the production of both hogs and beef cattle, which in turn has made Minnesota one of the major meat-packing states. The industry is especially important in Luverne, Worthington, Albert Lea, and Austin, home base of the Geo. A. Hormel & Company. Since its start in 1891, Hormel has grown from a small meat packer into a major national corporation that produces, in addition to meat products, an extensive variety of canned and frozen foods. South St. Paul, which was a major meat-packing center from the 1890s to the late 1960s, remains important as a livestock market. In 1995 its livestock receipts placed it second nationally behind Sioux Falls, South Dakota. Cattle, hogs, and sheep sold in South St. Paul are shipped to packing plants in Minnesota and its bordering states, as well as Illinois and Nebraska.

As diversified farmers have shown a remarkable ability to adapt to the land, they have also displayed an acute perception of changing market conditions. Modern farmers, like the pioneer farmers, seek to raise those things that command the greatest market value. Today, in terms of acres and yield, soybeans are Minnesota's second-ranking crop. Yet as recently as the Great Depression, soybeans were relatively scarce. They first appeared in Minnesota in 1917, when a farmer near Montevideo experimented with them. While he proved they would grow well, there was no apparent use or market for them at that time. But the drought and the

New Deal agricultural program that placed acreage ceilings on main crops, such as corn, wheat, and oats, caused more farmers to cultivate soybeans by the mid-1930s. Originally, they were raised mainly for fertilizer or forage, but the increasing national and international markets for soybean oil spurred cultivation and the construction of Minnesota's first soybean processing plant at Mankato in 1939. During and after World War II the explosive worldwide demand for soybean oil boomed cultivation in Minnesota to the point where in 1995 the state ranked third in soybean production behind Iowa and Illinois.

This 1956 photo shows the delivery and stockpiling of sugar beets at the American Crystal plant near Moorhead.
Courtesy of the Minnesota Historical Society

The search for new products and opportunities presented by consumer demands of an increasingly urbanized, industrialized society spurred the production of a great variety of crops nationwide. In Minnesota the major field crops have been supplemented with potatoes, sugar beets, flax, sunflowers, and vegetables. As crops like these increased, that branch of industry related to processing agricultural produce became more complex and varied. Since fresh produce is both bulky and perishable, it is usually processed close to the point of origin or, conversely, raised close to an existing processing area. As a result, sugar refineries have been developed principally in the Red River Valley and in vegetable processing plants in the main corn-soybean area of the south.

No other firm better exemplifies the growth of food processing than Green Giant, which made its giant and the giant's valley world-famous. The valley of the "Jolly Green Giant" is the Minnesota River Valley, where the Minnesota Valley Canning Company began modestly at Le Sueur in 1903 by canning sweet corn. Gradually the company expanded to other vegetables, and during the 1920s began marketing a new variety of peas under the trade name Green Giant. In 1928 the company used the name for its other products as well in a national advertising campaign that marked the beginning of an expansive period. The green giant on the label was a caricature of a rather ugly hunchbacked giant who seems to have been inspired by both Paul Bunyan stories and the fairy tales of the Brothers Grimm. Over the years the giant mellowed into a very happy, convincing ad man. The success of the label caused the company to change its name officially to Green Giant in 1950. After establishing a number of plants in Minnesota and other states to process a wide variety of vegetables, the company added an international division in 1961 and became recognized as one of the world's leaders in vegetable canning and packing. As a way of broadening its advertising appeal, the company in 1973 provided its Green Giant with a sidekick—the Little Green Sprout.

Like most of the other vegetable processors that sprang up in southern Minnesota, Green Giant was acquired by a larger corporation. In early 1979, the Pillsbury Company, famed for its flour, prepared doughs, frozen entrees, and restaurants, purchased Green Giant. After the transaction, the city of Le Sueur first lost Green Giant's corporate headquarters and later Pillsbury closed the processing plant there. Despite corporate changes the Green Giant tradition persists. Today travelers on the main highway bypassing Le Sueur are reminded of Green Giant's past by a prominent hilltop billboard featuring the Green Giant and the Little Green Sprout.

In the late twentieth century vegetable processing remains an important aspect of Minnesota's agribusiness. In 1994 Minnesota was the second and third ranking state, respectively, in the production of green peas and sweet corn.

As modern processing, like modern agriculture, became more varied, Minnesota's first food-processing industry, flour milling, was altered by new circumstances. After Minneapolis became the nation's leading flour producer, its annual output continued to rise to a peak of more than twenty million barrels for the crop year September 1, 1915–August 31, 1916. This growth was dominated by four major corporations, including Pillsbury and Washburn-Crosby, which had absorbed countless smaller companies in an age when consolidation affected all of the country's important industries. Despite consolidation, many small-town mills persisted, independent of the Minneapolis giants, in places such as Winona, Red Wing, and Mankato.

However, the large companies led the way in shifting operations to other parts of the nation. Foreseeing that Minneapolis flour milling

During the 1920s Robin Hood Mills, a subsidiary of International Milling Company, began operating flour mills in the western Canadian cities of Calgary, Alberta, and Moose Jaw, Saskatchewan.
Courtesy of the Minnesota Historical Society

would decline, Washburn-Crosby and Company started a mill in Buffalo, New York, in 1903. The anticipated decline came rather abruptly during the 1920s. By the end of that decade the Mill City produced only slightly more than half as much flour as it had at its zenith, and ranked third after Buffalo and Kansas City, Missouri. The decline resulted from a combination of forces that had been building for more than two decades. Soil exhaustion and ruinous black stem rust on the northern plains had caused a sharp reduction in production of the varieties of wheat best suited for bread flour. As this was occurring, Nebraska, Kansas, Oklahoma, and parts of Texas benefited from the development of a hard winter wheat that was just as desirable as hard spring wheat for flour making. Grain from this region could be more advantageously marketed and milled in Kansas City than in Minneapolis.

Changes in wheat culture were the main reason for the shift to Kansas City, but the rise of Buffalo was more complex. Lying between the Great Lakes shipping routes and the large flour market of the Northeast, Buffalo had traditionally been a flour-milling center, but it could not compete with Minneapolis until it was aided by policies of the federal government. Through a series of rulings, the Interstate Commerce Commission created price differentials in the shipping of bulk wheat and flour from west of the Great Lakes to Buffalo. Because it cost considerably more to transport flour than wheat, millers decided to construct plants at the greatest wheat depot closest to the most consumers: Buffalo, which also became a milling center for Canadian wheat. Under United States tariff regulations there was no import duty on Canadian wheat if the flour was exported. Since Buffalo was ideally situated with respect to both the Canadian shipping routes and the European market, it much more than Minneapolis or any other place benefited from the "milling-in-bond" principle.

The development of Buffalo and Kansas City as milling centers was led by Minneapolis-based companies that readily adapted to the changing conditions. Washburn-Crosby, the Pillsbury Company, and the International Milling Company, which was started in New Prague in 1892, all sent men, capital, and technical know-how to the new centers. But the headquarters of all the companies remained in Minneapolis, which became the nerve center of a national and international complex of terminal elevators, mills, and allied facilities. This outgrowth and extension of milling stimulated cosmopolitanism in Minneapolis as hundreds of businesspeople traveled widely in the nation and abroad and returned with new outlooks and perspectives.

As the leading millers were expanding outside Minnesota, they became concerned with diversification. Urbanization and increased demands for convenience foods created opportunities in the breakfast-cereal field. Washburn-Crosby in 1924 began marketing Wheaties, which soon became a household word throughout the new medium of radio. Several months before Wheaties was introduced, Washburn-Crosby and Company became the major financier of a Twin Cities radio station, which they named WCCO after the company's initials. Before the station passed to network ownership, the company used it to pioneer a then novel advertising technique—the singing commercial. On Christmas Eve, 1926, WCCO listeners were treated to a quartet singing the Wheaties ad to the melody of "She's a Jazz Baby," a refrain that later became familiar nationwide.

> Have you tried Wheaties?
> They're whole wheat with all of the bran.
> Won't you try Wheaties?
> For wheat is the best food of man.[1]

Through consolidation with some of its own subsidiaries and other milling companies, Washburn-Crosby became General Mills in 1928. The new name was intended to convey the impression that the company was no longer restricted to Minneapolis, but had become general because of its widespread holdings and the diversity of its products. General Mills typifies the modern companies that grew out of the old flour-milling firms. It continued milling and the marketing of Gold Medal flour but also branched out into breakfast foods, cake flours, quick dough mixes, frozen foods, and other products. In their continual quest for new products, General Mills and other companies began operating their own laboratories and developing a great awareness of consumer interest in the marketing of their wares.

In 1921 Washburn-Crosby and Company created one of the best-known fictional women in American history. Betty Crocker was an ad man's dream, inspired by the need to answer consumer inquiries with a human touch. Crocker was the surname of a former Washburn-Crosby official, and Betty was just a good American name.

Since her creation Betty Crocker has evolved to keep apace of society's styles, values, and images. But despite modifications in hair and dress styles, the first seven Betty images were of a fair-skinned, blue-

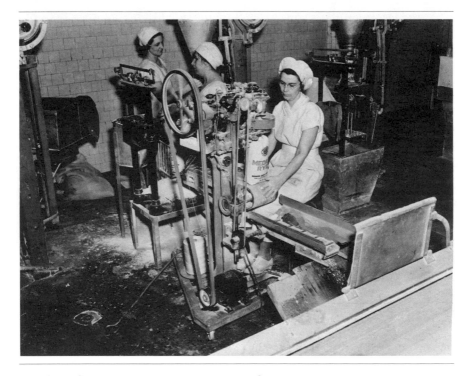

Packing flour was the last step in the manufacturing process. This three-woman
crew worked in the Minneapolis plant of General Mills about 1940. One filled
sacks, another weighed them, and the third sewed them.
Courtesy of the Minnesota Historical Society

eyed homemaker. Then, in September 1995, in anticipation of Betty's
seventy-fifth birthday, General Mills announced that it would remake
her to reflect a multiethnic society. The image of the 1996 Betty was to
be a computer composite of photos of seventy-five women (one for each
of Betty's years), who were to be selected primarily on the basis of how
well they demonstrated Betty Crocker characteristics, including enjoy-
ment of cooking and baking and commitment to family, friends, and
community.

The company's nationwide contest, open to all women at least eighteen years old, was, among other things, clever publicity. With more
than two hundred products bearing her name, Betty Crocker was
famous. The contest expanded that fame by giving her and General Mills
enough free publicity to make even the most important real-life celebrity
envious.

After great anticipation, the Betty for America's new society was revealed on March 19, 1996. Dressed casually in a sweater, the thirty-something, brown-haired Betty seemed to be more personable than any of her predecessors. She had "slightly darker skin color and eyes that have been transformed from blue to deep brown. She could be of Mediterranean descent, or perhaps Hispanic, maybe with a touch of American Indian."[2] Company officials were satisfied that this new Betty would be seen differently by various ethnic groups.

Although its leading flour millers helped develop other milling centers, the industry has remained important in Minnesota, but only after major adjustments. Over time Minneapolis lost its reputation as the Mill City. Its flour production of 1960 was more than 70 percent less than its greatest year, but to many farmers and other residents throughout the state it was still the Mill City. But the rapid growth of the "brainpower industries"—computer and instrument designing and manufacturing—soon helped the city shed its old image, and the term Mill City was heard only rarely by the 1970s.

Since its World War I period zenith, Minnesota's flour milling has declined both in terms of pounds produced and in its portion of the nation's total output. Nonetheless, production data for 1994 showed that Minnesota, with seventeen mills, had more daily milling capacity than any other state. American flour production has increased sharply, but the milling industry has been decentralized, with Minnesota, Kansas, New York, California, Missouri, Ohio, and Illinois as its main locations. As a result, Minnesota, even with the highest-ranked milling capacity, produced only about one tenth of the country's total. Minnesota's closest rival, Kansas, with Wichita, Topeka, and Buhler as significant milling centers, ground about 17 percent more wheat flour than Minnesota's 36.69 million hundredweights. But all of its nineteen mills produced only standard wheat flour, whereas of Minnesota's seventeen mills, four ground durum, a special wheat flour used for making pasta products, and three, rye. Significantly, Minnesota had one third of the country's durum mills and one fourth of its rye mills.

The leading flour-producing company in Minnesota and the nation was Con Agra, a large food-products conglomerate based in Omaha, Nebraska. Its Hastings mill in 1994 ranked as the largest in Minnesota and the fourth largest nationally. With other mills in New Prague and Wabasha, Con Agra was well ahead of its closest Minnesota challenger, ADM Milling Company, which mills in Minneapolis, but only slightly ahead of it nationally. Con Agra, ADM, and Cargill, which operates a mill in Mankato, were the big three nationally. General Mills, whose Kansas City, Missouri, mill is the fourth largest in the country, was the nation's fifth largest milling company, with a capacity only about 28 percent of Con Agra's.

Most of Minnesota's reputation as a verdant, scenic state rests on its northern forests. Lush though they may be, those forests have been greatly altered since the lumbermen's frontier. As recently as the 1930s, lumbermen were felling the last unprotected stands of white and red pine in the final surge of frontier extraction. Today, although a great deal of the state is wooded, the percentage of forested land has been reduced from a prefrontier 70 percent to about 30 percent. The virtual disappearance of the Big Woods and the farmers' incursion into the western and southern belts of the primarily coniferous forest zone account for most of the decrease. Even the remaining forest, which lies mostly in the fourteen northeastern and north-central counties, has been drastically changed since frontier days. Once the large conifers such as the white and red pine had been cut, such trees as the much faster-growing aspen, birch, poplar, and jack pine, which had been disdained by frontier lumbermen, proliferated. The drastic change in the distribution of trees is the main reason for the present nature of forest industries, which emphasize production of oriented strand board, pulp, and paper.

Minnesota's conversion from frontier lumbering to managed forest industries is illustrative of national trends. By the late nineteenth century, as the voracious demands of industry and population growth threatened depletion of natural resources, there was a growing public awareness nationwide that old ways had to be changed. Conservation measures advocated by some Populists and Progressives and other reformers were accepted in principle, but implementation was quite another matter, especially in Minnesota, where to a large extent the frontier still existed physically and the frontier mentality still ruled.

Nonetheless, even before frontier lumbering had peaked, Minnesota was pushed into the national conservation movement, not because of a great public awareness but rather because of the efforts of a small, far-sighted group that was concerned about the future as well as the present. As early as 1876 there were enough Minnesotans who saw the need for a planned program of forest use to organize the Minnesota State Forestry Association, one of the first groups of its kind in the nation. The association, working through civic groups and fraternal organizations, tried to win public acceptance of the necessary conservation measures. Although the association was effective in marshaling opinion, Minnesota's greatest conservation thrust came from one outstanding individual—Christopher Columbus Andrews.

Andrews, a Massachusetts lawyer, moved to St. Cloud before the Civil War and served as a brigadier general in the Minnesota Volunteers. In 1869, when Andrews was forty years old, President Ulysses S. Grant appointed him United States minister to Sweden and Norway. While

Christopher Columbus Andrews, an early advocate of forest planning, was principally responsible for promoting Minnesota's first reforestation projects.
Courtesy of the Minnesota Historical Society

serving in this post, Andrews, in the course of studying the Swedish economy, was impressed by that country's reforestation projects, in which he saw the future of Minnesota. Although Andrews was absent from the United States for a number of years during the 1870s and 1880s because of his Scandinavian assignment and his later service as consul general in Rio de Janeiro, Brazil, he was more influential than any other single Minnesotan in advocating forest planning.

At first many of Andrews's speeches and writings on the subject had little impact because there was still so much virgin forest. However, public awareness of the depletability of its timber resources was jolted by the disastrous Hinckley forest fire of September 1, 1894. The Hinckley catastrophe, in which more than four hundred people lost their lives, ranks as one of the greatest forest fires in the nation's history. The very nature of Minnesota, with its flat terrain, occasional drought years, and strong sweeping winds, was conducive to fires, and in 1894 those conditions were complicated by the carelessness of lumbermen who left stumps and piles of waste in their wake and by the indifference of frontier settlers toward minor fires. After the holocaust, Minnesotans responded with state aid to survivors, and in 1895 the legislature provided that the state auditor also serve as the state forest commissioner. The auditor was authorized to name a chief fire warden, who could appoint deputy wardens and who was to appraise the state's forest resources and promote reforestation projects. Although he was sixty-six years old, Andrews gladly accepted the position because it provided him at last with a real opportunity to put some of his ideas into practice.

Andrews served as chief fire warden for ten years and as forestry commissioner for six more years before being named secretary of the newly created state forestry board, an agency independent of the auditor's office. It was a difficult time. Conservationists, including governors John Lind, Samuel R. Van Sant, and John A. Johnson and President Theodore Roosevelt, helped popularize the conservation movement, but in Minnesota there was also strong opposition. However, Andrews was successful in achieving at least a philosophical acceptance of his beliefs that forests should occupy only land unsuited for agriculture, that annual cutting should never exceed annual growth, and that the forests should continually be renewed through reforestation. While Andrews was still chief fire warden the state created a School of Forestry at the University of Minnesota to help professionalize the new directions. The school, started only two years after the first of the nation's forestry schools, was headed for many years by Samuel B. Green, who, through his teaching, writing, and speaking, helped win acceptance of new forestry practices in Minnesota.

Responding to Andrews's urgings, the legislature authorized a state nursery, made state parks forest reserves, created several new parks with both conservation and recreation in mind, and greatly expanded the forest service through legislation of 1911. Partly because of the influence of Andrews and other Minnesota conservationists, the federal government reserved specified forest tracts under the Morris Act of 1902 and also, while Roosevelt was president, created two massive national forests in Minnesota—the Superior National Forest, which contained thousands of acres of virgin forest; and the Minnesota National Forest, which became the Chippewa National Forest in 1928. Although both were sizable originally, they have subsequently been enlarged and now comprise about one sixth of the state's total forested area. These achievements, although in keeping with the reform spirit of the times, were also prompted by the recurrence of forest fires. During every dry year the hundreds of minor fires did not greatly concern the public despite the history of the Hinckley fire. However, the destruction of Chisholm in 1908 and the villages of Baudette and Spooner two years later again aroused public concern and stimulated new forestry legislation. In 1914 Minnesota voters approved a constitutional amendment authorizing the state to set aside as state forests those public lands that were better suited for forests than for agriculture. A last stark reminder of the need for better forest management was provided by the catastrophic fires of October 12, 1918, in the cutover Cloquet–Moose Lake area. Even more disastrous than the Hinckley blaze, the fires destroyed 1,500 square miles, killed 453 people outright, displaced 11,382 families, injured or disrupted 52,371 people, and caused property losses of about $30 million.

Although conservationists made significant advances during the progressive era, resistance to their movement continued. They had to battle the apathetic, who still believed that Minnesota's virgin forests were not really threatened. Further, there was vocal and well-organized opposition from civic boosters, railroads, lumber companies, and land speculators who insisted that lumbermen were merely opening the way for farmers. Lumber companies, especially, wanted to sell their cutover land rather than have it remain on the tax rolls, so it was natural for them and others who believed that northern Minnesota could become another agricultural frontier to encourage cutover farming. Even the state of Minnesota

This 1903 street scene of International Falls illustrates the persistence of frontier
conditions in the extreme north of Minnesota.
Courtesy of the Minnesota Historical Society

was a major participant in the campaign. At the behest of Governor John
A. Johnson, who believed the state's population needed boosting, the
1905 legislature re-created the state Board of Immigration. During its
twenty-two-year tenure the agency heavily publicized the alleged agricultural advantages of the cutover lands through promotional literature,
exhibits, and itinerant agents.

Strangely enough, the claim that northern Minnesota could become
part of the farm belt was strengthened during the period 1880–1920
because there were many opportunities for farmers to sell produce locally
to lumbermen or miners. As a result, thousands of small farms were started in the least rocky portions of the old forest zone. As late as 1920, the
philosophical battle still raged between advocates of reforestation and
boosters of cutover farming about the best land use in the wasted forest
lands.

Conservationists won the argument as conditions changed in the
1920s. The rapid closing of frontier lumbering and the agricultural
depression ruined thousands of farmers, who simply abandoned their

land. These small farms in time passed to the state as tax-delinquent lands. By 1930 the situation had reached crisis proportions. About one seventh of the state's entire acreage was on the tax-delinquent rolls and about three fourths of those acres were in the old coniferous forest area. This circumstance prompted Governor Floyd B. Olson to appoint a land utilization committee, which recommended in 1932 that Minnesota recognize that most of the cutover land was suitable only for forests and that the state take steps to create more state forests with the aim of developing economic and recreational opportunities. The tax-delinquent lands helped expand existing forests and became the basis of twenty-six new state forests created during Olson's administration. These changes, which were augmented by New Deal reforestation work done by the Works Project Administration and the Civilian Conservation Corps and by later creations and expansions of state forests, have borne fruit in recent years.

In 1993 Minnesota had a total forest acreage of 16.7 million, of which nearly 90 percent was classified as timberland, meaning that it was potentially harvestable. Thirty-five percent of the timberland was of a type in which aspen dominated. There were nearly four times as much aspen type

This pioneer claim in Koochiching County, about 1920, was typical of the abortive efforts to establish commercial agriculture in the region.
Courtesy of the Minnesota Historical Society

as maple-basswood, the second ranking forest type. Following maple-basswood were black spruce, elm-ash, oak, and birch. The three kinds of pine—jack, red, and white—combined accounted for only 5 percent of the timberland, a telling reduction from their estimated 18 percent on the eve of frontier cutting. White pine, the former prince of the frontier forest, was by far the scarcest pine. It stood at only 63,000 acres, or the equivalent of an area about 10 miles square.

The principal owners of Minnesota's timberlands are private parties, the state and its political subdivisions such as counties and cities, the federal government, and various forest-industry companies. Logging companies that supply wood-products manufacturers commonly buy timber rights from individual land owners. Sales of timber rights on public lands are conducted on the basis of competitive bidding. The various governmental jurisdictions and two trade associations—the Minnesota Timber Producers Association and Minnesota Forest Industries, Inc.—cooperate in adhering to the principle of sustainable growth—annual cut should not exceed annual growth. Many of the several hundred members of the Minnesota Timber Producers Association, formed in 1937, are loggers and sawmill operators. Minnesota Forest Industries, Inc., consisting of primary manufacturers, has only nine members: Blandin Paper Company of Grand Rapids; Boise Cascade Corporation of International Falls; Champion International Corporation of Sartell; Hedstrom Lumber Company of Grand Marais; Hennepin Paper Company of Little Falls; Lake Superior Paper Industries of Duluth; the Potlatch Corporation, with plants at Cloquet, Brainerd, Bemidji, Cook, and Grand Rapids; Rajala Companies of Big Fork and Deer River; and Superwood Corporation (a subsidiary of Georgia Pacific), which has plants at Bemidji and Duluth.

Increasing demand for paper and wood products has propelled Minnesota's timber production to a record level. In 1993, 4,102,600 cords, the equivalent of 2.05 billion board feet, were cut. Well over half of this was aspen. A precise comparison to the record frontier cutting season of 1899–1900, when 1.11 billion board feet of logs were cut, is difficult, if not impossible, because of the lack of comparable data. About one eighth of the 1993 harvest was fuelwood, whereas the statistics for 1899–1900 evidently included only logs that were used for commercial lumbering. Since wood was the primary energy source for numerous homes, businesses, and even factories in 1900, obviously thousands of cords were used for fuel, but not counted then in timber production. Nonetheless, even if a generous allowance was made for fuelwood in

1899–1900, its production would fall well short of the current yield.

Although Minnesota's timber production has increased, its ranking among the states has dropped sharply from third place in its record frontier year. In 1991 Minnesota stood nineteenth in timber production. Among others, it was surpassed by nearby Wisconsin and Michigan, all of the southeastern states, and the Pacific Coast states.

The economic impact of Minnesota's forest industry is impressive. Considering both secondary manufacturing and primary processing, the industry in 1993 had 58,900 employees, a payroll of $2.2 billion, and gross sales of $7.3 billion. Data for 1994 show that the main use of all harvested timber was to make pulp and paper. Of the harvest, 32 percent was used for that purpose. The manufacturing of oriented strand board (OSB) consumed another 30 percent. OSB, a relatively new product, is made by combining slices of wood that have the approximate dimensions of sandwich meat with a strong adhesive and heat-compacting them into sheets the size and

Paper machines and just-manufactured rolls of paper in Boise Cascade Paper Mill,
International Falls, about 1968.
Courtesy of the Minnesota Historical Society

thickness of plywood. The advantages of OSB are that it is stronger than plywood of the same thickness and can be made from such trees as aspen, birch, and poplar, which are unsuitable for plywood manufacturing.

Potlatch is Minnesota's leading producer of OSB. Named after Potlatch, Idaho, its original location, the company has OSB plants at Bemidji, Cook, and Grand Rapids. Minnesota's lumber producers, led by Hedstrom Lumber Company and the Rajala Companies, used about one sixth of all timber. A survey conducted by the Minnesota Department of Natural Resources indicated that aspen, followed by oak and jack pine, were the main trees used in Minnesota's wood-products industry.

Minnesota's current high timber production is projected to increase in the foreseeable future, which is probably surprising to those who are concerned about the near depletion of virgin forests. Aside from the demands of a burgeoning population, there are several fundamental reasons for the recent surge in the forest industry. In the postfrontier era there has been a general acceptance of the premise that trees are really a long-range crop. Thus, through a combination of conservation, reforestation, disease and pest control, and managed cutting, forests have been restored and, with proper safeguards, can be sustained, if not expanded. Thanks to scientific experimentation, numerous new applications of wood products made from hitherto undesirable trees have been discovered. Like all industries, forestry has been revolutionized by technology, which now effectively enables loggers to cut most of the year and process and manufacture wood products faster and more efficiently.

Historically, lumbermen quickly accepted technological changes. The advent of trucks in the post–World War I years caused the demise of logging railroads. Use of trucks accelerated the cutting of isolated stands of virgin timber by making them more accessible at a much lower cost than extending logging railroads would have. The popularization of the chain saw in the late 1940s was a major breakthrough that eliminated much manual labor in timber harvesting. Although American loggers had experimented with gasoline-powered chain saws as early as 1905, the first portable chain saw was developed in 1927 by Andreas Stihl of Stuttgart, Germany. After Stihl's patents were released by the United States government during World War II, American firms copied them and began producing their own chain saws.

While the chain saw revolutionized cutting, it has generally been replaced by various cutting machines. Tractor-mounted hydraulic shears, which first appeared in the 1940s, were in common use by the late 1960s.

These machines, which can cut trees up to two feet in diameter, are especially useful for clear-cutting stands of relatively small trees on level terrain. The feller-bunchers in use today shear the trees near ground level while holding them upright by clamps above the shears, and then, if necessary, move them short distances so that they can be dropped without damaging adjacent trees. Loggers estimate that the use of feller-bunchers produces about three times as much timber in a given amount of time than cutting with chain saws. A survey of Minnesota loggers completed in 1993 indicated that nearly three fourths of their cutting was done by using feller-bunchers.

Some Minnesota loggers have replaced their feller-bunchers with a yet more sophisticated system of two machines—the harvester and the forwarder. Like the feller-buncher, the harvester grips the tree, but instead of shearing it off, cuts it near the ground with a power saw. The device then lays the tree down, delimbs it by hydraulically feeding it through steel knives, and then saws it into lengths preset on its computer controls. The computer also enables the operator to obtain a printout of production by type and amount of timber. Mounted on special wide-track tires, the harvester applies less pressure to the land than a footstep. Despite its large size the machine is surprisingly mobile and works effectively in lanes cut barely wider than it. Thus, the harvester, which only scantly damages the forest floor and remaining trees, is well suited for thinning tree plantations. Once the harvester has cut lanes, covered them with slash that will remain on the forest floor until it decays, and piled the sawed logs, it is followed by the forwarder. Equipped with hooks mounted on a swiveling crane and a large metal carrier, the forwarder picks up the logs and transports them to a truck rendezvous site.

Other than greatly increasing the harvesting rate, reducing the work force, and profoundly altering the social makeup of cutting crews, the feller-buncher and harvester have redefined the cutting season. With the capability of running well on unfrozen ground, the use of these machines generally means that the cutting season is closed only for a short time during and after the spring thaw until the ground becomes firmer and load restrictions that affect logging trucks are lifted. The winter months, however, are still the peak cutting period, because only then are such swamp-growing trees as black spruce and tamarack accessible.

As compared to their frontier predecessors, present-day loggers are able to increase production by using more of the tree. Those who cut the virgin forest usually would not use any tree part with a diameter of less than twelve inches. Today the minimum diameter for pulp purposes is four inches, and for sawlogs, depending on the type of tree, six to eight inches. The heavier use of small sawlogs in recent times has caused sawmill operators to become more innovative. By using extra-thin (eighty-five thousandths of an inch) blades, modern saws produce much less waste than the traditional blades, which were three eighths of an inch wide. Additionally, a laser-guidance system assures that the boards are cut precisely, resulting in less shaver planings and less sawdust. Less warping of boards, a long-standing source of waste, has been achieved by uniform drying in computerized kilns. This new cutting and drying technology has enabled mills to increase lumber production by as much as 40 percent.

A combination of environmental sensitivity and economic opportunity has led to the virtual elimination of waste materials. Planer shavings are commonly sold to poultry raisers for bedding. Bark from sawmills, paper mills, and oriented strand board plants, and sawdust, are used as supplementary energy sources at paper mills.

In a highly industrialized society in which environmental concerns are paramount, any business that uses a natural resource, including forest industries, is always in the public eye. In Minnesota, forests, especially stands of old-growth white pine, somehow represent the quintessential aesthetic environment. Thus, to some, any cutting of trees scars that environment. Harvesting trees and processing wood products is naturally interrelated with other environmental issues, such as soil erosion, water quality, and land management.

Concern about possible detrimental environmental impact by forest harvesting prompted a coalition of Minnesota environmental organizations to ask the state Environmental Quality Board in 1989 to undertake a Generic Environmental Impact Statement (GEIS). When completed in 1994, the GEIS resulted in an approximately six-thousand-page report that included detailed technical studies on all aspects of forestry and forest industries. The GEIS concluded that Minnesota's existing forestry practices were environmentally sound; that tree mortality from insects, disease, and old age exceeded harvests; that annual growth exceeded annual harvest; that harvesting could be increased; and that even with greater harvesting, the state by 2040 would have more forested area than it had in 1990.

While obviously implying that long-range planning and management were needed, the GEIS stopped short of calling for legislative action.

Consequently, a twenty-five-member GEIS Roundtable representing various constituencies met in 1994 to consider possible legislation. In keeping with its recommendation, the 1995 legislature by the Sustainable Forest Resources Act created the Minnesota Forest Resources Council. Its thirteen gubernatorially-appointed members were to represent organizations engaged in matters affected by forestry, including the environment, game management, conservation, forest industries, logging, private forest owners, and the Department of Natural Resources. Under the law, the council, which was constituted and staffed, has submitted a report to the governor and the legislature "on the status of the state's forest resources, and strategic directions to provide for their management, use, and protection."[3] Unavoidably, there will always be some tension, if not disagreement, between opponents and proponents of various timber-harvesting proposals, but the Forest Resources Council should provide an important forum for balancing environmental protection and use.

Although Minnesota's farms and forests contributed mightily to the state's development, they never achieved the national status of its iron resources. Since the opening of the Mesabi Range, Minnesota, by producing nearly two thirds of the country's iron ore, has far outstripped its closest rival. Not only was its ore plentiful, but it was rich, easily mined, and accessible to water transportation. But, like lumbering, iron mining had to undergo a difficult adjustment after the height of its exploitation. As the richest deposits were depleted, Minnesotans converted to mining the more plentiful, but poorer, taconite, the "mother ore" of the Mesabi Range.

Twentieth-century Minnesota mining has to a large extent been the story of the Mesabi, whose production far surpassed all other American iron regions and completely dwarfed the combined production of Minnesota's three other iron-ore locales—the Vermilion Range, the Cuyuna Range, and ore pits in the southeastern part of the state. The frontier phases of Vermilion and Mesabi mining had run their course by the time the first ore was shipped from the Cuyuna Range in 1911. The Cuyuna, a long, narrow range, stretched from near Brainerd in the central part of the state northeastward for about sixty-five miles, and it lay across an area that had already been settled by farmers. The discovery and opening of the Cuyuna Range was principally due to the persistence of Cuyler Adams, who first detected signs of magnetic ore in 1895 while surveying land. He worked for another sixteen years, surveying, core testing, and persuading mining companies to invest, before the first ore was mined.

Cuyuna sounds like an Indian name, but it was coined by Adams's wife, Virginia, by taking the first syllable of her husband's given name and adding it to Una, the name of their dog.

The ore from the Cuyuna, like that of the Vermilion Range, was hard and deep, so most of the early mines were developed underground. The Cuyuna ores were also comparatively rich in manganese, which proved to be very important to the United States during World War I, when its importation was limited.

Minnesota's fourth iron-ore area has never been referred to as a range because that ore (in the Spring Valley area in Fillmore County) was found in small pockets of ten to fifty thousand tons under cultivated land. In 1941 contractors took samples, and the next year they removed some sixty thousand tons. Because of the value of the land for crop purposes, the extraction was carefully done when the ground was not frozen. The valuable topsoil was scraped off and deposited so it could be respread later. Then the iron ore, which usually lay from just below the surface to depths of twenty feet, was scooped into trucks for shipment to a local washing plant, and later transshipped by rail. Usually the contractors simply paid the Fillmore County farmers a royalty of about twenty-five cents a ton for ore. Though insignificant when compared to the three iron ranges, this district was quite important during the 1950s. With the end of its mining in 1969, the Fillmore County district had produced slightly more than eight million tons, an amount equal to about one twelfth of the accumulated yield of the Vermilion Range.

Long before the Mesabi reached its full potential, miners discovered that some of the most accessible ore had to be improved before it could be used in blast furnaces. The richest ore—the so-called direct-shipment ore—was simply excavated and shipped to furnaces in Pittsburgh, Erie, and other manufacturing centers; but often adjacent ore had impurities such as clay, silica, other rocks, or excessive moisture. The Oliver Mining Company as early as 1907 experimentally removed such substances near the mining sites to produce a concentrated product with a higher ore content. Satisfied that crushing and washing (beneficiating) would improve the quality of the ore, in 1909 the company commissioned its district manager, John C. Greenway, to construct a concentrating plant at Trout Lake near the company's planned community of Coleraine. Within a short time other companies built concentrators, and by the mid-1920s about one third of Minnesota's iron ore was improved to a product called gravity concentrate before being sent east. By the late 1950s there were nearly eighty concentrating facilities spread along the Mesabi Range.

In terms of tonnage, the peak of Minnesota's iron production was attained in 1953, but in terms of numbers of men employed, the zenith was reached during World War I, when approximately eighteen thousand men worked the mines. By 1932, however, there were fewer than two thousand miners, a plunge caused by postwar production cutbacks, increased use of labor-saving machinery, and the onset of the depression.

The World War I era was noteworthy not only because of unprecedented production but also because of labor unrest fomented in part by the radical Industrial Workers of the World. There was also a renewal of Minnesota resentment against absentee mine owners. Such men as Tower, Oliver, and Carnegie had never been popular with those Minnesotans who saw evil in big business, and their type became less so during the time of progressive reforms. Animosity welled up again yet stronger during World War I because of the antibusiness stance of the militant Nonpartisan League and the general public belief that war profiteering was rampant.

The League's renewal of the antibusiness crusade stimulated a legislative review of iron-ore taxation, which was regarded as the public's most

An open-pit mine at Hibbing in 1924.
Courtesy of the Minnesota Historical Society

effective check on the excesses of the giant out-of-state steel corporations. Some of the postwar reaction was also caused by the belief that Minnesota had been bilked by the first iron-ore capitalists. Many Minnesotans remembered that Charlemagne Tower had convinced the state to levy ore duties of only a penny a ton in order to encourage range development. This original tonnage tax was discontinued in 1897 in favor of an ad valorem property tax based on the assessed valuation of unmined ore; but over the years influential groups and individuals argued that this tax too was insufficient. Proponents of heavier taxation contended that the steel companies were depleting Minnesota's heritage and that within a half-century or so the state would be left with only gaping holes as a stark reminder of its onetime wealth. Reasoning that iron ore (unlike the forests) could not be renewed, legislators concluded that mining should be subjected to what opponents called double taxation. Therefore, the 1921 legislature overwhelmingly passed an act instituting an "occupation tax," an imprecise description of a special tax on the tonnage of extracted ore. Although conservative Governor Jacob Preus had serious reservations about the measure, he signed it. Unlike the 1881 tonnage tax, this was a tax not in lieu of property taxes but in addition to them. To forecheck an anticipated challenge of the law's constitutionality, it was submitted to the voters of the state, who accepted it as a constitutional amendment in 1922.

The occupation tax remained controversial for years. Companies naturally claimed that it caused higher operating costs, which forced them to reduce the labor force and to charge higher prices for finished steel products. They also argued that the burden of double taxation would discourage further exploration and development. But the greatest and probably most justifiable ire of the companies was directed at the assessors of the iron-range communities, who used property-tax levies to support well-staffed municipal governments and some of the nation's finest public schools. The excesses of the assessors during the early 1920s finally forced the legislature to place ceilings on property-tax assessments in the range communities.

Despite some legislative relief, the iron-mining industry suffered during the Great Depression. Ore production, which averaged about 33 million tons annually in the 1920s, plunged to an all-time low of 2.2 million tons in 1932. However, the onerous ad valorem taxes on unmined ore remained high. In 1932 mine owners paid almost $16 million, compared to an annual average of about $18 million during the 1920s.

The desperate depression years, replete with massive unemployment and continued high taxes, caused increasing worries about the economic future of the iron ranges. Despite lowered ore production, the relatively imminent depletion of iron ore was apparent. Regional fears were also fueled by the cutting of the last sizable stands of virgin forests. Understandably, depression-ridden iron rangers living in a vast cutover area of gaping pits sought new solutions.

The initiative for change came from John Blatnik and Richard Kelly of the Chisholm Junior Chamber of Commerce. Parts of their area rehabilitation plan, first publicly revealed in 1938, were enacted by the 1941 legislature, with the strong support of Governor Harold Stassen.

The legislature accepted the premise that long-range iron mining was attainable only by turning to taconite, the Mesabi Range's low-grade iron ore. To encourage taconite production, the legislature, for taxation purposes, made a distinction between it and traditional iron ore. In freeing taconite from the combination of occupation and ad valorem taxes, the 1941 law specified that any future taconite producers would pay a production tax. In another long-range measure the legislature created the Iron Range Resources and Rehabilitation Board (IRRRB). The agency, whose authority encompassed the regions of all three ranges, was intended to promote employment in mining, forestry, and agriculture, and to stimulate the economy through new programs in such areas as vocational education and tourism.

The crisis atmosphere of 1941 was relieved by heavy iron-ore production during World War II and record production in the booming postwar period. But by the late 1950s prospects were bleak. Most of the high-grade ore was gone and the mining economy was suffering in a time of great national affluence. But there was also hope; some mining companies and political leaders were claiming that northern Minnesota could be saved by taconite.

Taconite was first discovered by a Michigan prospector in the early 1870s and appraised by Newton H. Winchell, Minnesota's state geologist, in the late 1880s and early 1890s. Winchell determined that the hard slate-gray to blackish sedimentary rock underlay the breadth of the Mesabi and contained narrow bands of low-grade magnetite. In his written reports Winchell identified the rock as "taconyte," a word he borrowed from other geologists. Winchell concluded that the taconite stratum was of a type first identified in the Taconic Mountains of western Massachusetts and Vermont. Winchell used the name to describe a whole era of sedimentary deposits, but generally his fellow geologists used it only when referring to the Mesabi's mother rock containing the low-grade ores. Without professional acceptance Winchell's designation became obsolete. Worldwide the word *taconite* defines low-grade iron ores similar to those on the Mesabi.

The first miners on the Mesabi were obviously aware of taconite, but they were interested only in the soft, rich pockets of ore. Not only was taconite hard, but its mineral bands contained only particles of iron that were only about one third as rich as the best Minnesota ores. As the mine owners became aware of the limited quantities of high-grade ore, however, they began to wonder about the commercial potential of taconite. Then, in 1913, a Mesabi land owner who was also a University of Minnesota regent sent taconite samples and the problem of their utilization to the newly organized Mines Experiment Station at the university. After that time the development of the taconite industry was principally due to the work of Edward W. Davis, an engineer with the Mines Experiment Station. Davis worked on principles and machinery for extracting the ore particles, and within a few years he had developed techniques for crushing and washing the rock and separating the ore. Employing these techniques at experimental plants at Duluth and later at Babbitt, he successfully extracted a moderately rich product from taconite. But, unfortunately, his experiments also proved that his process was plagued by a host of technical problems and that production was so costly, it was impossible for taconite to compete with direct shipment and concentrated ores. So the experimental plants were soon abandoned, but Davis continued his taconite research.

With state funds and, later, grants obtained from the IRRRB, he worked for twenty years developing a process that not only would crush the rock but would ultimately reduce it to a flourlike texture, something that had not been possible in the first plants. There were related problems to solve too, such as efficiently removing the ore particles by magnetic attraction and discarding the tons of waste, or tailings. By the time of World War II Davis had made enough progress to attract the interest of two new companies, Erie Mining Company and Reserve Mining Company, both of which had been formed by parent steel companies to supply them with iron ore. As more efficient processing steps were devised and refined, both companies became persuaded that commercial taconite production was feasible.

Reserve moved first and in 1946 announced that it would construct a taconite plant at Silver Bay on Lake Superior. The company built not only a large plant, which it named in honor of Davis, but a village for its workers as well. At last, in 1955, the first pellets were produced, and the next spring they were shipped eastward from the company's harbor alongside the plant. This installation and another taconite facility opened by the Erie Mining Company at Hoyt Lakes in 1957 were the culmination of Davis's long years of searching for effective ways of producing quality ore from taconite. The process entailed breaking huge rocks into smaller pieces and then pulverizing the pieces into the flourlike dust from which giant magnets pulled out the usable ore particles. The particles of ore had to be processed into a shippable product, so they were next mixed with a binding clay, and pellets about one fourth of an inch in diameter were formed. Once the pellets had been hardened by heat of over 2,000 degrees, they were stockpiled for shipment on ore carriers.

The techniques of producing taconite had been mastered, but the

Reserve Mining Company's Silver Bay plant was Minnesota's first commercial taconite processing facility.
Courtesy of the Minnesota Historical Society

The *C. L. Austin*, an ore carrier, was the season's first ship when it arrived at Silver
Bay on April 6, 1956.
Courtesy of the Minnesota Historical Society

process, especially when compared to earlier mining, was costly.
Consequently, Reserve and Erie, the steel companies, and many others
interested in the economic future of iron mining felt inhibited by the
state's mineral tax laws. Rapid depletion of other iron ores and the
impending financial doom for Minnesota's ranges gave rise to increasing
talk of the need to so something that would encourage the taconite industry. By 1960 there was a general recognition by Minnesotans that something had to be done, but understandably there was long and heated
debate over specifics. Some, especially the most liberal DFLers, opposed
any sort of concession to big business, and the arguments over tax reform
began to assume the characteristics of a classic confrontation between the
public and the robber barons of an earlier age. Finally, in 1963, the legislature banned an increase in taconite taxes for twenty-five years. This act
assured taconite producers as well as potential developers of copper and
nickel deposits that their tax rates would not exceed those of other

Minnesota manufacturers. Because there was an existing constitutional provision relating to iron-ore taxation, the question had to be submitted to the voters in the form of the "taconite amendment." Greatly concerned about public indifference, both major political parties and the Iron Mining Association of Minnesota, an association of various mining companies, launched an intensive publicity campaign to inform the electorate about the nature of taconite and the need for the amendment. The mining company association distributed thousands of sample packets containing taconite bits, finely crushed ore, and pellets so that people throughout the state were made tactually aware of the issue. In the election of 1964 voters overwhelmingly approved the amendment. Its passage proved to have the desired effect of increasing taconite production and stimulating the construction of new plants.

Before the amendment Minnesota had just two commercial taconite plants, with a combined annual production of about 18 million tons. By 1976 the two original plants had been expanded and six additional ones constructed. In 1967 taconite shipments for the first time exceeded iron-ore shipments, and nine years later they comprised more than three fourths of Minnesota's iron exports. As taconite became dominant, the mining of direct-shipment ore and the production of gravity concentrate were ended first on the Vermilion and Cuyuna Ranges. On the Vermilion Range the last direct ore was shipped in 1963, and the last gravity concentrate, four years later. Some production on the Cuyuna persisted into the 1980s, with the last exportation of gravity concentrate made in 1984. The Mesabi's last direct ore was extracted in 1984, and in 1995 it produced only 365,000 tons of gravity concentrate, compared to 45 million tons of taconite pellets.

Although taconite revived the range economy, it was a mixed blessing. It brought prosperity and renewed hope for the future, but it also brought controversy. The primary issue was the dumping of taconite tailings into Lake Superior at Reserve Mining's Silver Bay plant. Before Reserve began constructing the facility it requested permission from the federal and state governments to relocate a highway, erect a power plant with a tall smokestack, and construct a harbor. These requests were routinely granted, but state officials were troubled by Reserve's other request: permission to draw water from Lake Superior and, after using it in processing, return it and the suspended waste particles—the tailings—to the lake. The matter was debated for nearly a year before permits were granted, and when they were, there was included the proviso that the tailings should not pollute the lake.

By the late 1960s telltale signs—such as the brilliant aquamarine discoloration of the lake near the plant—were convincing proof to some that the tailings were indeed polluting. Subsequent investigations and vocal public concern caused the federal government; the states of Minnesota, Wisconsin, and Michigan; and the Minnesota-based Environmental Defense Fund to bring a lawsuit against Reserve in federal district court to halt the dumping of tailings into Lake Superior.

The proceedings, which were presided over by Judge Miles Lord, dragged on for nine months and produced so many headline stories that *Reserve Mining* and *taconite tailings* became household words in Minnesota. During the trial the plaintiffs alleged, among other things, that minute asbestos fibers contained in the tailings were a potential cancer hazard because they had been carried into the water supply of Duluth and other lakeshore communities. Both sides produced witnesses who testified at great length, and charges, countercharges, and defenses sometimes

This 1962 aerial view of Reserve Mining's taconite plant at Silver Bay shows the
large fan-shaped deposit of taconite tailings in Lake Superior.
Courtesy of the Minnesota Historical Society

became acrimonious. At last, in April 1974, Judge Lord ordered Reserve to halt the dumping of tailings into Lake Superior immediately. However, in a series of legal moves the company appealed the decision to the Eighth Circuit Court of Appeals in St. Louis and even asked that the court remove Lord as trial judge because of his alleged bias in favor of the plaintiffs. In separate actions the court ordered Lord's removal, which had the effect of making him a hero to many Minnesotans, and compelled Reserve to find an on-land disposal site. Despite threats that it might terminate its Minnesota operations, Reserve at last, in 1978, reluctantly accepted an on-land site on its railroad line seven miles from the Silver Bay plant.

The opening of the new site, appropriately named Milepost 7, in the summer of 1980 ended one of the bitterest environmental clashes in recent history and seemingly revived the Silver Bay economy. But the promise of enduring prosperity for Silver Bay and other range communities was shattered by the recession of 1982. As the steel industry suffered nationwide, it had to compete with imported iron in an emerging global economy. In the depths of the recession, taconite-pellet production in 1982 was only about 23 million tons, a precipitous drop from the high of 56 million tons in 1979. For the period 1982–90, iron mining, whose worth dropped by almost a third, was the only sector of Minnesota's economy that declined. The plight of the industry was accentuated when compared to the overall gain of 79 percent in the state's gross product during that time.

The recession was a crushing blow to long-suffering iron rangers. Massive layoffs and plant closings created the most desperate crisis since the Great Depression. The Butler Taconite Plant near Nashwauk, which was closed in 1985, and Reserve Mining were the principal casualties. Having spent $370 million to ready Milepost 7 and make air-quality improvements, Reserve was ill-prepared for an economic disaster. It declared bankruptcy in 1986, and operations at Silver Bay were shut down for four years until Cyprus Northshore resumed taconite-pellet production. After its acquisition by Cleveland-Cliffs, Inc., in 1994, Cyprus Northshore was renamed Northshore Mining Company.

The Mesabi's boom and bust cycles are in keeping with the history of mining areas worldwide. During the gradual recovery since the gloom of the early 1980s, the recession has become the standard gauge in assessing the status of taconite. Mining companies and their trade association, the Iron Mining Association of Minnesota, regularly compare prerecession, recession, and postrecession production. Pellet production for 1995 was the highest since 1980.

Since the recession Minnesota's taconite producers and their customers, the blast-furnace steel manufacturers, have strived to meet the challenges of foreign iron ore, domestic minimills that recycle used steel, and less demand for steel. To cope with these new realities, Minnesota's seven taconite companies have shifted to larger equipment, more plant automation, and the development of new products. To more efficiently remove the overburden from taconite deposits and haul crude ore from the mine sites to crushers, producers have resorted to bigger shovels and massive trucks. The largest trucks, which cost about $1.5 million each, have wheels twelve feet in diameter and a capacity of about 250 tons, or approximately 100 cubic yards.

Within the noisy, dusty plants where taconite is finely crushed, formed into pellets, and baked, automation reigns. The lines of huge machines have an eerie appearance. They move all day, every day, seemingly without human guidance. Usually workers are not to be seen on the line, and when they are it is to repair some machine problem that has been detected by computers monitored from a central control room. Computerization has resulted in better controls and the production of more uniform pellets. Automation includes some use of robotic devices, such as machines to wash floors, a task formerly done by people, and computer-controlled automatic loading and unloading of the railroad cars used to export pellets. Because of technology, about half of a taconite plant's employees are actually engaged in such service activities as equipment maintenance and repair. Their work stands in sharp contrast to the nostalgic image of frontier miners, an image that is reinforced by the gigantic statue of a muscular miner armed with pick and shovel that stands alongside the highway at Ironworld Discovery Center, near Chisholm.

Fittingly, the statue represents a way of life that gave way to technological advances. Accommodation to new machines has become a key characteristic of iron-range culture. Since 1982 the taconite industry's work force has been roughly halved from its prerecession employment of twelve thousand workers.

By way of new products the taconite makers have developed alternatives to the traditional acid pellets, which required the addition of limestone (a fluxing agent) at the blast furnaces. While acid pellets are still made, the companies to varying degrees manufacture both flux and semiflux pellets. By adding crushed limestone transported from Michigan they enable steelmakers to eliminate a step at the blast furnaces. A more recent product that holds considerable promise is direct reduced iron (DRI). Rather than being pelletized, DRI is shaped into briquets, which are about four inches long with the thickness and width of common charcoal briquets. Their advantage is twofold: they are easier to ship, and they have an iron content of about 95 percent, compared to 65 percent in the pellets. Despite the advantages of DRI, its large-scale production is on hold. The National Steel Pellet Company of Keewatin has proven its feasibility, but the extent of future production will depend on steel manufacturers who specify the products they want from taconite plants.

In the mid-1990s Minnesota's taconite industry is in its best financial condition since the recession. The seven taconite plants—at Keewatin (National Steel Pellet Co.), Hibbing (Hibbing Taconite Co.), Mountain Iron (U.S. Steel Group), Eveleth (Eveleth Mines), Virginia (Inland Steel Mining Co.), Hoyt Lakes (LTV Steel Mining Co.), and Silver Bay (Northshore Mining Company)—are all operating at near capacity. Generally, their products are marketed in the same fashion as iron ore had been traditionally. Pellets are usually shipped by rail to Lake Superior and then carried eastward by ore carriers from the ports of Taconite Harbor, Silver Bay, Two Harbors, Duluth, and Superior, Wisconsin. However, about half of National Steel Pellet Company's shipments go directly by rail to blast furnaces near St. Louis, Missouri.

Although production has been increasing, the taconite industry is still beset with problems. The continuing soft market for steel products has caused steel prices and the price of taconite to lag behind inflationary advances in the general economy. As a result, Minnesota's taconite industry's income in 1995 was approximately 20 percent lower than its prerecession levels. Relative to the state's entire economy, the worth of the taconite industry continues to decline. In 1995 it stood at only 0.6 percent of the state's gross product.

Nonetheless, taconite is vitally important to the economy of northeastern Minnesota. Given their troubled history, residents of the Mesabi Range are understandably cautious about their economic future. Having experienced the depletion of high-grade natural ore, they obviously contemplate the ultimate loss of taconite. Of necessity, any projections about taconite's future are based on current assumptions. Those who make long-range predictions generally estimate that raw taconite should last for at least another two hundred years. Those of a more pessimistic nature, who are inclined to place more emphasis on worldwide market conditions, tend to believe that the taconite industry could be ended much sooner, not by depletion of the natural resource but rather because of complex economic factors.

The fragility of an economy heavily dependent on taconite has long been apparent. Consequently, the IRRRB has sought to diversify Mesabi Range activities by promoting tourism. In 1977 it opened the Iron Range Interpretative Center, an impressive state-of-the-art facility that portrays the geology and history of Minnesota's three ranges. With the addition of an entertainment complex in 1986, the center became Ironworld USA, and recently Ironworld Discovery Center. Picturesquely located at the brink of abandoned open pit mines, Ironworld, which includes a significant research center of both published and unpublished historical materials, has become a major tourist attraction. To stimulate winter tourism, the IRRRB in 1983 acquired the Giants Ridge ski facility near Biwabik. With its thorough remodeling and an aggressive program of encouraging regional snowmobiling, the agency has added to the wintertime appeal of the Mesabi Range.

Partially with the aim of making the ranges more attractive, the 1977 legislature added a Mineland Reclamation Division to the IRRRB. The division, based at Ironworld, produces millions of seedlings in its own nursery. Its reforestation of former mine sites and other places has been extensive. By 1991 its employees had planted more than 1.5 million trees. The division has also converted numerous mines and pits, which have filled with water naturally, into prime recreation areas by stocking them with fish and establishing swimming beaches, campgrounds, and parks. Its efforts and the various tree-planting projects by taconite companies are at least having the effect of partially restoring the range environment to its original timbered condition.

As agriculture, forestry, and iron mining have been transformed, Minnesota's economy has been greatly altered by the emergence of the high-technology industry. High technology, as defined by the federal Bureau of Labor Statistics, includes thirty-six industries that employ many engineers and scientists and manufacture, among other things, computers, drugs, electronic and medical devices, and laboratory equipment.

Minnesota's high-technology industry has been especially important since the nation's entry into World War II, but its best-known company—3M—dates from the early twentieth century. Minnesota Mining and Manufacturing Company, as it was formally named for most of its history, was started at Two Harbors in 1902 by a small group of businessmen.

Operating on the mistaken assumption that there was a nearby deposit of corundum, they intended to mine it and manufacture abrasives. Even though the corundum mine never materialized, Lucius P. Ordway, a St. Paul millionaire general manager of a plumbing firm, and a partner saw great potential in manufacturing sandpaper. After acquiring the company in 1905, Ordway and his associate produced sandpaper in Duluth for only four years before moving their business to St. Paul, which had the marked advantage of a dryer climate.

Thanks to the salesmanship of William L. McKnight, a former South Dakota farm boy, the establishment of a company research laboratory, and the development of an abrasive cloth, 3M's sales boomed during the World War I period. Out of its continual quest for new products, 3M developed an abrasive for wet sanding, which was first marketed in 1921. Then, during the 1920s, the company greatly expanded its sales base by complementing its line of abrasives with masking tape and other adhesives. Because of its diversified products, which by the Great Depression included roofing granules, resins, and film, 3M actually expanded during the hard times. As a major defense contractor during World War II, the company developed and supplied such products as reflectorized tape and nonslip sheeting.

Honeywell, Minnesota's second-ranking high-technology firm, can trace its beginning to the invention of a spring-powered thermostat by A. M. Butz of Minneapolis in 1885. The first company organized to produce and sell the instrument failed, but after its reorganization as the Electric Thermostat Company in 1889, it obtained financial backing from William R. Sweatt, a Minneapolis manufacturer of wooden wheelbarrows. Sweatt became owner of the firm during its long period of financial difficulties, but sales increased sharply after Sweatt developed a time-clock thermostat in 1905. By 1912, when the company's name was changed to the Minneapolis Heat Regulator Company, it was on a solid foundation. As a manufacturer of thermostats for coal furnaces, the company was independent until its merger in 1927 with the rival Honeywell Heating Specialties Company of Wabash, Indiana, owned by Mark Honeywell. Headquartered in Minneapolis, the new firm was originally named the Minneapolis-Honeywell Heat Regulator Company.

Like 3M, Honeywell emphasized diversification through its own research and development program. By the start of World War II Honeywell was a significant producer of automatic controls used in a variety of heating, air-conditioning, and industrial applications. Its

Round thermostats ready for final checkout and packaging at Honeywell's plant in
Golden Valley, about 1960.
Courtesy of the Minnesota Historical Society

sales nearly quadrupled from the merger until World War II, a remarkable achievement considering the long depression that detrimentally
impacted the overall economy. With its technical experience the firm
moved naturally into World War II military contracting, which included guidance systems for bombers. This wartime work, in turn, paved
the way for Honeywell's development of missile-guidance systems during the cold war.

   After World War II Minnesota's high-technology industry was augmented significantly by the manufacturing of computers and medical
devices. In the computer field, Control Data (currently named Ceridian)

had the most impact. Organized in 1957 by William C. Norris, Control Data was an outgrowth of Minnesota's pioneering years in the computer field. In 1945, Norris, an electrical engineer who had served as a naval intelligence officer during World War II, recognized the potential government market for computers. Norris, who became famous for his insights into the future, was the key idea man of Engineering Research Associates (ERA), organized in Minneapolis in early 1946.

As one of the nation's first computer companies, ERA sold its first system to the federal government in 1950, and after additional government sales entered the commercial market in 1954. ERA's early success had attracted the attention of Remington Rand, the massive corporation that had entered the computer field in 1949. When ERA was sold to Remington Rand in 1951, the value of its original shares had increased by 8,000 percent. As the leading computer manufacturer, Remington Rand faced increasingly stiff competition from International Business Machines (IBM). Consequently, Remington Rand was sold to Sperry Gyroscope Company in 1955, and the new company, Sperry Rand Corporation, named Norris to head its computer sector—the Univac Division of Sperry Rand.

After heading Univac for two years, Norris decided to form his own company with the aim of manufacturing computers that were different from those made by Univac and IBM. By 1969, after Norris had engineered a number of key acquisitions, Control Data's sales topped one billion dollars and the company had a workforce of forty thousand worldwide. As Control Data grew, many other Twin Cities computer hardware and software firms were formed, some by administrators and engineers, who had first entered the field with Norris and ERA. The rapid rise of the high-technology industry was evident by labor statistics for 1980, when about fifty thousand, or nearly one sixth of Minnesota's industrial employees, worked for 3M, Honeywell, Univac, and Control Data.

The computer industry, like flour milling of an earlier age, stimulated the creation of allied high-technology industries such as the making of medical devices. Minnesota's emergence as a major hub for the manufacturing of medical devices came about through a combination of circumstances. The state's electronics and computer businesses offered invaluable practical training for engineers and technicians, who could easily move into medical technology. Years of medical research at the world famous Mayo Clinic in Rochester and the University of Minnesota medical school also contributed, as did engineering education offered by the University of Minnesota and the importance of the Twin Cities as a financial center with capitalists willing to invest in new ventures.

Medtronic, which became the largest of several hundred medical technology companies in the state, was started in Minneapolis by Earl Bakken in 1949. After Bakken developed an external battery-powered heart pacemaker in 1958 and an implantable pacemaker two years later, the firm grew rapidly. Medtronic's meteoric rise led to the creation of many other medical technology companies, which were quite often started by former Medtronic employees.

As relatively new ventures heavily dependent on continually developing new products, Minnesota's high-technology businesses have been particularly vulnerable to changing market conditions. Since 1980 domestic and foreign competition and the great expenditures for research have forced major adjustments. During the 1980s Honeywell lost money on its computer division and both Control Data and Medtronic were forced to restructure and downsize.

Despite these setbacks high technology remains an important component in Minnesota's diverse economy. In 1995 three high-technology firms—3M, Honeywell, and Medtronic—were among the top ten of Minnesota's largest publicly held companies. With 70,687 employees, 3M was the leader. Honeywell, with 50,100, and Medtronic, with 10,700, ranked eighth and tenth, respectively. The others in the top ten reflect not only the character of current business but of society as well. They were Norwest Corporation (banking), First Bank System, St. Paul Companies (insurance and investment services), Dayton Hudson (general-merchandise retailer), United Health Care (health-maintenance organizations), Northwest Airlines, and General Mills.

The nature of Minnesota's economy in the late twentieth century can also be understood by looking at data compiled by the Minnesota Department of Trade and Economic Development. For 1990, Minnesota's gross state product (GSP) was slightly over $100 billion, an increase of 79 percent over an eight-year period. At 22 percent, manufacturing was the largest single sector. The heavy interdependence of people in an increasingly complex, urbanized society was evident from the contribution of services, which, at slightly over 17 percent of the GSP, ranked second to manufacturing. Finance, insurance, and real estate combined was the source of nearly 17 percent, as were wholesale and retail trade. The total for the three levels of government—state, local, and federal—was nearly 11 percent of the GSP.

Minnesota's current economy is illustrative of the continuity and change in the state's history. Agriculture, forestry, and mining, although greatly changed by new economic circumstances and technology, continue to be significant. But most of the diversity in the late-twentieth-century economy has resulted from increasing metropolitanism and the development of the high-technology industry.

1 0

MAINSTREAM POLITICS

SINCE 1948 MINNESOTA'S two major political parties have mirrored national trends. While the DFL has generally been regarded as one of the most liberal elements in the national Democratic Party, some of its most successful politicians have adapted well to the increasingly conservative mood of the state and the nation. Likewise, Minnesota's Republican Party has been carried along in the national conservative reaction against progressive Republicanism. While the two parties have distinct ideologies, they have been forced to appeal to a large centrist constituency of independents, who are more likely to be persuaded by issues or personalities than by party allegiance.

When the DFL established itself as a bona fide rival of the Republicans in 1948, the ideologies of Hubert H. Humphrey and Harold Stassen best symbolized their parties. Humphrey quickly established himself as a leader of the most liberal Democrats nationally, and Stassen's gubernatorial successors, Edward J. Thye and Luther W. Youngdahl, were dedicated to continuing progressive Republicanism.

As Stassen's national appeal faded, Humphrey was the central figure in Minnesota politics for the three decades before his death in 1978. As a freshman senator he expressed himself clearly, frequently, and sometimes at great length on a wide range of national and international affairs. By the mid-1950s, early in his second term, he was already recognized as a presidential possibility. In 1960, as his second senatorial term drew to a close, Humphrey made a bid for the Democratic Party presidential nomination but was outshone in the primaries by the well-financed John F. Kennedy of Massachusetts. During the early part of his third term he was

Vice president Hubert H. Humphrey spoke at St. John's University, Collegeville, Minnesota, on May 7, 1966.
Courtesy of the Minnesota Historical Society

continually in the national and international limelight, because of his role as Senate majority whip and his championship of the Civil Rights Act, the Peace Corps, and the Food for Peace program. Humphrey was a logical choice for the vice presidential nomination in 1964, although President Lyndon B. Johnson, who had succeeded to the presidency after Kennedy's assassination on November 22, 1963, flirted with other running-mate possibilities, including Minnesota's other senator, Eugene J. McCarthy.

Humphrey's election to the vice presidency enhanced his presidential prospects but also intertwined his political career with those of Eugene J. McCarthy and Walter F. Mondale more closely than ever. Mondale, who as a college student had worked in Humphrey's 1948 senatorial campaign, was appointed by DFL Governor Karl F. Rolvaag to serve the remainder of Humphrey's third senatorial term. At the time of his appointment he was the most respected member of the Democratic-Farmer-Labor Party's younger generation. Friends and critics alike agreed that Mondale's political career had been idyllic. In 1960, at the age of thirty-two, he was appointed Minnesota attorney general by DFL Governor Orville L. Freeman, and he was subsequently elected to the post for two more terms. As attorney general Mondale became widely known as a champion of consumer rights. Much of the time during the early 1960s he was more newsworthy than any other state official, including the governor. Although Mondale was given his second big break with the senatorial appointment, it was soon apparent that he had a solid base of public support. He was elected to a full term in 1966 and was easily reelected in 1972, even though Richard M. Nixon defeated Democrat George S. McGovern in the presidential contest in Minnesota by a wide margin.

Humphrey as vice president initially benefited from the president's domestic accomplishments and was regarded nationally as the natural successor to the popular Johnson. But Humphrey unavoidably became associated with the increasing public distrust of the Johnson administration—a circumstance that put him and his onetime Minnesota ally, Eugene J. McCarthy, on a collision course toward the bitter Democratic Party split of 1968. The battle lines were drawn when McCarthy on November 30, 1967, announced that he would launch a campaign against American involvement in Vietnam. The declaration had great public appeal because of rapidly growing disillusionment with the country's role in Southeast Asia. Certainly McCarthy's stature as a congressional leader added significance to his crusade. After serving five terms in the House of Representatives he had been elected to the Senate in 1958, defeating Edward J. Thye, the two-term Republican incumbent who had succeeded Stassen as governor. During his first term McCarthy addressed a variety of domestic and foreign issues and became known as one of the

During his bid for the Democratic presidential nomination in 1968, Senator Eugene McCarthy spoke at St. John's University, Collegeville, Minnesota.
Courtesy of the Minnesota Historical Society

most liberal members of the Senate. He became yet better known nationally in 1964 because of Johnson's consideration of him as a vice presidential possibility, and he was easily reelected to the Senate.

To those who wanted things spelled out, McCarthy was enigmatic. Like Humphrey he had taught in college for a time, which in some circles helped establish the DFL as the party of the professors. But unlike Humphrey, whose public utterances tended to be flamboyant and verbose, McCarthy spoke slowly, calmly, and philosophically. In part because of his mannerisms and in part because he offered questions, not answers, he struck some of his followers as a modern Socrates—a man with profound insight into society's malaise. At a time when the "establishment" defended American intervention in the Vietnam War, McCarthy appealed to many young people, especially college-age students, who took up his anti-establishment cause. During his anti-Vietnam crusade McCarthy was seen by his supporters as a humane philosopher who hoped to save the nation from yet greater tragedy, but many opponents believed that his stance was nothing more than a vendetta against Johnson for the coquetry of 1964.

McCarthy shocked the nation by easily winning most of New Hampshire's national convention delegates in the first primary of 1968. That success led Senator Robert F. Kennedy of New York to declare himself for the presidency, and Johnson was soon forced to announce that he would not run for reelection. Johnson's retirement opened the way for Humphrey, and Kennedy's assassination set the stage for a Democratic national convention in Chicago featuring two Minnesotans as the frontrunners for the presidential nomination.

The acrimonious rivalry of the Humphrey-McCarthy forces was reflected in Minnesota's precinct caucuses. Party regulars who were well acquainted with the long public service of both men tended to support Humphrey, but McCarthy showed great strength among college students and did particularly well in such outstate college communities as Marshall, Winona, Mankato, St. Cloud, and Moorhead. The contest in Minnesota was significant not because Humphrey captured most of the delegates but because the conflicting philosophies over Vietnam created such animosities that even the winner was assured of losing some support. This grassroots struggle in Minnesota was indicative of the schism that later emerged within the national Democratic Party.

In Chicago Humphrey easily won the presidential nomination on the first ballot, thus becoming the first Minnesotan to run for the presidency as a major party candidate. But Humphrey could not disassociate himself from Johnson's Vietnam policy, and when Chicago police used strong-arm tactics to quell demonstrating anti-Vietnam protesters and Humphrey refused to criticize them, the regular party lost much support. The disaffection of vociferous McCarthy supporters did not seem to be a decisive issue during most of the campaign because the polls regularly showed Humphrey to be far behind Republican candidate Richard M. Nixon. But Humphrey campaigned tirelessly and enthusiastically, like a "Happy Warrior" in the Al Smith tradition, and in the end lost the election by only 500,000 votes out of 70 million cast. There can be little doubt that the decision would have been different if those who were influenced by the Vietnam dilemma had voted for their party's candidate. McCarthy did not actively campaign, nor did he announce his support for Humphrey until just a week and a half before the election, when he gave his onetime friend and fellow builder of Minnesota's Democratic-Farmer-Labor Party an endorsement that at best was perfunctory.

In a sense, both Humphrey and McCarthy lost in 1968. With his defeat Humphrey was temporarily out of public office, but he was easily elected to the United States Senate in 1970, taking the seat left vacant when McCarthy chose not to run. It is very unlikely that McCarthy could have been reelected even if he had run after having challenged his party in 1968 and, in the minds of many, having ruined the presidential aspirations of his fellow Minnesotan. However, some believed that, in the long range, McCarthy would be favorably remembered because of his opposition to American involvement in Vietnam. Albert Eisele concluded that his "stand against the Vietnam War in 1968 was a singular act of courage that grows larger in retrospect and guarantees him a secure place in the history of his country."[1]

In 1972, Humphrey's presidential ambitions were undercut by George S. McGovern's well-executed campaign. McGovern of South Dakota was overwhelmed by Richard M. Nixon, failing even to carry his home state in the general election. But as the Nixon administration was devastated by the Watergate scandal, which led to Nixon's resignation in 1974, Humphrey again became a party favorite. Those who contemplated 1976 presidential possibilities also often mentioned Walter F. Mondale, and Mondale did launch a short, abortive bid for the nomination in 1974. His withdrawal, prompted by his expressed aversion to the rigors of campaigning, appeared to have seriously damaged his chances for higher office. But the sudden emergence of the moderate Jimmy (James Earl) Carter, a former Georgia governor, as the Democratic Party's favorite presidential candidate created a new opportunity, because of Carter's need to garner the support of northern liberals, including organized labor. By June 1976, after his nomination was assured, Carter began carefully screening potential running mates. After receiving the nomination at the New York City convention, he announced Mondale as his choice for vice presidential candidate. Mondale's place on the ticket somewhat soothed traditional New Deal liberals who thought Carter was too conservative, and the Georgia-Minnesota connection provided the desirable sectional balance. Nonetheless, no ticket could strongly unify the factionalized Democratic Party, whose many constituencies had difficulty working together.

Walter F. Mondale was the second Minnesotan to serve as vice president of the United States.
Courtesy of the Minnesota Historical Society

Despite his earlier aversion to the campaign trail, Mondale worked hard and effectively among party regulars. He appealed especially to organized labor and blacks in the major industrial states and participated in the historic first debate between vice presidential candidates when he faced the conservative Kansas Senator Robert J. Dole, President Gerald R. Ford's running mate. Polls indicated that Mondale was regarded as an asset to the ticket, and with the Carter-Mondale victory of November 2, 1976, he became the second vice president from Minnesota.

Because of his affliction with cancer, a factor that probably generated some sympathy votes and aided in his easy reelection to the Senate, Humphrey was inactive for most of the campaign season. But Eugene J. McCarthy, as the Independent Party candidate, threatened to undermine Carter and Mondale. When the election proved to be a close contest, contrary to early polls showing Carter-Mondale far ahead of Ford-Dole, the McCarthy candidacy—which appealed mostly to those inclined to vote for Carter and Mondale—was galling to many Democrats. As in 1968, they were puzzled by McCarthy. To some he seemed to be just the Democratic counterpart of Stassen, to others he appeared to be an embittered man, but to his supporters he offered calm reason in a campaign bereft of thoughtful discussion of the issues by the presidential candidates of the major parties. The closeness of the election, which seemed a dead heat on election eve, magnified McCarthy's importance. His candidacy denied Carter and Mondale the electoral votes of four states and narrowed their victory margin over Ford, who had succeeded Nixon, and Dole.

After a promising start the Carter administration was soon plagued by a host of problems. Carter's tendency to find the middle ground made him appear uncertain and indecisive, and his Washington outsider stance offended many Democratic congressional leaders. The increasing antigovernment and antitax mood of the nation was compounded by high inflation and high unemployment. Late in the Carter administration foreign-affairs crises rivaled the bad economic news for public attention. Carter's response to the Soviet invasion of Afghanistan in December 1979 failed to evoke an outpouring of American patriotism. During a decided heating of the cold war Carter offended farmers by banning grain exports to the Soviet Union, and he lost further support by barring American athletes from participating in the 1980 Olympic Games in Moscow. As the nation wrested with the Soviet crisis it had to endure the ignominy of the Iranian hostage crisis. Carter's failure to win the freedom of Americans held by the fundamentalist Iranian government doomed his presidency.

After they were nominated for reelection, Carter and Mondale had to face the challenge of a reinvigorated Republican Party, which had taken a turn to the Right in the late 1970s. Led by the ticket of Ronald W. Reagan of California and George H. Bush of Texas, the Republicans exploited the economic and foreign policy woes of the Carter administration. The Reagan surge late in the campaign led to a landslide Republican victory.

Mondale was nominated by the Democrats to face the immensely popular Reagan in 1984. As a decided underdog he attracted much attention by selecting Geraldine A. Ferraro, a New York congresswoman, as his running mate. Ferraro, as the nation's first woman vice presidential candidate, added an element of excitement to an otherwise lackluster campaign. Mondale's warnings about the hazards of deficit spending and his advocacy of a tax increase won him plaudits for political courage, but failed to blunt Reagan's easy reelection. Like McGovern in 1972, Mondale won only one state, but he, at least, had the satisfaction of carrying his home state. The presidential election of Democrat Bill (William J.) Clinton, former Arkansas governor, in 1992 gave Mondale an opportunity to return to government service. In the summer of 1993 Clinton selected him to be the nation's ambassador to Japan.

Although Humphrey, McCarthy, and Mondale have been the most conspicuous Democratic-Farmer-Labor politicians, others have served in important national positions as well. Eugenie M. Anderson of Red Wing, who, like Humphrey and McCarthy, was a pioneer in the Democratic-Farmer-Labor Party, was the first woman in the nation's history to hold ambassadorial rank. She was ambassador to Denmark from 1949 to 1953 and later served as minister to Bulgaria and as a representative on the United Nations Trusteeship Council. Orville L. Freeman, after three terms (1955–61) as governor, was the secretary of agriculture in the Kennedy and Johnson administrations. His initiatives in that position included the feed-grain reduction program and an extension of the Agricultural Trade Development and Assistance Act. During the administration of President Lyndon B. Johnson, Walter W. Heller of the University of Minnesota chaired the President's Council of Economic Advisers. Robert S. Bergland of Roseau was the secretary of agriculture during Carter's administration. As a four-term (1971–77) congressman from northwestern Minnesota, he was a frequent critic of Nixon's agricultural policies, which, he charged, favored big producers. Under his administration, the Department of Agriculture emphasized continuation of the federal government's price-support system, which he believed was the most effective way of achieving the long-standing Democratic goal of sustaining relatively small family farms.

The fame of Humphrey, McCarthy, and Mondale can easily leave the impression that Minnesota has been basically a one-party state, but in reality a number of Minnesota Republicans have gained national prominence. Even though he ceased to be a serious presidential aspirant after 1952, Harold Stassen was recognized as one of the nation's most prominent Republican politicians during the Eisenhower presidency (1953–61). During the 1950s, Congressman Walter H. Judd of Minneapolis was one of the national leaders in the China lobby—that group which urged strong United States support of Chiang Kai-shek's exiled Republic of China and the containment of the Communist regime of mainland China. Judd, a medical doctor who had served as a missionary in China, became an influential figure during the Eisenhower presidency. He reached the pinnacle of his career in 1960 when he delivered the keynote address at the Republican National Convention. But after a ten-term career in the House of Representatives, changing voter moods and the appeal of the youthful Donald M. Fraser unseated him in 1962.

During his first term Richard M. Nixon brought some Minnesotans into prominent government positions. James D. Hodgson, who was born in Dawson in 1915, was named secretary of labor in 1970. Hodgson had been educated at the University of Minnesota and worked for the Minnesota Department of Employment before moving to California in 1941, where he subsequently held a variety of labor relations and personnel positions with the Lockheed Aircraft Corporation. Maurice H. Stans, a native of Shakopee, was appointed secretary of commerce in 1969 when he was sixty years old. After finishing high school in his hometown, Stans was educated at Northwestern University in Evanston, Illinois. Following a career in accounting, he entered government service. During the Eisenhower presidency he served successively as deputy postmaster general, deputy director, and director of the Bureau of the Budget. During the Kennedy-Johnson years, when the Democrats controlled the White House, he was an officer in California and New York financial institutions. In 1972 Stans resigned to become the financial director of the Committee to Reelect the President. As Nixon's chief fund-raiser he was tainted by the Watergate scandal, and later, in a humiliating end to his public career, pleaded guilty to Watergate-associated misdemeanors.

In his efforts to make the Supreme Court more conservative, Nixon appointed two Minnesotans to it. In 1969, Warren E. Burger, a native of St. Paul, was named the court's fifteenth chief justice, and the next year, Harry A. Blackmun, who had spent most of his Minnesota years in Rochester and the Twin Cities, was also named to the court. Not surprisingly, the media commonly dubbed them "the Minnesota Twins."

Warren E. Burger was chief justice of the United States Supreme Court, 1969–86.
Courtesy of the Minnesota Historical Society

Both had profound effects, but hardly in the way Nixon anticipated. Burger, who had gained a reputation as a law-and-order conservative judge while serving on the federal Court of Appeals for the District of Columbia, 1956–69, was expected to embody the "strict constructionist" policy on which Nixon had campaigned in 1968. However, instead of rejecting the activist philosophy of the Earl Warren court, Burger, who served as chief justice until his resignation in 1986, proved to be more liberal than Nixon anticipated. The Burger court reaffirmed First Amendment rights, expanded women's protections against sexual discrimination, and upheld busing as a means of desegregating public schools.

Blackmun, who was appointed to the court from the Court of Appeals for the Eighth Circuit and served until his retirement in 1994, became famous for writing the majority opinion in the case of *Roe v. Wade.* In that landmark 1973 decision the court held that a woman's right to an abortion during the first trimester of pregnancy was a private matter that could not be regulated by states. For the second trimester, states were limited to regulating abortions, but did not have the authority to ban them until the third trimester. In reversing a century-old tradition of government opposition to abortion, the decision was hailed by women's rights activists and other liberals. Blackmun, who may have been influenced by his long-standing interest in medicine and his work as the legal counsel of the Mayo Clinic, had rigorously studied the medical and ethical implications of the decision before the court acted. Ironically, *Roe v. Wade,* which initially seemed to resolve a troublesome issue, proved to have the opposite effect. The decision itself became an issue between its liberal supporters and conservatives, who soon began advocating a constitutional amendment to ban abortions.

After Burger and Blackmun were appointed to the Supreme Court and Humphrey's and McCarthy's 1968 activities were still fresh in the public mind, Minnesota had a national reputation for producing political leaders. In 1972 political scientist Neal R. Peirce, echoing a common refrain, noted that "man for man, it would be hard to name a state which has contributed as many men of stature and depth to national political life in the postwar era as Minnesota."[2] Such an observation was more easily made than explained. Perhaps Minnesota's political activism was a natural byproduct of the long era of agrarian discontent; perhaps Scandinavians, the state's most politically active ethnic group, were more inclined than others to seek solutions to life's problems through politics and government.

Harry A. Blackmun, who served as a justice on the United States Supreme Court, 1970–94, wrote the majority opinion in the landmark case of *Roe v. Wade*. *Courtesy of the Minnesota Historical Society*

Whatever the elusive reasons, there can be little doubt that Minnesota not only had national political impact during the active Populist, Progressive, and Farmer-Labor days but earned even more recognition for political contributions in the post–World War II period.

Part of the widespread recognition of Minnesota as a progressive state has been based on relatively recent changes in state government. Stassen's election in 1938 ushered in a sixteen-year period of continuous Republican control of the governorship. In 1946, when Edward J. Thye, Stassen's successor, was elected to the United States Senate, Luther W. Youngdahl was elected governor. Reelected in 1948 and 1950, the popular, progressive

Youngdahl championed humane and moral policies. Accepting the premise that government should actively participate in improving the human condition, Youngdahl's program stressed welfare services, expanded public housing and public health enhancements, and increased support for education and care of the mentally ill and physically disabled. Not too surprisingly, he came to be best remembered for his antigambling and antiliquor stances. Despite strenuous opposition, Youngdahl convinced the legislature to tighten bans on slot machines and other illegal gambling devices and toughen enforcement of liquor sales laws.

Before reaching the midpoint of his third term, Youngdahl resigned to accept a federal district judgeship in Washington, D.C. The reasons for this move are somewhat obscure, but speculation includes the notion that Democratic President Harry S. Truman wanted to help the DFL by getting Youngdahl out of the state as well as the belief in some circles that Youngdahl did not want to be thrust into the role of heading the state "Stassen for President" campaign in 1952.

Those traditional Republicans who regarded Youngdahl as being too liberal were hardly delighted with their party's embracement of political newcomer Dwight D. Eisenhower, the former World War II general. Minnesotans, after voting Democratic in five successive presidential elections, chose Eisenhower in 1952 and again in 1956.

Eisenhower's immense popularity, however, stemmed from his personal charm rather than his political affiliation or philosophy. Thus, there was really nothing significantly inconsistent about Minnesotans electing Orville L. Freeman as the state's first DFL governor in 1954. Freeman's election and reelection in 1956 and 1958 established a virtual parity between the DFL and Republican Parties. Reflecting the influence of both the New Deal and Luther W. Youngdahl's social programs, Freeman during his first two terms sought and generally achieved increased funding for education, welfare, and worker's compensation; reorganization of state government; and fairness in minority employment.

At various times during Freeman's governorship, the state's most publicized DFLer was Coya G. Knutson, the flamboyant congresswoman from the Ninth District, which included the Red River Valley. Elected in 1954 and reelected two years later, Knutson holds the distinction of being the only Minnesota woman ever elected to Congress. A native North Dakotan, she graduated from Concordia College in Moorhead, Minnesota, in 1934 and then studied at the Juilliard School of Music in New York City. After teaching briefly in North Dakota, she moved to

Minnesota. In 1940, while teaching high school at Oklee, she married Andrew Knutson. While teaching and helping her husband in his hotel and café business, she became active in the Red Lake County DFL.

After being recruited by county DFL leaders, she was elected to the state House of Representatives in 1950 and reelected in 1952. Although she challenged the party by running for Congress without its endorsement, Knutson easily defeated four men in the primary election and then upset the veteran Republican incumbent in the general election.

In Congress Knutson championed liberal economic and social causes. As the first woman to serve on the House Agriculture Committee she was an

The only Minnesota woman ever elected to Congress, Coya G. Knutson promoted
liberal economic and social causes.
Courtesy of the Minnesota Historical Society

early and ardent booster of the Food Stamp Bill, which, she believed, would help the poor and her family-farm constituency. She was also a key sponsor of the Student Defense Loan Program and the Equal Rights Amendment. Knutson's legislative actions were in keeping with her party's progressive tradition, but she proved to be somewhat of a maverick. In 1956 she broke with the state DFL over its endorsement of presidential candidate Adlai E. Stevenson. She not only campaigned for Stevenson's rival, Estes C. Kefauver, but openly criticized the bossism of the state party.

After that campaign her DFL opponents were openly critical of her unorthodox style and even her attire. This estrangement led to an event that attracted national attention in 1958 as she was seeking a third term. The media delighted in reporting the famous "Coya, Come Home" letter in which her husband, who had remained in Oklee, publicly urged her to leave Washington and resume her wifely duties in small-town Minnesota. Although the timing and tenor of the letter suggested a political setup, both her DFL and Republican opponents took advantage of it. Despite lingering bad publicity, she was only narrowly defeated by Republican Odin Langen in the general election. Later, her husband testified at a hearing of a special United States House elections subcommittee that Coya's DFL primary opponents were mainly responsible for convincing him to write the letter.

Freeman's bid for a fourth term as governor was ruined by a series of economic crises in the late 1950s. A national steel strike, which caused a sharp drop in iron-ore production, resulted in massive unemployment in mining communities, which traditionally supported the DFL. Freeman's handling of the meat packers' strike in Albert Lea, the most acrimonious of several strikes in the state, undermined the DFL's prolabor image. Believing that the strike posed a public danger, Freeman called in the National Guard preparatory to closing the plant. The governor's seeming ineptness, which attracted heavy media coverage, was underscored by a federal court–mandated plant reopening.

With his recent difficulties fresh in the public mind, Freeman in 1960 was defeated by Elmer L. Andersen, a former state senator. Andersen, a progressive Republican in the Stassen tradition, had a contentious term. Although he was a strong advocate of public education and expanded social programs, much of his term was fraught with legislative debate over the need to redraw congressional district boundaries after the results of the 1960 census caused the state's allocation to the House of Representatives to be reduced from nine to eight.

Andersen was also in the awkward position of having his principal rival, Karl F. Rolvaag, as lieutenant governor. Until a 1972 constitutional amendment was passed, candidates for governor and lieutenant governor were not required to run as a ticket or even to be of the same political party. Rolvaag, son of the famous novelist Ole Rölvaag and a key member of the DFL's inner circle during its early years, had served as lieutenant governor during Freeman's three terms. Somehow the public disenchantment with Freeman did not extend to him.

As expected, when Andersen sought reelection in 1962, he was opposed by Rolvaag for the first four-year gubernatorial term in state history. To assure more continuity in that office, voters had approved a constitutional amendment doubling the length of a gubernatorial term. The promise of this new, longer term gave the Andersen-Rolvaag contest special significance.

For those who wanted immediate results, the election was a major disappointment. The initial tally indicated a virtual tie, but the canvassing board report issued slightly more than three weeks after the election showed that Andersen had won, but only by 142 votes out of about 1.24 million cast. Pending the outcome of a recount, Andersen continued in office after the January 8, 1963, inauguration date. Finally, in March, after a laborious process of eliminating defective ballots, the three-judge recount panel announced that Rolvaag had eked out a 91-vote victory, the narrowest in state gubernatorial history.

During his somewhat abridged term, Rolvaag, whose image seemed bland as compared to the exuberant Hubert Humphrey, failed to inspire public confidence. This caused key DFLers to worry about retaining the governorship. In the Minnesota equivalent of a palace coup, forty party leaders in 1965 met secretly at Sugar Hills, a northern Minnesota resort, to contemplate the 1966 election. After extensive complaining about Rolvaag they concluded that he was not reelectable and, for the sake of the party, should not run. The secret of Sugar Hills was soon leaked and subsequent media publicity revealed the DFL's internal strife.

Rolvaag angrily responded by announcing his candidacy for a second term. But within hours he was challenged by Lieutenant Governor Alexander M. Keith, the favorite of the Sugar Hills group. Keith, of Rochester, who preferred to be publicly identified as A. M. "Sandy" Keith, was only thirty-five years old when he became lieutenant governor in 1963. Much of his appeal was generational. At a time when many people were smitten with the youth and vigor of the late president John F. Kennedy, the handsome, outgoing Keith symbolized the dawning of a new age for the DFL.

Understandably, many DFLers resented the attempted dumping of Rolvaag, whose roots extended to their party's beginning. Delegates to the state convention carried their animosities through twenty contentious ballots before endorsing Keith. Visibly upset, Rolvaag challenged Keith in the primary. Benefiting from a marked Republican crossover vote, Rolvaag swept to victory. But the high cost of the DFL schism was soon obvious. In the general election Rolvaag was defeated by Republican Harold LeVander, a South St. Paul attorney.

Although DFLers tried to portray LeVander as a conservative, he was progressive in the essential questions of the day—public education, the environment, social programs, and regional governance. While the governor and the conservative-dominated legislature favored expansion of state programs, they recognized the need for additional revenue. Since the state already had a steep graduated income tax and high property taxes, the most likely additional revenue source was a sales tax. However, LeVander had campaigned on the pledge that he would not support a sales tax unless it was supported by a public referendum. This declaration put him on a collision course with members of his own party who had long favored such a tax as a way of at least deferring increases in the income tax and promoting some property-tax relief.

In legislative debates liberal DFLers vigorously attacked the proposed sales tax, whose burden, they charged, would fall the heaviest on those least able to pay. Recognizing that some liberal votes were necessary to pass the measure, its conservative proponents agreed that certain of life's necessities—food, clothing, and medicine—would be exempted. LeVander, true to his campaign promise, vetoed two sales-tax measures, which opened him to DFL charges that his vetoes were not sincere because he actually favored the tax. The sales tax obviously could not have passed without support from some DFLers, who believed additional state revenue was vital. However, in the area of political rhetoric, the DFL tried to cast LeVander and conservative legislators as tax raisers and themselves as saviors of the common people because of the exemptions in the 1967 sales-tax measure.

During LeVander's administration a notable advance was made in the area of regional governance by the creation of the Metropolitan Council, a response to the transformation of the Twin Cities into a metropolitan area. With the post–World War II impact of the automobile and the resultant proliferation of suburbs, Minneapolis and St. Paul lost residents as the counties in which they were located gained dramatically. Minneapolis's peak population of 521,718 was reached in 1950. However, the federal censuses of 1960 and 1970 showed 482,872 and 434,400, respectively. During the same twenty-year period Hennepin County grew from 676,579 to 960,080. Although St. Paul was more stable than Minneapolis, a similar pattern was evident there. The capital city's record population of 313,411, attained in 1960, was a gain of only about 2,000 over a decade. But by 1970, the city's population stood at 309,980. However, from 1950 to 1970 Ramsey County's population rose from 355,332 to 476,255.

By 1967 the seven-county metropolitan area of Anoka, Carver, Dakota, Hennepin, Ramsey, Scott, and Washington Counties had 132 incorporated cities and villages and 68 townships within its 3,000-square-mile area. As the populations of Minneapolis and St. Paul were declining and that of their suburban ring increasing, it had become increasingly obvious that the traditionally independent local jurisdictions had to have centralized planning. During the 1960s the most pressing metropolitan-area problems were sewage disposal; unplanned growth, which resulted in urban sprawl; the need for a metropolitan-wide transit and transportation system; open space preservation, which many local governments were reluctant to undertake because it lowered their tax bases; growing fiscal disparities between communities; and solid-waste disposal.

To varying degrees, some of these matters, which had been evident for years, had caused some metropolitan cooperation. A voluntary planning association in the 1920s failed for lack of financial support, but the legislature in 1933 created the Minneapolis–St. Paul Sanitary Sewer District. To force regional airport planning a 1943 law established the Metropolitan Airports Commission. The Metropolitan Area Sports Commission, which was authorized to construct and manage a stadium in Bloomington, the principal southern suburb, was started in 1956. It was mainly responsible for the acquisition of the major-league baseball Minnesota Twins and the professional football Minnesota Vikings. During Freeman's administration the legislature in 1957 moved toward more general planning by forming the Twin Cities Metropolitan Planning Commission, the main predecessor of the Metropolitan Council. That body was quite similar to a council of government, an agency that performed planning services for its member governments. It studied problems, reported to the legislature, but had no implementation authority. A year after beginning the planning commission, the legislature, responding to the menace of the state's major pest, established the Metropolitan Mosquito Control District.

By 1967 a more favorable political climate made it possible for the state to deal with metropolitan issues. Part of the stimulus for a new planning agency came from the federal government, which in 1966 required that all grant applications had to be reviewed by a substate agency. Since the Twin Cities Metropolitan Planning Commission could not be held politically accountable, legislators were reluctant to continue using it for reviewing. Strong support for a new regional agency came from the Citizens League, the leading organization in lobbying the legislature and stimulating public interest. Another vital circumstance was the reapportionment of the legislature. Historically, rural legislators had higher priorities than metropolitan planning, but because of the United States Supreme Court's one-person, one-vote decision, their numbers were lessened. Responding to a suit a federal court ordered Minnesota to reapportion its legislature in accordance with the Supreme Court's ruling. In 1966 Governor Rolvaag twice vetoed reapportionment measures for failing to achieve equitable reapportionment, but finally the balky lawmakers shifted eleven House and five Senate seats to the metropolitan area. As a result of this action, the metropolitan area had almost half of the legislative seats.

The act creating the Metropolitan Council had strong bipartisan support because of the continuing sewage-disposal question, which was aggravated by septic-tank pollution. Most legislative debate was not concerned with the need for the council, but rather with its nature and with such details as whether its members should be appointed or elected. Legislators were determined to create something unique, so they did not consider either a full-fledged unified metropolitan government or a council of government (COG). The nation's first COG had been formed in the Detroit metropolitan area in 1957. By 1965 there were ten, and within another five years more than three hundred. To Minnesota's lawmakers their main shortcoming was that memberships of governments within their areas were voluntary.

With the intention of developing comprehensive planning and coordination for the seven-county metropolitan area, the legislators carefully delineated the nature of the Metropolitan Council. The resultant agency, whose members were to be appointed by the governor, was not a general-purpose metropolitan government, a COG, or a local government. Rather, it was an agency that reported to the state. Yet its creators bestowed it with considerable power, because it was authorized to review local government plans and ultimately to approve or reject them.

Within its first two decades the Metropolitan Council's authority was defined by about a dozen laws, which had the overall effect of increasing its power in such areas as park and open-space planning, housing, mass transit, solid and hazardous waste, sewage disposal, and airport and sports-facilities planning. The Metropolitan Council has certainly met, if not exceeded, the expectations of its founders. It has been widely hailed for its innovation and has been nationally and internationally studied by societies coping with rampant metropolitanism.

LeVander's decision not to seek reelection opened the way for the resurgence of a surprisingly unified DFL, which seemingly had relegated the recent Keith-Rolvaag and Humphrey-McCarthy battles to the dustbins of history. The party was certainly helped by McCarthy's unwillingness to seek a third senatorial term. To many people both inside and outside the DFL, McCarthy was the villain of 1968, who had denied the presidency to a fellow Minnesotan. His voluntary removal gave Humphrey an unchallenged opportunity to reenter the Senate. Humphrey easily won his fourth Senate election in 1970 and his immense popularity also helped the DFL recapture the governorship.

In naming its gubernatorial candidate, the DFL displayed its second generation. All the serious contenders and the eventual nominee, Wendell R. Anderson, were relatively young men who had not been associated with the first great DFL success in 1948. Anderson, of St. Paul, who was only thirty-seven years old, had enjoyed great success in both athletics and politics. He was an All-American hockey player at the University of Minnesota and a member of the 1956 United States Olympic team. He was first elected to the state House of Representatives in 1959, the year before he was admitted to the Minnesota bar. After serving four years in the House, he emerged as one of the Senate's leaders during his eight years in that body.

To the surprise of many, Anderson defeated the Republican nominee, Douglas M. Head, a progressive who was the incumbent state attorney general, in the general election and then faced the challenge of working with a conservative legislature for the first half of his first term. In 1972 the DFL for the first time gained control of both legislative houses, but by then Anderson had achieved what came to be publicized as "the

Minnesota Miracle." During the campaign he had endorsed a Citizens League proposal to raise some taxes with the aim of shifting more of the costs of public elementary and secondary education from localities to the state.

Changes enacted in 1971 had the overall effect of increasing state power while diminishing the role of localities. Some taxes, including the consistently popular "sin taxes" on liquor and cigarettes and corporate and personal property taxes, were increased and a penny was added to the existing three-cent sales tax. With $558 million in new revenue, the state was able to increase state aid for education from 43 to 70 percent within a biennium and to lower property taxes by about one-tenth. The revised school-aid formula, by virtue of narrowing disparities between rich and poor districts, had significant social consequences. Anderson and the DFL naturally took credit for these major changes, and Republican efforts to dub the governor "Spendy Wendy" had little impact.

In 1973 the legislature abandoned its sixty-year experiment with non-partisanship. The idea of restoring party designations had been generally endorsed by DFL leaders since it was advocated by Governor Freeman. Subsequently, the League of Women Voters recommended repeal of the 1913 law, and during the 1960s, party-designation planks were included in both DFL and Republican platforms. Critics attacked nonpartisanship as being essentially hypocritical, because conservative and liberal caucuses were really composed of Republicans and DFLers, respectively. Both parties also believed the change would help discipline the occasional mavericks, who resisted party affiliation. However, the 1973 act was mainly supported by DFLers, who had actually changed their name from the Liberal Caucus to the DFL Caucus in 1969. After DFLers gained control of both legislative chambers for the first time in the election of 1972, they sensed a political advantage in using party designations.

Anderson's early success and his personal popularity not only gave the DFL unprecedented control but also attracted national publicity for the state. Minnesota, which has consistently ranked near the top in national quality-of-life surveys, was featured in *Time* magazine of August 13, 1973. With a cover showing Anderson, garbed in a lumberjack shirt, holding up a fish at a state lake and an article story titled "Minnesota: A State That Works," the North Star State's glories were revealed to millions of readers. Along with the many plaudits for the state's progressiveness, vibrant economy, and friendliness, *Time* extolled Anderson, whose future, it ventured, "may be larger than Minnesota." Anderson was described as a possible vice presidential candidate in 1976 who as a young midwestern Protestant governor "might elegantly complement a Ted Kennedy candidacy."[3] Subsequent events underscored the hazards in speculating about the future.

Women's influence was significant in Minnesota's politics and society by the time of Anderson's governorship. The women's movement was fueled by some events of the turbulent 1960s. Some women's groups, notably the American Association for University Women and the Business and Professional Women's Clubs, which had sought an Equal Rights Amendment to the federal constitution as early as the Truman administration, convinced President John F. Kennedy to establish the President's Commission on the Status of Women. That action, along with the Equal Pay Act of 1963 and the Civil Rights Act of 1964, which, among many other things, outlawed sexual basis discrimination, affected all states.

In 1965 Governor Rolvaag, at the urging of the President's Commission on the Status of Women and state women's groups, created a Minnesota Commission on the Status of Women. Significantly, a study done by that organization in its first year concluded that widespread discrimination against women existed in such areas as employment, equal pay, maternity benefits, and admission to professional schools at the University of Minnesota.

Nationwide, the women's movement was spurred by the formation of the National Organization for Women (NOW) in 1966, and by women's roles in the black civil rights movement and the anti–Vietnam War protests. In Minnesota DFL women who had supported McCarthy in 1968 were particularly outspoken about the Vietnam issue. The Minnesota NOW chapter, which was dedicated to winning legislative ratification of the Equal Rights Amendment, was formed in 1970. That organization, with essential support from the recently organized DFL and GOP feminist caucuses, enlisted strong bipartisan support for the measure, which was approved by the legislature in 1973, the year after Congress passed it. Minnesota's quick and enthusiastic acceptance of the amendment, which ultimately failed to be ratified by the required thirty-eight states, helped reinforce the state's progressive reputation.

As the women's movement raised public consciousness of women's contributions, roles, and history, more women began to run for and win political office. In 1970 there was only one woman serving in the Minnesota legislature, but five years later there were eight. In 1974, with the election of DFLer Joan Anderson Growe as secretary of state, Minnesota for only the second time in its history had a woman constitutional officer. Historian Marjorie Bingham attributed Minnesota's extensive activity in the women's movement in the early 1970s to "a progressive attitude toward reform; strong 'traditional' women's groups that provided networks and experience; a large university located in a metropolitan area; a high level of women's education; economic prosperity; and several private foundations, like the Northwest Area and Amherst H. Wilder foundations, which provided funding for innovative programs."[4]

In 1974, when Wendell R. Anderson was swept into a second term by a better than two to one margin over his Republican opponent, the GOP nationally was in disarray. As the most significant outcome of the Watergate scandal, President Richard M. Nixon resigned effective August 9, 1974. His party suffered the consequences in the elections of 1974 and 1976. The political fallout from Watergate caused the progressives who still dominated the GOP in Minnesota to disassociate themselves somewhat from the Republican image. In 1975 they formally changed the Minnesota's party's name to Independent Republican.

The GOP rebounded from Watergate far faster than was generally anticipated in 1974. In Minnesota this resurgence was aided by a colossal DFL blunder after the election of Carter and Mondale. When Mondale resigned his Senate seat preparatory to assuming the vice presidency, Governor Anderson resigned, and his successor, former lieutenant governor Rudolph G. Perpich, appointed him to complete Mondale's term. Meaningful public reaction, whose real impact was delayed until the election of 1978, was extremely critical of this pragmatic arrangement.

Coincidentally, when Anderson ran for a full term in 1978, both of Minnesota's seats in the Senate were open because of Humphrey's death on January 13, 1978. Governor Perpich appointed Humphrey's widow, Muriel, to the Senate until the election in November 1978 of a replacement for the four remaining years of Humphrey's term.

The unusual situation of both Senate seats being contested simultaneously, combined with the election of state officers, gave the IRs a marvelous opportunity as Watergate was dimming in the public mind, conservatism was rapidly becoming more appealing, and many Minnesotans were still irked by Anderson's caper. The IRs achieved a smashing victory—dubbed "the Minnesota Massacre" by some of the media—in the general election by winning both Senate positions and the governorship. Rudolph E. Boschwitz, a millionaire plywood merchant and longtime party activist, bested Anderson, and David F. Durenberger defeated Robert Short for the remainder of the Humphrey term. Albert H. Quie, who had represented Minnesota's First District in Congress for slightly more than ten terms, was chosen governor over Perpich.

The election results dealt with public rejection of the "ins" and acceptance of the "outs" as well as political philosophy. Both the IR and the DFL had liberal and conservative wings. Durenberger, who had served as Governor LeVander's executive secretary, was a progressive with backing from a number of "Democrats for Durenberger" and Independents. Boschwitz's conservatism was masked by his just-plain-Rudy image, replete with characteristic plaid shirts and homey radio and television ads. Quie, a Stassen-type progressive, had long been known as a champion of public education. Significantly, IR unity transcended the different ideologies of its candidates. While Anderson and Perpich were endorsed candidates, they had both been wounded by the senatorial appointment.

In the other Senate race, Durenberger was aided by a bitter DFL battle between the liberal Donald M. Fraser, who had served in the national House of Representatives for eight successive terms, and businessman Robert E. Short, well remembered for bucking the party to run with Rolvaag in 1966. Fraser had satisfied DFL liberals with his congressional votes, and as the endorsed candidate took a strong environmental stand by supporting the Boundary Waters Canoe Area Act of 1978, by which Congress banned logging, mining, and snowmobiling and curtailed motorboating in three wilderness areas within the Superior National Forest. While Fraser's stance pleased wilderness advocates, it offended many northern Minnesotans, who believed in development rather than wilderness preservation and resented what they regarded as interference from Twin Cities elitists. The overriding impact of the wilderness issue was evident by the primary results. Out of 511,087 ballots, Short won by only a 3,451-vote margin, with the greatest rejection of Fraser occurring in the traditionally DFL-dominated counties closest to the designated wilderness. For example, in St. Louis, the most populous county containing part of the Boundary Waters Canoe Area, Short outpolled Fraser by 38,090 to 14,062. Conversely, voters in metropolitan Hennepin County favored Fraser by 82,972 to 41,980 votes. Short also benefited from support from antiabortionists and thousands of IR crossover votes, only to fall easy prey to Durenberger in the general election.

Among other things, the 1978 election demonstrated that the GOP was taking a sharp turn to the Right. Long resentful of Stassen and

Eisenhower progressivism, many staunch conservatives had not had a hero since 1964, when Arizona Senator Barry M. Goldwater was the Republican presidential candidate. However, in 1976 a significant portion of Minnesota's delegation to the GOP National Convention showed their strong endorsement of western conservatism by supporting former California governor Ronald W. Reagan's presidential bid. Although incumbent President Gerald R. Ford was nominated, Reagan and California both gained stature in the conservative movement.

Conservatism, with its dedication to traditional laissez-faire economic policies, was intensified in the 1970s by several developments. California's famous Proposition 13 of 1978, which imposed property-tax reductions, fueled an antitax rebellion nationwide. Conservatives emphasized that reducing government income was the most effective way of eliminating bureaucratic waste and mismanagement and needless social programs. Moral aspects of conservatism featured strong reactions to the alleged liberal excesses of the sixties with respect to gay and women's rights and permissiveness in treating criminals and controlling drug use. Likewise, especially the antiabortion evangelical Christian component of the conservatives targeted the Supreme Court, mainly because of its *Roe v. Wade* decision.

During Quie's administration new militantly conservative legislators fought to reduce taxes. While sympathetic to modest income-tax reductions, Quie did not want to risk jeopardizing support for public education and major social programs. At any given time Quie had more problems with some members of his own party than with DFLers. Philosophical differences over the proper role of government were complicated because inflation regularly boosted individuals into higher income-tax brackets and by the arcane art of revenue forecasting.

As a way of limiting the income-tax burden Quie supported automatic inflation adjustments, which would have the effect of raising bracket ceilings and save taxpayers from being arbitrarily subjected to a higher percentage tax. Indexing, as the adjustments were called, was enacted by the legislature in 1979 after lengthy and sometimes heated debate. The gentlemanly Quie, who obviously would have been more comfortable in a consensus-building environment, seemed shocked by the legislature's angry rhetoric. As state revenues and expenditures were subjected to intense scrutiny, revenue forecasting became all-important. When some of the Quie administration's overly optimistic projections were unrealized, the state was confronted with budget crises that forced cutbacks in state agencies and educational institutions.

Conservative impact during Quie's governorship reflected national trends. Reagan's election as president in 1980 helped prove the popularity of the determination to shrink government revenues. The lessons of Quie's difficulties and Reagan's success were not lost on politicians such as former governor Rudy Perpich, who realized that to make a comeback he had to adjust to the new realities of the early 1980s. Thus, Minnesotans in 1982 were introduced to the new Rudy. As Anderson's

Rosalie E. Wahl, appointed in 1977, was the first woman to serve on the
Minnesota Supreme Court.
Courtesy of the Minnesota Historical Society

successor Perpich had been noted for several uniquenesses. A native of Hibbing, he was the state's first Roman Catholic governor, the first governor from the iron range, and, in a state noted for the success of its Scandinavian-American politicians, a second-generation Croatian-American.

After his defeat in 1978 an embittered Perpich left politics and, for a time, Minnesota. As a vice president of World Tech, Inc., a subsidiary of the Twin Cities–based Control Data Corporation, Perpich represented the firm in Eastern Europe. This experience, he was able to claim, had given him a greater understanding and appreciation of the world of business, which he could put to good use as governor. His corporate association also helped to ameliorate Perpich's earlier reputation as a doctrinaire antibusiness DFL liberal.

The characteristically unconventional Perpich challenged Attorney General Warren R. Spannus, the DFL-endorsed gubernatorial candidate, in the primary and won. Perpich had taken the unprecedented step of naming a woman, Marlene Johnson, who had distinguished herself as an officer in various business organizations, to be his running mate. With broadened appeal to business, women, and the DFL antiabortionists, he easily defeated his Republican opponent in the 1982 general election. With their party's support, Perpich and Johnson were reelected by a wide margin four years later. During his second elected term Perpich gained the distinction of becoming the longest-serving governor in the history of Minnesota.

Defying a precise ideological label, Perpich blended conservatism and liberalism. Stressing economic growth, he became the state's greatest salesman. At a time when the legislature regularly debated improving the state's "business climate," Perpich fought to keep businesses in the state and to attract new enterprises. His promotion of a megamall in Bloomington, which resulted in the Mall of America, attracted much attention, as did his unsuccessful efforts to lure General Motor's Saturn automobile plant to Minnesota and to open a chopstick factory for the Chinese market in his hometown. Perpich did more than any previous governor to bring women into his administration and the court system. He frequently appointed women to head state government departments, and in 1977 he appointed the first woman—Rosalie E. Wahl, a professor of law at William Mitchell College of Law—to the state supreme court. By the time he left office in January 1991, women were in a majority on the court. While generally satisfying the business community, Perpich retained support of organized labor by vetoing several legislative attempts to curtail workers' benefits.

Although Perpich was the dominant figure in Minnesota politics during most of the 1980s, the GOP fared well. Durenberger was reelected to the Senate by wide margins in 1982 and 1988, and conservatives were especially pleased by the election results of 1984. Reagan mounted a serious challenge to Mondale for Minnesota's electoral votes and Boschwitz turned back the challenge of DFL Senate candidate Joan Anderson Growe. Growe's nomination was indicative of the increasingly significant role of women in the DFL. Prior to her nomination, party leaders agreed that their candidate should be a woman. In the legislature an additional infusion of what was coming to be called the Christian Right enabled the GOP to win a narrow majority in the House of Representatives, thereby setting off renewed calls to slash taxes and cut welfare programs.

Strong antitax sentiment was a major factor in forcing the legislature to seek alternative revenue sources. State taxes on some forms of legalized gambling and a state lottery emerged as the most appealing possibilities. Until the 1980s Minnesota had a well-established reputation as an antigambling state. The state's constitutional ban on gambling was modified somewhat by a 1945 law that permitted nonprofit bingo by charitable, fraternal, and religious organizations. This so-called "church bingo" was the only form of legalized gambling when Governor Youngdahl declared war on slot machines and roulette wheels. The bingo law, under a 1978 act, was amended to permit paddlewheels, tipboards, and raffles, and in 1981 pull-tabs were legalized.

Advocates of expanded gambling first promoted pari-mutuel betting on horse racing. They contended that the addition of the "sport of kings" would not only enrich recreational opportunities for Minnesotans but would also be a significant revenue source and would stimulate a state "horse industry." Curiously, their model was a horse track in Winnipeg, Manitoba, Canada, that was on the verge of bankruptcy.

Following an intense media campaign, voters were persuaded to amend the state constitution in 1982 to permit pari-mutuel betting on horse racing. Canterbury Downs, the track opened at Shakopee in 1985, was initially successful, but by the end of its fifth season had failed financially. Much of its decline was caused by competition from bingo parlors on Indian land, which had likewise been authorized in 1982.

As Canterbury Downs was struggling, gambling was expanded greatly by the beginning of a state lottery and a series of state contracts with Indian tribes to permit casino gambling on reservations. The lottery, which was authorized by a constitutional amendment approved in 1988, was started in April 1990. Casino gambling on reservations resulted from the congressional passage of the Indian Gaming Regulatory Act of October 17, 1988, which was intended to promote tribal economies. Minnesota was the first state to negotiate agreements with tribes that were authorized by the law.

The rapid gambling surge profoundly and rapidly changed Minnesota society. By 1990 the state ranked fourth after Nevada, New Jersey, and South Dakota in per capita gambling sales. The popularity of gambling was evident in a recent poll that showed that 87 percent of Minnesota's adults had participated in some form of gambling, with Indian casino gambling as the leading type, a position it had held since 1991. The state's seventeen Indian casinos offer the advantages of year-round operation, Vegas-type gambling, celebrity entertainment, restaurants, and sometimes nearby lodging. As the casinos, especially those easily accessible from the metropolitan area, have boomed, there has been continued strong participation in the lottery and other forms of legalized gambling, which until 1985 were called charitable gambling. Canterbury Downs, which has been the big loser, has changed ownership three times. However, with new owners and a new name—Canterbury Park—and temporary tax relief from the legislature, it shows some promise of becoming a profitable venture.

Recent legislatures, reflecting a somewhat cautious public mood, have been reluctant to authorize additional forms of gambling, such as pull-tabs, in bars and off-track horse-race betting parlors. Although hesitant to legalize more types of gambling, Minnesotans relish what they have. A recent survey by the *St. Paul Pioneer Press* showed that Minnesotans waged $3.5 billion annually at Indian casinos and $1.2 billion on other forms of gambling, excluding the lottery and pari-mutuel betting. In assessing the scope of gambling, the paper observed that "People make more visits to casinos than they do Twins and Vikings games, the symphony and the theater combined. They bet nearly twice as much money as the state spends on public education. And they're not about to stop."[5]

Allied effects of gambling include attraction of tourists and, as critics are fond of observing, the operation of six state-subsidized compulsive-gambling treatment centers. Concern about the long-range future of gambling prompted the recent legislative creation of the Governor's

Advisory Council on Gambling to study its social and economic impact.

Although Perpich himself had misgivings about gambling, its explosion will always be associated with his administration. But Perpich will also be remembered as a hard-working, imaginative promoter whose sometimes quixotic notions took their political toll. His standing in the polls dropped sharply after his reelection in 1986. His public image suffered, in part because of his quarreling with the media. In 1988 at the governor's mansion he crankily responded to media questioning about his family's lifestyle and speculation about whether he was coloring his graying hair. Well known for his eccentricities, he amazed even his many critics by successfully negotiating a visit to Minnesota in 1990 by Soviet President Mikhail Gorbachev. Despite considerable DFL opposition, Perpich prevailed in the primary election, but was defeated by the moderate Independent Republican candidate Arne H. Carlson in the general election.

Carlson, copying the Perpich model, selected a woman—Joanell M. Dyrstad, former mayor of Red Wing—as his running mate. Although Carlson favored abortion rights, his victory resulted mainly from public disenchantment with Perpich. Significantly, as the voters were rejecting Perpich they also voted out Republican United States Senator Rudy Boschwitz. Boschwitz, a fiscal conservative who had served twelve years in the Senate, fell to political newcomer Paul D. Wellstone, a Carleton College political science professor. Considering the impressive conservative gains starting in 1978, Boschwitz's defeat was surprising. Wellstone's enthusiastic, upbeat campaign and a major tactical error by Boschwitz were decisive factors in the close contest. In retrospect, both the gubernatorial and senatorial elections, which featured thousands of split ballots, seemed to be influenced primarily by a pronounced antiincumbent vote rather than by political ideologies.

Subsequent events made Boschwitz's defeat seem even more aberrational than it did in 1990. Dominance of Independent Republican precinct caucuses by the Christian Right and other dedicated conservatives in 1994 led to the party's endorsement of Allen Quist for governor. Quist, from St. Peter, who had served in the state House of Representatives for three terms, 1983–89, forced Carlson to shift more to the Right. Before facing Quist in the primary election, Carlson selected Joanne E. Benson of St. Cloud as his running mate. His ostensible reason for replacing Dyrstad with Benson was that Dyrstad wanted to run for the United States Senate seat being vacated by the retiring David

Durenberger. However, there was a widespread belief that Benson was chosen because she was more conservative than Dyrstad on the abortion issue, and would better help curb Quist's bid. Appealing to Independents and moderate Independent Republicans, Carlson and Benson won the primary by a two-to-one margin.

In the primary, Dyrstad's Senate bid was thwarted by conservative Rod Grams, a former Twin Cities television news anchorman who was serving in his first term in the national House of Representatives. Running an effective campaign against the bigness of the federal government, Grams outpolled Ann Wynia, the DFL nominee, in the general election.

Swept into office as part of the loudly trumpeted "Republican Revolution of 1994," Grams soon emerged as one of the Senate's most conservative members. He stood in sharp contrast to Wellstone, who had established a record for himself as one of the most liberal senators. Grams's victory, further anticipated conservative gains, and the belief that the embarrassment of Watergate was far behind them were all reasons that stimulated the IRs to change their party's name back to Republican at their 1995 convention.

While public attention was focused on Wellstone and Grams, Minnesota women achieved unprecedented political stature. Benson was the third successive woman to be elected lieutenant governor, and in 1993 Sharon Sayles Belton was elected mayor of Minneapolis, thereby gaining the distinction of being the first woman and the first black to hold that position. Increasing numbers of women were elected to the legislature. In 1995–96 they comprised nearly one fourth of its total membership.

In Minnesota and nationwide, Republicans tended to regard their 1994 successes as a foretelling prelude to the presidential-year elections of 1996. But President Clinton, by shifting closer to the center, demonizing conservatives on social and environmental issues, and the government shutdown of 1995, rebounded sharply. Throughout the 1996 campaign he regularly led GOP nominee Robert J. Dole in Minnesota polls by more than twenty points and was easily reelected by winning Minnesota's vote and that of thirty other states and the District of Columbia on November 5, 1996.

While there was little suspense in the presidential campaign, Minnesota's senatorial contest was fiercely contested between the incumbent Wellstone and challenger Rudy Boschwitz. Boschwitz, who had alienated staunch conservatives, failed to win Republican endorsement,

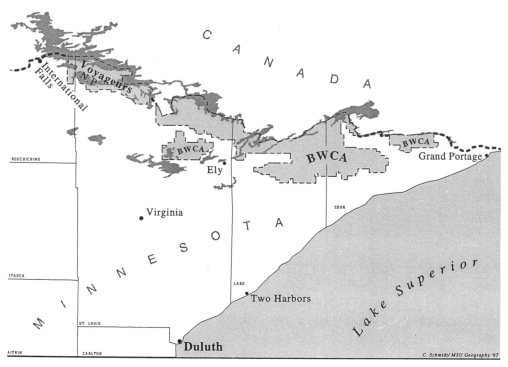

Boundary Waters Canoe Area and Voyageurs National Park

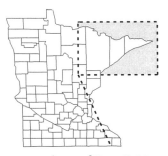

Area of Detail Map

C. Schmidt/ MSU Geography '97

but had enough support to block the endorsement of the most conservative aspirant at the state convention. Boschwitz was campaigning against Wellstone even before easily winning the primary and becoming the Republican candidate.

During his campaign Boschwitz worked hard to attract the support of Independents and moderates in both parties by portraying himself as a commonsensical fiscal conservative who opposed federal welfare programs, and Wellstone as the quintessential ultraliberal who was outside the political mainstream of the 1990s. Wellstone countered that the federal government had to have a social conscience. Appealing particularly to women, senior citizens, and lower- and middle-income voters, Wellstone surged late in the campaign to win decisively. The candidacy of the Reform Party's Dean M. Barkley, who garnered 7 percent of the vote, probably helped to widen Wellstone's margin. Wellstone's victory did not result from a liberal resurgence since 1994. Rather, many swing voters seemed to have been offended by what they perceived as Boschwitz's highly negative campaign. So, as in the first Boschwitz-Wellstone contest of 1990, the outcome was not determined primarily by political ideologies.

Throughout the senatorial campaign, environmental issues that undoubtedly have implications for a future well beyond the political careers of Boschwitz and Wellstone commanded public attention. The controversies involved the wilderness status of two areas in northernmost Minnesota—the Boundary Waters Canoe Area (BWCA) and Voyageurs National Park. The BWCA, comprising 1,075,000 acres (about 1,680 square miles) within Superior National Forest, evolved from a series of federal administrative decisions, congressional acts, and presidential executive orders after the General Land Office first reserved half a million acres from private acquisition in 1902. These actions had the cumulative effect of creating and expanding three roadless areas in which motors, including those of aircraft, were banned. In 1958, after increasing public support for the wilderness concept, the roadless areas and some adjoining and nearby tracts were designated as the Boundary Waters Canoe Area.

The rapid pace of urbanization nationally boosted public support for wilderness preserves—areas where there would be no permanent residents and the solitude of nature would be assured by banning motors. After the congressional passage of the Wilderness Act in 1964, its strongest supporters campaigned to extend the wilderness concept in the BWCA. Their efforts to further restrict access of motorboats and snowmobiles nat-

urally conflicted with those of many local fishing guides and resort owners. The clash of the wilderness proponents and multiple-use advocates
was not only acrimonious but split Minnesota's congressional delegation
and contributed to the Minnesota Massacre of 1978—the defeat of
prominent DFLers who supported wilderness expansion.

Despite the political fallout in Minnesota, the federal Boundary
Waters Canoe Act of 1978 was a major triumph for wilderness supporters. It provided that motorboat use was to be cut from 62 to 24 percent
of the BWCA's water area and that only two permanent snowmobile trails
into Canada could remain open. Because it was generally believed that the
changes would detrimentally affect local businesses, the law promised
them some financial relief to adjust to the new reality. Since the BWCA
Act the motor ban had been extended to several portages as a result of
court decisions.

Voyageurs National Park, centered on the Kabetogama Peninsula
between Rainy and Kabetogama Lakes, was created by Congress in 1975.
Consisting of approximately 218,000 acres, most of the park was established as a virtual roadless area accessible only by watercraft or snowmobiles. Most local residents have long favored a multiple-use park that they
insist would better stimulate their economy. But various environmental
organizations have contended that much of the park should be granted
wilderness status. In 1991 the National Park Service prepared a study featuring various wilderness scenarios for the park, and in the spring of 1996
Representative Bruce F. Vento, of Minnesota's fourth congressional district (St. Paul and nearby suburbs), proposed that most of the
Kabetogama Peninsula be designated as wilderness.

Vento's idea clashed with the goals of his DFL colleague—
Representative James L. Oberstar, who has represented Minnesota's
eighth congressional district since 1975. Oberstar, in supporting his multiple-use constituents in the BWCA and Voyageurs National Park areas,
advocated a partial reversal of wilderness policies. He proposed to permit
complete motorboat access to four major BWCA lakes that were only partially open under the 1978 law and to allow trucks to transport boats on
three portages. To assure local interests, a strong role in determining
BWCA and Voyageurs policies and management, Oberstar further proposed that separate oversight councils be created for both areas. Oberstar's
plans were supported by Senator Grams, who introduced a companion
measure in the Senate.

Possible consideration of the Oberstar and Grams bills in an election year was not lost on Senator Paul D. Wellstone, who would certainly have lost political support if he either supported or opposed them. Finessing the issue, Wellstone got the Federal Mediation and Conciliation Service to referee the deliberations of separate committees for the BWCA and Voyageurs. The committees, with representatives of both wilderness and multiple-use advocates, began meeting in September 1996. Their deliberations, which have been characterized by hard-line stands on both sides, have become regular media fare. President Clinton's announcement that he would veto any bill that opened the three key BWCA portages to truck use at least forestalled congressional acceptance of that specific proposal until after the 1996 election.

The fate of wilderness in the BWCA and Voyageurs revived interest in the politics of environmentalism to a degree not seen since the dumping of taconite tailings into Lake Superior by Reserve Mining. Predictably, the quarrel has sectional overtones. Most multiple-use supporters live near the BWCA and Voyageurs, and most wilderness advocates are from the Twin Cities metropolitan area. Consequently, many local multiple-use believers bitterly complain about outside interference by urbanites who speed away on modern highways from fast-paced metropolitan life to an environment reminiscent of the pre–industrial age. Statewide, recent polls have indicated that 70 percent of Minnesotans support the present status of wilderness in the BWCA.

Aside from the obvious environmental question, the Grams and Oberstar bills touch on the essence of determining public policy in a federal union. Local involvement in making and implementing policies, its supporters claim, is fundamentally democratic. However, critics have been quick to respond that both the BWCA and Voyageurs National Park are federal reserves, which should be managed by central government policies without local interference. In an era in which federal government bashing has become especially fashionable in areas where most of the land is owned by the United States, there seems to be no easy solution. Since the BWCA wilderness is the most heavily visited wilderness area in the nation, the economic stakes over its use are extremely high.

In a broad sense, the wilderness controversy exemplifies the dilemma of modern Minnesota, which, like that of the nation, hangs suspended between the past and the future. Science and technology over the years have extended nature's resources and made them more usable; conservation and preservation have saved some last vestiges of natural and wilderness areas, and yet even the most ardent wilderness advocates recognize that many of the good and beautiful things in present society exist not because resources were conserved but because they were used. The question remaining today, then, is not a simple one of either totally preserving what is left or using it up, but rather of arriving at a balance between the two. The problem, though national and international in scope, is particularly significant in Minnesota, where metropolitanism and wilderness are but hours apart.

Using the recent past as their guide, demographers predict that urbanization in Minnesota will accelerate. As this occurs, more and more of the state's residents will live in an urban corridor extending from St. Cloud on the northwest through the Twin Cities to Rochester on the southeast. Many members of this likely twenty-first-century society will undoubtedly relish the idea of being able to at least temporarily transform themselves physically and spiritually by experiencing the wilderness. Minnesota's history has set its direction. Future Minnesota society, with experience gleaned from its past, will have to make decisions that aim to keep nature and technology and people's needs and desires in balance.

NOTES

INTERLUDE: THE VIKING MYTH

1. Erik Wahlgren, *The Kensington Stone: A Mystery Solved* (Madison: University of Wisconsin Press, 1958), 3.
2. Hjalmar Holand, "The Kensington Rune Stone Abroad," *Records of the Past* 10 (September–October 1911), as quoted in Milo M. Quaife, "The Myth of the Kensington Rune Stone: The Norse Discovery of Minnesota," *New England Quarterly* 7 (December 1934): 619.
3. Quaife, "Myth of Kensington Rune Stone," 619–20.
4. Wahlgren, *Kensington Stone*, 5.
5. Thomas R. Henry, "The Smithsonian Institution," *National Geographic* 94 (September 1948): 343.
6. Blegen, in his book *The Kensington Rune Stone: New Light on an Old Riddle* (St. Paul: Minnesota Historical Society, 1968), 124, refers to tapes that he had never heard but that he believed would clarify the origins of the stone. A transcript of part of those tapes, strongly supporting the hoax rumor, was published in "The Case of the Gran Tapes: Further Evidence on the Rune Stone Riddle," *Minnesota History* 45 (Winter 1976): 152–56.
7. Brigitta Linderoth, "The Kensington Stone: A Review Essay," *The Old Northwest* (1984), 10:477.
8. "Some Points of Controversy," in *The Quest for America* (New York: Praeger Publishers, 1971), 155–74; and "Viking Hoaxes," in *Vikings in the West*, Eleanor Guralnick, ed. (Chicago: The Archaeological Institute of America, Chicago Society, 1982), 53–76.
9. Wahlgren, *Kensington Stone*, 181.

CHAPTER 2: EUROPEANS IN THE WILDERNESS

1. Louise Phelps Kellogg, *The French Régime in Wisconsin and the Northwest* (Madison: State Historical Society of Wisconsin, 1925), 78.
2. [Pierre Esprit Radisson], *The Explorations of Pierre Esprit Radisson,* ed. Arthur T. Adams (Minneapolis: Ross & Haines, 1961), 134.
3. Quoted in Kellogg, *French Régime,* 113.
4. Pierre Esprit Radisson. "The Western Lakes Region in Summer," in *With Various Voices: Recordings of North Star Life,* comps. Theodore C. Blegen and Philip D. Jordan (St. Paul: Itasca Press, 1949), 4.
5. Kellogg, *French Régime,* 242.
6. Kellogg, *French Régime,* 350.
7. Theodore C. Blegen, *The Land Lies Open* (Minneapolis: University of Minnesota Press, 1949), 57.
8. *The Journal of Jonathan Carver and Related Documents, 1766–1770,* ed. John Parker (St. Paul: Minnesota Historical Society Press, 1976), 132.
9. J[onathan] Carver, *Travels through the Interior Parts of North America, in the Years 1766, 1767, and 1768,* 3rd ed. (London, 1781; reprint ed., Minneapolis: Ross & Haines, 1956), 105.
10. Carver, *Travels,* 55.
11. Carver, *Travels,* 100.
12. Carver, *Travels,* 121.
13. "The Narrative of Peter Pond," in *Five Fur Traders of the Northwest,* ed. Charles M. Gates (Minneapolis: University of Minnesota Press, 1933; reprint ed., St. Paul: Minnesota Historical Society, 1965), 56.

CHAPTER 3: AMERICAN ASCENDANCY

1. Hunter Miller, ed., *Treaties and Other International Acts of the United States of America* (Washington, D.C.: Government Printing Office, 1931–48), 2:97.
2. William Watts Folwell, *A History of Minnesota,* 4 vols., rev. ed. (St. Paul: Minnesota Historical Society, 1956–69), 1:98.
3. Henry R. Schoolcraft, *Narrative Journal of Travels Through the Northwestern Regions of the United States* (Albany: E. & E. Hosford, 1821), 251.
4. J. C. Beltrami, *A Pilgrimage in America* (1828; reprint ed., Chicago: Quadrangle Books, 1962), 413.
5. [Henry R. Schoolcraft], *Schoolcraft's Expedition to Lake Itasca: The Discovery of the Source of the Mississippi,* ed. Philip P. Mason (East Lansing: Michigan State University Press, 1958), 35.
6. [Schoolcraft], *Lake Itasca,* 35.
7. H. H. Sibley, "Reminiscences: Historical and Personal," in *Minnesota Historical Society Collections* (St. Paul: The Society, 1872), 1:466–67.

CHAPTER 4: MINNESOTA'S QUEST FOR EMPIRE

1. J. Fletcher Williams, *A History of the City of Saint Paul and the County of Ramsey, Minnesota*, Minnesota Historical Society Collections (St. Paul: The Society, 1876), 4:465.

2. Williams, *Saint Paul*, 85.

3. Williams, *Saint Paul*, 111.

4. Quoted in Williams, *Saint Paul*, 113.

5. Quoted in Milo M. Quaife, ed., *The Convention of 1846*, State Historical Society of Wisconsin Collections (Madison: The Society, 1919), 17:565.

6. "Memorial of the Citizens of Minnesota," March 28, 1848, *Sen. Misc. Doc.* 98, 30th Cong., 1st sess.

7. "Organization of Minnesota Territory," in Minnesota Historical Society Collections (St. Paul: The Society, 1872), 1:55.

8. *Minnesota Pioneer* (St. Paul), February 13, 1850, 3.

9. *Minnesota Pioneer*, March 6, 1850, 2.

10. Quoted in Folwell, *History of Minnesota,* 1:304.

11. Quoted in Russell W. Fridley, "When Minnesota Coveted Canada," *Minnesota History* 41 (Summer 1968): 77.

CHAPTER 5: TRIALS OF STATEHOOD

1. John B. Thompson, "Southern Opposition to Statehood," in *With Various Voices*, 94–95.

2. Quoted in Folwell, *History of Minnesota*, 2:212.

3. Nathaniel West, *The Ancestry, Life and Times of Hon. Henry Hastings Sibley, LL.D.* (St. Paul: Pioneer Press Publishing Co., 1889), 263.

4. Quoted in Folwell, *History of Minnesota*, 2:176n.

5. Quoted in William E. Lass, "The Removal from Minnesota of the Sioux and Winnebago Indians," *Minnesota History* 38 (December 1963): 364.

CHAPTER 6: PEOPLING THE LAND

1. Quoted in Harold F. Peterson, "Early Minnesota Railroads and the Quest for Settlers," *Minnesota History* 13 (March 1932): 34.

2. *Minnesota Pioneer*, June 5, 1851, quoted in Mary Wheelhouse Berthel, *Horns of Thunder: The Life and Times of James M. Goodhue, Including Selections from His Writings* (St. Paul: Minnesota Historical Society, 1948), 86–87.

3. Hans Mattson, *Reminiscences: The Story of an Emigrant* (St. Paul: D. D. Merrill Co., 1892), 110.

4. Quoted in George M. Stephenson, "When America was the Land of Canaan," *Minnesota History* 10 (September 1929): 247.

5. Stephenson, "Land of Canaan," 238.

6. Quoted in Helen Clapesattle, "When Minnesota was Florida's Rival," *Minnesota History* 35 (March 1957): 215.

7. Brewer Mattocks, *Minnesota as a Home for Invalids* (Philadelphia: J. B. Lippincott Co., 1871), 147.

CHAPTER 7: THREE FRONTIERS

1. G. W. Schatzel, "The Wheat Fields of Minnesota," in *With Various Voices,* 143.

2. Quoted in Charles Byron Kuhlmann, *The Development of the Flour-Milling Industry in the United States with Special Reference to the Industry in Minneapolis* (Boston: Houghton Mifflin Co., 1929), 119.

3. Quoted in William G. Edgar, *The Medal of Gold: A Story of Industrial Achievement* (Minneapolis: The Bellman Co., 1925), 106–107.

4. Quoted in Edgar, *Medal of Gold,* 112.

5. Quoted in Everett E. Edwards and Horace H. Russell, "Wendelin Grimm and Alfalfa," *Minnesota History* 19 (March 1938): 22.

6. *Minnesota Pioneer,* April 8, 1852, as quoted in Berthel, *Horns of Thunder,* 81.

7. Quoted in Agnes M. Larson, *History of the White Pine Industry in Minnesota* (Minneapolis: University of Minnesota Press, 1949), 70.

8. *St. Paul and Minneapolis Pioneer Press,* December 24, 1880, as quoted in Minnesota Department of Conservation, Division of Forestry, *A History of Forestry in Minnesota with Particular Reference to Forestry Legislation* (St. Paul, 1965), 7.

CHAPTER 8: A LEGACY OF PROTEST POLITICS

1. Quoted in John D. Hicks, *The Populist Revolt: A History of the Farmers' Alliance and the People's Party* (Minneapolis: University of Minnesota Press, 1931; reprint ed., Lincoln: University of Nebraska Press, Bison Books, 1961), 160.

2. Quoted in Martin Ridge, *Ignatius Donnelly: The Portrait of a Politician* (Chicago: University of Chicago Press, 1962), 150.

3. Quoted in Rhoda R. Gilman, *Minnesota: Political Maverick,* component of *Minnesota Politics and Government: A History Resource Unit* (St. Paul: Minnesota Historical Society, 1975), 26.

4. "Populist Party Platform," in Henry Steele Commager, ed., *Documents of American History,* 2 vols., 7th ed. (New York: Appleton-Century-Crofts, 1963), 1:593.

5. Theodore Christianson, *Minnesota, the Land of Sky-Tinted Waters: A History of the State and Its People,* 5 vols. (Chicago: American Historical Society, 1935), 2:195.

6. Carl H. Chrislock, *The Progressive Era in Minnesota, 1899–1918* (St. Paul: Minnesota Historical Society, 1971), 9.

7. Christianson, *Minnesota,* 2:287.

8. Quoted in Christianson, *Minnesota,* 2:291.

9. Quoted in Christianson, *Minnesota,* 2:291.

10. *Minneapolis Journal,* June 18, 1912, as quoted in Gilman, *Minnesota: Political*

Maverick, 35.
11. George H. Mayer, *The Political Career of Floyd B. Olson* (Minneapolis: University of Minnesota Press, 1951), 3.
12. Mayer, *Political Career of Floyd B. Olson*, 301.
13. Chrislock, *Progressive Era*, 196.
14. James M. Shields, *Mr. Progressive: A Biography of Elmer Austin Benson* (Minneapolis: T. S. Denison & Co., 1971), 3.

CHAPTER 9: THE DIVERSE ECONOMY

1. Quoted in James Gray, *Business Without Boundary: The Story of General Mills* (Minneapolis: University of Minnesota Press, 1954), 160.
2. *Star Tribune* (Minneapolis), March 20, 1996, 1.
3. *Minnesota Statutes, 1995*, Ch. 89A.03, Subd. 6.

CHAPTER 10: MAINSTREAM POLITICS

1. Albert Eisele, *Almost to the Presidency: A Biography of Two American Politicians* (Blue Earth, Minn.: The Piper Company, 1972), 445.
2. Neal R. Peirce, *The Great Plains States of America: People, Politics, and Power in the Nine Great Plains States* (New York: W. W. Norton & Co., 1972), 147.
3. *Time*, August 13, 1973, 35.
4. Marjorie Bingham, "Keeping at It: Minnesota Women," in Clifford E. Clark, Jr., ed., *Minnesota in a Century of Change: The State and Its People Since 1900* (St. Paul: Minnesota Historical Society Press, 1989), 459.
5. "Minnesota's High-Stakes Game," St. Paul *Pioneer Press*, March 12, 1995, 1.

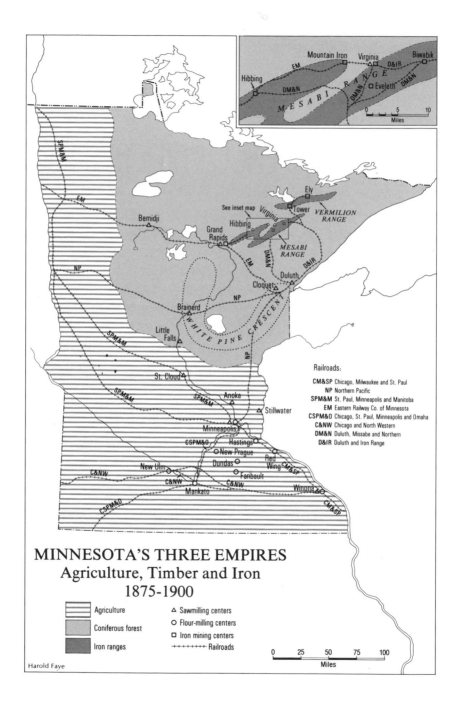

Mountain Iron Virginia Biwabik

Hibbing EM D&IR

DM&N MESABI RANGE Eveleth DM&N

0 5 10
Miles

Ely
Tower VERMILION
See inset map Virginia RANGE
Bemidji Hibbing
Grand MESABI
Rapids RANGE
Duluth
Cloquet
Brainerd
Little WHITE PINE CRESCENT
Falls
St. Cloud
Anoka
Stillwater
Minneapolis
CSPM&O Hastings
New Prague
New Ulm Dundas Red
Faribault Wing
Mankato Winona

Railroads:

CM&SP Chicago, Milwaukee and St. Paul
NP Northern Pacific
SPM&M St. Paul, Minneapolis and Manitoba
EM Eastern Railway Co. of Minnesota
CSPM&O Chicago, St. Paul, Minneapolis and Omaha
C&NW Chicago and North Western
DM&N Duluth, Missabe and Northern
D&IR Duluth and Iron Range

MINNESOTA'S THREE EMPIRES
Agriculture, Timber and Iron
1875-1900

▤ Agriculture	△ Sawmilling centers
▦ Coniferous forest	○ Flour-milling centers
▨ Iron ranges	□ Iron mining centers
	+++++++ Railroads

0 25 50 75 100
Miles

Harold Faye

SUGGESTIONS FOR FURTHER READING

Bibliographies and Indexes:

Blatti, Jo, comp. *Women's History in Minnesota: A Survey of Published Sources and Dissertations*. St. Paul: Minnesota Historical Society Press, 1993.

Brook, Michael, comp. *Reference Guide to Minnesota History: A Subject Bibliography of Books, Pamphlets, and Articles in English*. St. Paul: Minnesota Historical Society, 1974

——— and Sarah P. Rubinstein, comps. *A Supplement to Reference Guide to Minnesota History: A Subject Bibliography, 1970–80*. St. Paul: Minnesota Historical Society Press, 1983.

Ross, Carl, comp. *Radicalism in Minnesota, 1900–1960: A Survey of Selected Sources*. St. Paul: Minnesota Historical Society Press, 1994.

Saucedo, Ramedo, comp. *Mexican Americans in Minnesota: An Introduction to Historical Sources*. St. Paul: Minnesota Historical Society, 1977.

Taylor, David Vassar, comp. *Blacks in Minnesota: A Preliminary Guide to Historical Sources*. St. Paul: Minnesota Historical Society, 1976.

Reference Works:

Holmquist, June Drenning, and Jean A. Brookins. *Minnesota's Major Historic Sites: A Guide*. 2d ed. St. Paul: Minnesota Historical Society, 1972.

————, Sue E. Holbert, and Dorothy Drescher Perry, comps. *History Along the Highways: An Official Guide to Minnesota State Markers and Monuments.* St. Paul: Minnesota Historical Society, 1967.

Toensing W [aldemar] F., comp. *Minnesota Congressmen, Legislators, and Other Elected State Officials: An Alphabetical Check List, 1849–1971.* St. Paul: Minnesota Historical Society, 1971.

Upham, Warren. *Minnesota Geographic Names: Their Origin and Historic Significance.* With an introduction by James Taylor Dunn. Reprint, St. Paul: Minnesota Historical Society, 1969.

———— and Rose Barteau Dunlap, comps. *Minnesota Biographies, 1655–1912.* Vol. 14 of *Collections of the Minnesota Historical Society.* St. Paul, 1912.

White, Bruce M., and others. *Minnesota Votes: Election Returns by County for Presidents, Senators, Congressmen, and Governors, 1857–1977.* St. Paul: Minnesota Historical Society, 1977.

General Histories:

Blegen, Theodore C. *Minnesota: A History of the State.* With a new concluding chapter by Russell W. Fridley. Rev. ed. Minneapolis: University of Minnesota Press, 1975.

Christianson, Theodore. *Minnesota, the Land of Sky-Tinted Waters: A History of the State and Its People.* 5 vols. Chicago: American Historical Society, 1935.

Clark, Clifford E., Jr., ed. *Minnesota in a Century of Change: The State and Its People Since 1900.* St. Paul: Minnesota Historical Society Press, 1989. (Seventeen scholarly essays on a variety of cultural, economic, political, and social topics.)

Folwell, William Watts. *A History of Minnesota.* 4 vols., 1920–29. Rev. ed. St. Paul: Minnesota Historical Society, 1956–69.

Gilman, Rhoda R. *The Story of Minnesota's Past.* St. Paul: Minnesota Historical Society Press, 1989.

Heilbron, Bertha L. *The Thirty-second State: A Pictorial History of Minnesota.* 2d ed. St. Paul: Minnesota Historical Society, 1966.

Biographies, Scholarly Monographs, and Others:

Anderson, Gary Clayton. *Kinsmen of Another Kind: Dakota-White Relations in the Upper Mississippi Valley, 1650–1862.* Lincoln: University of Nebraska Press, 1984.

————. *Little Crow, Spokesman for the Sioux.* St. Paul: Minnesota Historical Society Press, 1986.

———— and Alan R. Woolworth, eds. *Through Dakota Eyes: Narrative Accounts of the Minnesota Indian War of 1862.* St. Paul: Minnesota Historical Society Press, 1988.

Atkins, Annette. *Harvest of Grief: Grasshopper Plagues and Public Assistance in Minnesota, 1873–78.* St. Paul: Minnesota Historical Society Press, 1984.

Blegen, Theodore C. *The Kensington Rune Stone: New Light on an Old Riddle.* With a bibliography by Michael Brook. St. Paul: Minnesota Historical Society, 1968.

Bray, Edmund C., and Martha Coleman Bray, trans. and eds. *Joseph N. Nicollet on the Plains and Prairies: The Expeditions of 1838–39 with Journals, Letters and Notes on the Dakota Indians.* St. Paul: Minnesota Historical Society Press, 1976.

Bray, Martha Coleman. *Joseph Nicollet and His Map.* Philadelphia: The American Philosophical Society, 1980.

Brink, Carol R. *The Twin Cities.* New York: Macmillan, 1961.

Carley, Kenneth. *The Sioux Uprising of 1862.* 2d ed. St. Paul: Minnesota Historical Society, 1976.

Carroll, Francis M., and Franklin R. Raiter. *The Fires of Autumn: The Cloquet–Moose Lake Disaster of 1918.* St. Paul: Minnesota Historical Society Press, 1990.

Chrislock, Carl H. *The Progressive Era in Minnesota, 1899–1918.* St. Paul: Minnesota Historical Society, 1971.

————. *Watchdog of Loyalty: The Minnesota Commission of Public Safety During World War I.* St. Paul: Minnesota Historical Society Press, 1991.

Crouse, Nellis M. *La Verendrye: Fur Trader and Explorer.* Ithaca, N.Y.: Cornell University Press, 1956.

Davidson, Gordon Charles. *The North West Company.* 1918. Reprint, New York: Russell and Russell, 1967.

Davis, E[dward] W. *Pioneering with Taconite.* St. Paul: Minnesota Historical Society, 1964.

Densmore, Frances. *Chippewa Customs.* Reprint of original 1929 edition, with a new introduction by Nina Marchetti Archabal, St. Paul: Minnesota Historical Society Press, 1979.

Drache, Hiram M. *The Day of the Bonanza: A History of Bonanza Farming in the Red River Valley of the North.* Fargo: North Dakota Institute for Regional Studies, 1964.

Dunn, James Taylor. *The St. Croix: Midwest Border River.* Reprint, St. Paul: Minnesota Historical Society Press, 1979.

Eisele, Albert. *Almost to the Presidency: A Biography of Two American Politicians.* Blue Earth, Minn.: The Piper Company, 1972. (Humphrey and McCarthy, with good coverage of their 1968 split.)

Featherstonhaugh, George W. *A Canoe Voyage up the Minnay Sotor.* Reprint of the original 1847 edition, with a new introduction by William E. Lass, St. Paul: Minnesota Historical Society, 1970.

Gieske, Millard L. *Minnesota Farmer-Laborism: The Third Party Alternative.* Minneapolis: University of Minnesota Press, 1979.

———— and Steven J. Keillor. *Norwegian Yankee: Knute Nelson and the Failure of American Politics, 1860–1923.* Northfield, Minn.: The Norwegian-American Historical Association, 1995.

Gilman, Carolyn. *The Grand Portage Story.* St. Paul: Minnesota Historical Society Press, 1992.

————. *Where Two Worlds Meet: The Great Lakes Fur Trade.* St. Paul: Minnesota Historical Society Press, 1982.

Gilman, Rhoda R. *Minnesota: Political Maverick* (part of *Minnesota Politics and Government: A History Resource Unit*). St. Paul: Minnesota Historical Society, 1975.

————, Carolyn Gilman, and Deborah M. Stultz. *The Red River Trails: Oxcart Routes Between St. Paul and the Selkirk Settlement, 1820–1870.* St. Paul: Minnesota Historical Society, 1979.

Gladden, James N. *The Boundary Waters Canoe Area: Wilderness Values and Motorized Recreation.* Ames: Iowa State University Press, 1990.

Gluek, Alvin C., Jr. *Minnesota and the Manifest Destiny of the Canadian Northwest: A Study in Canadian-American Relations.* Toronto: University of Toronto Press, 1965.

Gray, John Morgan. *Lord Selkirk of Red River.* Toronto: Macmillan Co. of Canada, 1964.

Hall, Robert A., Jr. *The Kensington Rune-Stone Is Genuine: Linguistic, Practical, Methodological Considerations.* Columbia, S.C.: Hornbeam Press, 1982.

————. *The Kensington Rune-Stone: Authentic and Important.* With the collaboration of Richard Nielsen and Rolf M. Nilsestuen. Lake Bluff, Ill.: Jupiter Press, 1994.

Hansen, Marcus L. *Old Fort Snelling.* 1918. Reprint, Minneapolis: Ross & Haines, 1958.

Haynes, John Earl. *Dubious Alliance: The Making of Minnesota's DFL Party.* Minneapolis: University of Minnesota Press, 1984.

Helmes, Winifred G. *John A. Johnson, the People's Governor: A Political Biography.* Minneapolis: University of Minnesota Press, 1949.

Holand, Hjalmar R. *The Kensington Stone: A Study in Pre-Columbian American History.* Ephraim, Wisc.: Privately printed, 1932.

————. *A Pre-Columbian Crusade to America.* New York: Twayne Publishers, 1962.

Holmquist, June Drenning, ed. *They Chose Minnesota: A Survey of the State's Ethnic*

Groups. St. Paul: Minnesota Historical Society Press, 1981.

Jarchow, Merrill E. *The Earth Brought Forth: A History of Minnesota Agriculture to 1885.* St. Paul: Minnesota Historical Society, 1949.

Johnson, Elden. *The Prehistoric Peoples of Minnesota.* Rev. 2d ed. St. Paul: Minnesota Historical Society, 1978.

Jones, Evan. *Citadel in the Wilderness: The Story of Fort Snelling and the Old Northwest Frontier.* New York: Coward-McCann, Inc., 1966.

Kane, Lucile M. *The Falls of St. Anthony: The Waterfall That Built Minneapolis.* Rev. ed. St. Paul. Minnesota Historical Society Press, 1987.

———— and Alan Ominsky. *Twin Cities: A Pictorial History of Saint Paul and Minneapolis.* St. Paul: Minnesota Historical Society Press, 1983.

————, June D. Holmquist, and Carolyn Gilman, eds. *The Northern Expeditions of Stephen H. Long: The Journals of 1817 and 1823 and Related Documents.* St. Paul: Minnesota Historical Society Press, 1978.

Keillor, Steven J. *Hjalmar Petersen of Minnesota: The Politics of Provincial Independence.* St. Paul: Minnesota Historical Society Press, 1987.

Kellogg, Louise Phelps. *The British Régime in Wisconsin and the Northwest.* Madison: State Historical Society of Wisconsin, 1935.

————. *The French Régime in Wisconsin and the Northwest.* Madison: State Historical Society of Wisconsin, 1925.

Kjaer, Iver. *Runes and Immigrants in America: The Kensington Stone, the World's Columbian Exposition in Chicago and Nordic Identity.* Minneapolis: The Center for Nordic Studies, University of Minnesota, July 1994.

Kohl, Johann Georg. *Kitchi-Gami: Life Among the Lake Superior Ojibway.* Reprint of the original 1860 edition, with a new introduction by Robert E. Bieder, St. Paul: Minnesota Historical Society Press, 1985.

Kuhlmann, Charles Byron. *The Development of the Flour-Milling Industry in the United States with Special Reference to the Industry in Minneapolis.* Boston: Houghton Mifflin, 1929.

Larson, Agnes M. *History of the White Pine Industry in Minnesota.* Minneapolis: University of Minnesota Press, 1949.

Larson, Bruce L. *Lindbergh of Minnesota: A Political Biography.* New York: Harcourt Brace Jovanovich, 1971.

Lass, William E. *Minnesota's Boundary with Canada: Its Evolution Since 1783.* St. Paul: Minnesota Historical Society Press, 1980.

Lewis, Finlay. *Mondale: Portrait of an American Politician.* New York: Harper & Row, 1980.

Macabee, Paul. *John Dillinger Slept Here: A Crooks' Tour of Crime and Corruption in St. Paul, 1920–1936*. St. Paul: Minnesota Historical Society Press, 1995.

Marling, Karal Ann. *Blue Ribbon: A Social and Pictorial History of the Minnesota State Fair*. St. Paul: Minnesota Historical Society Press, 1990.

Martin, Albro. *James J. Hill and the Opening of the Northwest*. New York: Oxford University Press, 1976. Reprint, with a new introduction by W. Thomas White, St. Paul: Minnesota Historical Society Press, 1991.

Mayer, George H. *The Political Career of Floyd B. Olson*. Minneapolis: University of Minnesota Press, 1951. Reprint, with a new introduction by Russell W. Fridley, St. Paul: Minnesota Historical Society Press, 1987.

Meyer, Melissa L. *The White Earth Tragedy: Ethnicity and Dispossession at a Minnesota Anishinaabe Reservation, 1889–1920*. Lincoln: University of Nebraska Press, 1994.

Meyer, Roy W. *Everyone's Country Estate: A History of Minnesota's State Parks*. St. Paul: Minnesota Historical Society Press, 1991.

————. *History of the Santee Sioux: United States Indian Policy on Trial*. Lincoln: University of Nebraska Press, 1967.

Millett, Larry. *Lost Twin Cities*. St. Paul: Minnesota Historical Society Press, 1992.

Mitau, G. Theodore. *Politics in Minnesota*. Rev. 2d ed. Minneapolis: University of Minnesota Press, 1970.

Morlan, Robert L. *Political Prairie Fire: The Nonpartisan League, 1915–1922*. Minneapolis: University of Minnesota Press, 1955. Reprint, with a new introduction by Larry Remele, St. Paul: Minnesota Historical Society Press, 1985.

Murray, Stanley Norman. *The Valley Comes of Age: A History of Agriculture in the Valley of the Red River of the North, 1812–1920*. Fargo: North Dakota Institute for Regional Studies, 1967.

Nilsestuen, Rolf M. *The Kensington Runestone Vindicated*. Lanham, Md.: University Press of America, 1994.

Nute, Grace Lee. *The Voyageur*. 1931. Reprint, St. Paul: Minnesota Historical Society, 1955.

O'Connell, Marvin R. *John Ireland and the American Catholic Church*. St. Paul: Minnesota Historical Society Press, 1988.

Proescholdt, Kevin, Rip Rapson, and Miron L. Heinselman. *Troubled Waters: The Fight for the Boundary Waters Canoe Area Wilderness*. St. Cloud, Minn.: North Star Press of St. Cloud, 1995.

Rector, William G. *Log Transportation in the Lake States Lumber Industry, 1840–1918*. Glendale, Calif.: Arthur H. Clark, 1953.

Ridge, Martin. *Ignatius Donnelly: The Portrait of a Politician*. Chicago: University of

Chicago Press, 1962. Reprint, St Paul: Minnesota Historical Society Press, 1991.

Schloff, Linda Mack. *"And Prairie Dogs Weren't Kosher": Jewish Women in the Upper Midwest Since 1855*. St. Paul: Minnesota Historical Society Press, 1996.

Searle, R. Newell. *Saving Quetico-Superior: A Land Set Apart*. St. Paul: Minnesota Historical Society Press, 1977.

Shannon, James P. *Catholic Colonization on the Western Frontier*. New Haven, Conn.: Yale University Press, 1957.

Shrewsbury, Carolyn M., and Homer E. Williamson, eds. *Perspectives on Minnesota Government and Politics*. 3d ed. Edina, Minn.: Burgess Publishing Co., 1983.

Solberg, Carl. *Hubert Humphrey: A Biography*. New York: W. W. Norton & Co., 1984.

Stevens, Wayne Edson. *The Northwest Fur Trade, 1763–1800*. Urbana: University of Illinois, 1928.

Stuhler, Barbara. *Gentle Warriors: Clara Ueland and the Minnesota Struggle for Woman Suffrage*. St. Paul: Minnesota Historical Society Press, 1995.

———. *Ten Men of Minnesota and American Foreign Policy, 1898–1968*. St. Paul: Minnesota Historical Society, 1973

——— and Gretchen Krueter, eds. *Women of Minnesota: Selected Biographical Essays*. St. Paul: Minnesota Historical Society Press, 1977.

Tester, John R. *Minnesota's Natural Heritage: An Ecological Perspective*. Minneapolis: University of Minnesota Press, 1995.

Vennum, Thomas, Jr. *Wild Rice and the Ojibway People*. St. Paul: Minnesota Historical Society Press, 1988.

Wahlgren, Erik. *The Kensington Stone: A Mystery Solved*. Madison: University of Wisconsin Press, 1958.

Walker, David A. *Iron Frontier: The Discovery and Early Development of Minnesota's Three Ranges*. St. Paul: Minnesota Historical Society Press, 1979.

Warren, William W. *History of the Ojibway People*. Reprint of the original 1885 edition, with a new introduction by W. Roger Buffalohead, St. Paul: Minnesota Historical Society Press, 1984.

Waters, Thomas F. *The Streams and Rivers of Minnesota*. Minneapolis: University of Minnesota Press, 1977.

Watkins, Bonnie, and Nina Rothchild. With a foreword by Gloria Steinem. *In the Company of Women: Voices from the Women's Movement*. St. Paul: Minnesota Historical Society Press, 1996.

Woods, Thomas A. *Knights of the Plow: Oliver H. Kelley and the Origins of the Grange in Republican Ideology*. Ames: Iowa State University Press, 1991.

INDEX